Emasculation of the UNICORN

DI503767

Emasculation

of the

UNICORN

The Loss and Rebuilding of Masculinity in America

C.T.B. Harris, Ph.D.

NICOLAS-HAYS INC.
York Beach, Maine

First published in 1994 by
Nicolas-Hays, Inc.
P. O. Box 612
York Beach, ME 03910-0612

99 98 97 96 95 94
10 9 8 7 6 5 4 3 2 1

Distributed to the trade by
Samuel Weiser, Inc.
P. O. Box 612
York Beach, ME 03910-0612

Copyright © 1994 C. T. B. Harris
All rights reserved. No part of this publication may be reproduced or trans-
mitted in any form or by any means, electronic or mechanical, including pho-
tocopy, without permission in writing from Nicolas-Hays, Inc. Reviewers
may quote brief passages.

Library of Congress Cataloging-in-Publication Data

Harris, Clifton Tumlin Bud,
    Emasculation of the unicorn : the loss and rebuilding of
masculinity in America / by C.T.B. Harris.
        p.   cm.
    Includes bibliographical references and index.
    1. Masculinity (Psychology)—United States.   2. Men—United
States—Psychology.   I. Title.
HQ1090.3.H38   1994
155.3′32—dc20
                                                            93–47195
ISBN 0–89254–028–1   CIP
MV

Cover is a painting titled "Unicorn in Winter." Used by permission
of Sandra Darling, represented by The Blue Lantern Studio, 4649
Sunnyside Avenue North, Seattle, WA 98103.

Typeset in 11 point Palatino

Printed in the United States of America
The paper used in this publication meets the minimum requirements of the
American National Standard for Permanence of Paper for Printed Library
Materials Z39.48–1984.

Contents

PART I: MASCULINITY IN AMERICA

PART II: THE FAIRY TALE: AN ELEMENTAL BLUEPRINT FOR DEVELOPING MASCULINITY

PART III: TRANSFORMATION AND THE
REBUILDING OF MASCULINITY

Acknowledgments

A book such as this one is the product of many years of personal experience and reflection. A special thanks is due to the men, women and children with whom it has been my privilege to know and work with in my professioanl practice. Beyond them stand my friends and family members, and the mentors and teachers I have encountered over my lifetime.

My intellectual debt to Dr. C. G. Jung and Dr. Marie-Louise von Franz is especially keen, as they led me into the fairy tale as an illumination of the psyche and human experience. The writings of Helen Luke, Marion Woodman and Laurens van der Post have been rich sources of personal inspiration to me, as well as springs of creativity bringing life to the works of the intellect. My training experience at the C. G. Jung Institute in Zurich, its faculty and the analysts there have been of particular importance in the development of this book and my life. The many publications and the research from the Center for the Application of Psychological Type in Gainesville, Florida have helped me tremendously in understanding the practicality of this area in Jungian psychology.

Dr. Richard J. Riordan at Georgia State University deserves special mention as the first person to be responsive to my efforts at writing. Betty Lundsted, the editor at Nicolas-Hays, has been helpful and creative with a sense of humor that made the process of turning the manuscript into a book challenging and fun. Julia Bridger and Marion Hansen led the host of typists who converted my handwriting into readable form. In addition, John White, my agent, had tireless faith in his efforts to bring my work and the market together.

Over the years many people have read and commented upon the manuscript and offered me their support. I wish to thank them all. Among them were Barbara Stone, Nell Staples, Jim and Donna Phillips, Nancy Adams Grimes, Walt and

Audrey Shropshire, Theron Raines, Don Carroll, Maurice Shade and Sam Scoville.

My children, Clif, Marjorie and Betsy deserve a special thanks as does my wife, Massimilla, for enduring my restless pursuit of writing and publishing. My niece, Rebecca, was, for me, a candle representing the spirit of life and she inspired my associations with that image in the book. In a few brief years she taught us all a lot. Of course my parents, my brother and sister and my place in a family that has devoted itself to the task of bringing boys into manhood for almost a hundred years have shaped many of my notions. I am grateful to them all.

The last word of acknowledgement goes to Dr. Dirk Evers in Zurich. He nurtured my early work, challenged and corrected me when it was called for, and supported me when I needed it on this project and others. Thanks, Dirk, for your help and inspiration.

◊ ◊ ◊

The following publishers have given permission to use quoted material from copyrighted works.

Excerpt of "The Tinder Box" reprinted from *The Classic Fairy Tales* by Iona and Peter Opie, copyright © 1974 and used by permission of Oxford University Press.

The cartoon strip "Blondie" by Young and Drake on page 209, reprinted with special permission of King Features Syndicate.

Material from *The Manticore* by Robertson Davies, copyright © 1972, reprinted with permission of Viking Penguin, a division of Penguin Books USA, Inc.

Material from the article titled "Blows to the Spirit: A Dialogue Between Ken Kesey and Robert Stone" by Ken Kesey and Robert Stone are reprinted by kind permission of *Esquire Magazine* and the Hearst Corporation.

Foreword

During the Middle Ages the unicorn symbolized the creative masculine spirit, so fierce and powerful that only a virgin could tame him and only then through deception.

Unicorns, being strong and wild, are usually associated with the lion, the eagle, and the dragon. Ancient stories of the unicorn exist in almost every culture: in the world of the Old Testament, in Persia, India, China, as well as in the West. In one legend the unicorn was so strong and independent it refused to enter the ark and swam throughout the flood. Further, the horn of the unicorn signified health, strength and happiness, and to drink from it cured or provided immunity to incurable diseases.

The unicorn represented male vitality, the rampant masculine and penetrating force of the masculine spirit. The virgin represented his passive feminine aspect. Through the virgin's deception, the unicorn was delivered into the hands of human hunters who killed it and allowed its red blood to flow. From this betrayal and killing the unicorn was transformed and resurrected; he became the powerful energy contained in the virgin's holy garden next to the tree of life.

In our culture we have failed in the transformation of the masculine spirit. We began with that powerful, creative spirit, and somewhere along the way we emasculated it. Now the unicorn, that wondrous masculine symbol, is sentimentalized into being a stuffed toy living in cutesy toy departments or filling the forest of aisles in stationery and card shops, and our culture is left with a marshmallow animal with a limp horn.

To talk of unicorns and transformation takes us into the realm of metaphors so we can examine the evolution and development of human consciousness. The mental landscape of metaphors—dreams, stories, myths, fairy tales—deals with the eternal truths of human nature and maturation, and not with the literal truths of a particular spot in linear time. From the perspective of Jungian psychology, the process of the evolution of consciousness is eternal and takes place through the continuous cycle of transformation. We call this eternal process an archetypal process, and we can choose how we will participate in this process—consciously or unconsciously.

Trying to participate consciously allows us to participate in our own destiny, as well as participating in that of humankind. If we remain unconscious we become the victims of our own history and our own development.

Looking back to the good old days is always dangerous and easily becomes regressive. So I want to be clear that using ancient wisdom does not mean returning to the psychological landscape of the past: King Arthur and his court, the unicorn, the virgin and the hunter, Jesus and his followers, are right now and always have been. They represent eternal psychological and spiritual truths that we must struggle to define, redefine, and experience at each new level of consciousness and civilization that we attain. Paradoxically, these stories can also guide and comfort us. They represent developmental (archetypal) patterns in the maturation of the human psyche. When we are stuck, wounded, or in chaos, they can help us find the right thread to guide us on our way.

In this book I am looking at the need to transform the state of masculinity in our era. Currently this transformation is failing and we remain stuck and fragmented in this vital psychological area. In fact, this is how many men feel today, and women, too, as we all have these inner components. (I will discuss all of these concepts later in the book.) When we are in such a state of psychological confusion and fragmentation, we must begin once more the search for the "Holy Grail." The Grail is the symbolic container of the psycho-spiritual contents that will nourish and renew our lives and that we have lost touch with, allowing the foundation stones of our deepest values to disappear into the unconscious, as Avalon faded into the mists (as has happened throughout history as civilization has progressed from level to level).

If we choose not to journey and search, we allow ourselves and our culture to fall further into the confusion and fragmentation. Eventually nature will take its course and we will hit bottom and a new direction will result. The only problem in this solution is, as we see with alcoholics, that hitting bottom can be extremely painful and dangerous—and has just as good a chance of being destructive as of being healing or redemptive. Moreover, we may simply bounce back to the opposite extreme, setting the whole process up to repeat again, signifying that we have learned little from our pain.

Unicorn-ness and what it represents, virgin-ness and what it represents, deception, taming, and integrating (death and rebirth or transformation) and what it represents, are all segments of the cycle of growth that each person must experience and that each level of civilization must go through. When we speak of the unicorn and the virgin, we are speaking of two great sets of psychological opposites, the masculine and feminine principles, symbolized in many forms, eternal antagonists, seeking balance and reconciliation, and embodied in all of us.

To many people, the process of transformation seems to be the most intriguing area in which to work. However, the mystery of this process easily traps us in a paradox, because we are virtually incapable of *willingly* or *intellectually* understanding the mechanism of transformation. When the transformation process is off track for some reason, we are, in contradiction to what appears most logical, forced to work on more clearly defining the opposites involved at this time, and then grounding them in our living experience. As we live this separation and embrace the resulting tension (being aware of it and even suffering from it without being forced to repress or deny it or moving to precipitant action) involved in the process, the transformation will begin to work on its own, as an archetypal process. In other words, we must labor to discover and embrace the paradoxes of life. As we are able to accept and embody them, we prepare the foundation for the archetype of transformation to move us to a new attitude, a new level of consciousness that will either be different from (or beyond) a goal that we could have planned. In Jungian psychology, we call this process the transcendent function. Christianity often calls it grace.

In reality it is not the mechanism of transformation that has developed a problem. One or both of the opposites has lost its ground, resulting in a corresponding loss of psychological perception and identity that becomes reflected in an increasing degree of one-sidedness of some sort. Instead of struggling to embrace both sides of our living contradictions, we have lost touch with one side and are clinging blindly to the other. One could say that the problem of the transformation of masculinity in American lies metaphorically in uni-corn-ness and virgin-ness.

Personally and collectively, our old worlds are tangible and solid, and we have learned to live in them. The world of the future is elusive, fluid, often made from the light of dreams, or is beyond our imagination. It may also seem a prospective nightmare, a cloud battered by violent winds, a world torn by love, hate, hope, luck, fate, or God. This is as true for a 6-year-old going to the first grade as it is to a 70-year-old facing the twilight of life and the prospect of death.

It is no wonder that we cling to the old world, often homesick and wanting someone to provide concrete steps into the future for us. Our emotional and spiritual institutions, overhelmed by the growth of science and technology, no longer service our need for self-understanding. In our search for security and happiness, we are tempted to look for easy, concrete answers. This tendency creates the danger of self-help books, such as this one. If we yield to this temptation, then self-help becomes *self-avoidance*, and we attempt to replace experience with techniques and jargon provided by outer authorities.

One person who read this manuscript said that he became increasingly aware of his inadequacy, how far he had "fallen," and how could he possibly come up to this "performance." To feel this way is to miss the point of the book entirely. This is not meant to be a "how-to" book. This book is meant to deepen understanding and to challenge our own thinking and feeling so that developing our own "how-to" becomes an informed part of our vital conscious experience. To follow formulas, even in the sense of following, by imitation, a man such as Christ, tends to lead us to forget, or never even discover our own deepest meanings.

Jung clearly pointed out that without the intervention of consciousness our end is as dark as our beginning. He goes further, quoting the Codex Bezae apocryphal insertion at Luke 6:4 to emphasize this point: "Man if indeed thou knowest what thou doest, thou art blessed: but if thou knowest not, thou art cursed, and a transgressor of the law."[1] Dr. Jung continues in another place, "Before the bar of nature and fate, unconsciousness is never accepted as an excuse; on the contrary, there are very severe penalties for it."[2]

It is in this spirit, to help us know and understand ourselves better, that I offer this book, my exploration into the current state of masculinity in America and its psychological meaning.

---

[1] The *Codex Bezae* is a 5th century format of the gospels. This quote is not from Luke 6:4 in current biblical texts, but was an insertion at Luke 6:4 noted in the *Codex Bezae*. It was later deleted by scholars probably because it had to do with self-responsibility and the "law"—a prerogative the church wanted to retain. See *The Portable Jung*, edited by Joseph Campbell and translated by R. F. C. Hull. (New York: Viking Penguin, 1976), p. 637.

[2] Campbell, Joseph, ed. *The Portable Jung*, translated by R. F. C. Hull. (New York: Viking Penguin, 1976), p. 637.

Author's Note

A few years ago, I attended a party in Zurich, and several friends had heard I was writing a book. They asked what it was about. I answered by saying it was something about whatever happened to masculinity in America. Overhearing our conversation, a woman—a minister studying to become a Jungian analyst—exclaimed, "How about the whole world!"

This book is about men, and the nature of its content reflects a masculine perspective. A sexist view is not intended, nor implied. Indeed, I hope this book will be interesting and helpful to women, especially those with sons, those struggling to have relationships with men, and those interested in psychology. Male emasculation is as much a loss to women as it is to men.

The case histories presented in this book are intended for illustrative purposes. To protect those who have labored to understand, to work through and integrate their struggles, I have fictionalized ancillary information and made composites of individual cases. The resulting illustrations represent real-life experiences while obscuring the identity of any one person.

Any similarity between these illustrations and an actual family or individual is purely coincidental.

Emasculation of the UNICORN

PART
I

MASCULINITY
IN AMERICA

1

WHAT HAPPENED
TO OUR MANHOOD?

> Why didn't anyone tell us that if women got
> strong men would get doubly weak—as if in
> spite?
>
> —Isidora Wing in Erica Jong's
> *Parachutes and Kisses*.[1]

Since the turn of the century the values of modern man have
been increasingly questioned. As our attention has evolved
in the direction of personal growth, fulfillment and the
search for meaning in our lives, we must wonder what is the
future of manhood in our society. As men in a world that is
increasing in complexity, compulsiveness, and stress on
every level, we may also wonder what our culture is doing
to us and what it is demanding from us. Is the women's
movement, a marketing economy, or new-age psychology,
developing androgyny as men's fate, desire, salvation, or
damnation? As men we must figure out what we need individually for healthy alternatives, better frames of reference,
deeper self-understanding and finer discrimination. We
need this information for our own psychological, spiritual,
and physical health, and we need it in order to develop
healthy relationships. In turn, we also need to go a step fur-

---

[1]Erica Jong, *Parachutes and Kisses* (New York: Signet, 1984), p. 13.

ther and attempt to understand how the development of individual manhood affects our culture.

Primitive cultures had an advantage over modern cultures. Their men were initiated into masculine identities through solemn ceremonies and rites. These rites and ceremonies took boys out of the world of women and mothers, cleansed them, emptied them, and ushered them through a symbolic death of childhood into rebirth as well-defined men. But these times are gone and are not likely to return. Later, as culture developed past the era of hunters, apprenticeships became an important way of training boys into the tasks of manhood. Boys worked under more knowledgeable men, in the world of men, until they had achieved the skills necessary to work as men. This apprenticeship training continued in western cultures until very recent times. The apprenticeship system was even prevalent in the more intellectually oriented professions of law, medicine, and higher education.

In our century, the personal relationships between boys and men have changed dramatically. The swift development of technology, mass production, rapid communication, and scientific management has made skills gained from mass education and training necessary for most jobs. Even farming has become mechanized and scientific. As a result of these changes, men work in more specialized environments, and boys must master a fundamental body of knowledge before even *approaching* the world of work. Both boys and girls are now institutionally trained and educated. They are, by and large, not connected with their father and the world of men until they reach late adolescence. These fathers are also separated from their children because most of our current work situations do not mix with individual, family, and community life. Young boys have not been tutored, mentored, fathered, or initiated into the world of men or work for several generations. Fathers have become vague and shadowy figures in their sons' eyes. This makes the transition from boyhood to manhood a frightening and confusing experience for today's young men. No clear traditions and ceremonies mark the way. Only a little guidance comes from real men, with no way to know when one has really reached manhood.

In America the issue of becoming a man has suffered additional traumas. In a little over two hundred years our culture has evolved from a few colonies trying to survive in a wilderness to being the world's dominant power in technology, science, and other modern areas. Throughout every decade of American life, men have been faced with drastic change. Over the past century the changes have been so great that fundamental definitions of what it meant to be a man had to be revised for almost every generation.

If we look back a mere fifty or sixty years we can get a dramatic sense of a few ways our culture and history have affected men. The Great Depression of the 1930s wounded American men in a way that is difficult to understand today. I remember clearly how this wound showed itself in my life during the 1950s. When I was in high school, the primary concern of my father and my high school counselors was that I prepare for a career that would ensure a secure job and protect my family. But in the 1940s, World War II exploded and affected all of our families and our economy, creating a burst of technology and mass production, as well as employing women in these areas for the first time. It was also the last major conflict where we had a pure sense of who was right and who was wrong, with the clear ideal that each man who performed individual acts could also make a noticeable contribution. Moreover, we had the luxurious feeling that as a country we were number one, and the world counted on us. Since then, that sense of moral stability has faded.

In the 1950s we ended a confusing war in Korea. It was the first war we could not win. Things became more complex. The organization man, so-called "scientific management," and technology reached their zenith. Middleclass men became homogenized in the company world. Families became isolated as the suburbs developed in neat little rows of square lots, and companies moved men and their families over the country as the organizations needed them. To refuse a move threatened a man's career, meaning that he must also fear the company while he was devoting his life to it. The 1950s was a period of economic growth and security, but a major event threatened our American masculinity. Technology—our god—turned out to be fickle; the Russians proved that when they exploded bombs as big as ours and sent rockets into space.

The 1960s ushered in a decade of tragedies. The symbol (shallow though it was) of our heroism, President Kennedy, was shot down on our streets. This assassination was followed by the murder of Martin Luther King, Jr., who represented non-violent social change and the best in our spiritual leadership. New hope was dashed again with the murder of Robert Kennedy. President Johnson's pursuit of ostensibly heroic goals for the "Great Society" in the United States and his efforts in Southeast Asia to curb Communist conquest were both in the larger-than-life American tradition, but his efforts floundered, leading him to retire from public life.

For over twenty-five years American masculinity had been extroverted—a can-do culture of men out to build a better world and a better nation. It was a masculinity of assertion, rationality and ideas, achieving through technology, scientific management, and idealism, apparently intending to build a better culture and a better world. In the 1960s—in less than a decade—this apparent energy and idealism began to quiver.

Young people changed their values; they began to rebel, they listened to rock music, they smoked dope and dropped out. Many American men found they did not know their own sons and daughters. When women's liberation began, men found they did not know their wives, either. They were doubly confused because they had been raised by women, taught by women and often thought they were doing whatever good men should in the eyes of women. They had little understanding that they were raised in an outdated patriarchy that, paradoxically, had been taught to us by a supporting matriarchy (which the patriarchy also feared). Masculinity became confused, withdrawn and defensive.

Men Today

My interest is not in historical and sociological facts but in how the movement of history and society has affected the masculine personality and spirit in our culture. What kind of men are we now? This is a difficult question to answer because it is difficult to explain many individuals in a few generalizations.

Realizing that society's members include exceptions, I am going to discuss several types of masculine personalities drawn from the works of other authors as well as my own personal clinical experience. Obviously, men are complex and multifaceted, and I will not provide examples of every type of man in our culture. However, my perspective is grounded in Jungian psychology. As I will explain later in the book, and as some of you may know, the Jungian point of view emphasizes the perspective that everyone has both masculine and feminine components in their personality. From this, it follows that the general health or "dis-ease" of the masculine (or feminine) spirit directly affects us all.

In the introduction to his book on fathers, Andrew Samuels, a Jungian analyst, makes the following comments:

> Analysts are beginning to meet a new kind of man. He is a loving and attentive father to his children, a sensitive and committed marital partner, concerned with world peace and the state of the environment; he may be vegetarian. Often, he will announce himself as a feminist. He is in fact a wholly laudable person. But he is not happy—and bids fair to stay miserable until either the world adjusts to him or he manages truly to integrate his behavioral and role changes at a level of psychological depth. Otherwise this man, casualty of a basically positive and fruitful shift in consciousness, will stay a mother's boy. He is a mother's boy because he is doing what he is doing to please women.[2]

---

[2]Andrew Samuels, *The Father: Contemporary Jungian Perspectives* (London: Free Association, 1985), p. 3.

Samuels makes these provocative observations and then does little to help us understand what these observations mean in a personal way.

The poet Robert Bly explains his perception of this new kind of man more fully. Bly calls these men the "soft male."[3] Bly says he has encountered these men throughout the country, and they sometimes seem to make up at least half of his audiences. He describes them as young men who have begun to see their own feminine side and pay attention to it, but he also concludes that while many of them are life-preserving, they don't seem to be *life-giving*. They have no energy and they are unhappy.

Dr. Dan Kiley, in his bestselling book *The Peter Pan Syndrome*,[4] discusses another type of current man, one who has never grown up and whose emotional life is stunted. The Peter Pan type has difficulty relating and often leaves relationships for no apparent reason. His personality is involved in a narcissistic lifestyle focusing in early adulthood on "I want" and in later years on "I should." While young he often appears as a sensitive but intelligent underachiever. He may have talents but during this time he is generally confused, as evidenced by an unsound educational and work history. He pursues his fantasies, whatever they suggest. As he grows into his 30s, he is likely to go to the opposite extreme and become a workaholic. Many Peter Pans appear personable and successful, but underneath have a feeling of bland despair. Surprisingly, they need the dependency of a woman to assuage their own insecurity. Even later, when they are successful and have families they pursue acceptance by others as a way to final self-acceptance. Alas, their successes prevent them from relating fully to women and children and merely cover their depression and inability to believe in themselves. The popu-

[3]See Keith Thompson, "What Men Really Want," an interview with Robert Bly, in *New Age Magazine* (May, 1982), p. 32.
[4]Dr. Dan Kiley, *The Peter Pan Syndrome: Men Who Have Never Grown Up* (New York: Avon, 1983).

larity of Kiley's book and my own experience indicates that this is a common personality type in today's male.

During the last decade, I have encountered another type of man in my practice: the *maternal man*. His attitude toward his wife appeared maternal because he was supportive, directing, nurturing, and enveloping like an overreacting mother— although, paradoxically, he was also often patriarchal and patronizing. This type of male reflects the grey and life-threatening hold the culture can have on us. This is an aspect of the matriarchy supporting the patriarchy that I mentioned earlier. This man is attempting to remain in control and simultaneously do the right thing, the expected thing. He is also *very* afraid of women's anger.

Most of these men have evolved into the second type of manipulative man that I will discuss in the next few paragraphs. Maternal men usually espouse the concepts of women's liberation fully. They want their wives to go back to school or get a job—to fulfill herself and all her potentials *in the latest cultural* fashion. The maternal man is anxious to come to therapy with his wife so she can grow, whether she wants to or not. He does not realize that he is putting her in a double bind between herself and his feminist cultural ideals. He is also reluctant to examine his role and how he makes intimacy in a relationship with a woman actually impossible. These men seldom come on their own for therapy until after a divorce. They are usually feeling hopeless and depressed. Their common complaint is, "I supported her in every way I could. Now I feel like I was her parent and she grew up and left home." Well, they are right. As soon as the wife began to grow, she was no longer satisfied to be a daughter-wife and forced her husband to choose: either end the relationship or open himself to mature masculinity and his own feminine side.

A fourth category of man is one I call the *pseudo-liberated* man. He is simply an opportunist, and he may be either single or married. The single type has learned to develop a facade of sensitivity, the little-boy qualities that he swaps for sex and occasionally for money. Most of these types put so much energy into appearing sensitive that they aren't too good at making a living. They often like older women. Yes, they are good sex partners. In fact, they need lots of sex and often like to make love for hours. They like to touch, to hug and they are good at massage. This is wonderful in bed, but what about the rest of their lives? In clinical situations, usually the woman involved with such a man comes in wondering why he will not commit to the relationship after all this time and lovemaking. Or she may wonder why he needs other women, because this type is never quite faithful. His problems, unfortunately, are sad and deep. He has an underlying depression and cannot define and stand for things that are important to him in relationships and life.

The married man in this category is somewhat different. He is frequently having a problem with impotence. His response to the women's movement is to enthusiastically agree with all its claims and to consciously accept the guilt for the mistreatment of women by men. He preaches women's liberation, discusses it avidly at social gatherings and vociferously supports his wife's going back to school in a nonthreatening area, or her "little job." If she gets serious about pursuing a career he will "sure be glad when someone else brings in a little money around here." In essence, he gives with one hand and takes away with the other. Many of his basic attitudes are untouched. If his career calls for a move, he'll make it for the good of the family no matter what it does to her schooling or career.

Both of these types are difficult for women to deal with. They seem to offer a promise of understanding, sensitivity and relationship, but can never fulfill the promise with advancement in the real world. Both types have adopted behaviors to bring about certain results. The first type may be a little more exploitive, but both are secretly looking for ways to protect themselves and to get what they want. The truth is, both also have a lot of underlying anger toward women—but, more important, toward the feminine in themselves.

Erica Jong, reflecting her view of a wide variety of modern men and women in her novels, makes some caustic but also penetrating comments about certain categories of modern men.

> The "eligible" man at a swell New York dinner party was likely to be a terminal neurotic, so wounded by one, two, three or four ex-wives that he was unlikely to ever trust a person of the female persuasion again; and so burdened by outrageous debts or labyrinthine legal and tax problems, that he had little time for the ideal woman he claimed to be seeking even in the unlikely event she might cross his path.[5]

She also comments dramatically at times about the high rate of impotence in men and how rapidly men appear to be burning their life-force and their sex-force. Many of the men in her novels are hurt, withdrawn, sulky and childish. Of course, these comments mirror her imagination and perception as a novelist. But I have heard these same comments echoed enough in my office to take them seriously.

For years the image of the hardhat, beer-drinking, pickup-truck-driving construction and blue-collar worker carried the macho fancy of American masculinity. As an image, they were not confused by "women's lib." They kept right on whistling and making comments when a woman walked by no matter how mad it made the readers of *Ms.* magazine. Now there is growing evidence that this group of men, in reality, is in full emotional retreat—tuning out with increasing alcoholism and drug addiction[6]—giving us another category of men, the *blue-collar addict*.

Large companies have become desperate enough to give free drug tests, and small companies live in fear of who will

---

[5]Erica Jong, *Parachutes and Kisses* (New York: Signet, 1984), p. 142.
[6]J. Castro, "Battling the Enemy Within: Companies Fight to Drive Illegal Drugs Out of the Workplace," in *Time Magazine* (International edition), March 17, 1986, p. 52.

show up for work and what condition they will be in. Of course, blue-collar addicts are stoned off the job as well, creating problems in their marriages, families, and relationships. There is no social level left that has not experienced a loss of masculine tradition and the arrival of enormous emotional difficulties for men.

There is another man around who also reflects these same traumas and culture shocks, who is a little more traditional in form and not as extreme as any of the previous types. His group seems small, but I hope growing. He is confused but honestly struggling to understand the issues. Many of these men come to therapy because of their wives or families and then stay for themselves. They are unhappy—often confused, bewildered and hurt by all that has happened, but they have not given up or "adjusted." Often they do not know whether to try to adapt, to try to compromise, or to chuck it all and live defensively pursuing only uncommitted sex. However, they care too much to accept the easy answers. They want to be good husbands, good fathers, good lovers, and they want their struggles and unhappiness appreciated and respected. By and large they are still looking to women and to the culture to give them the answers. Nevertheless, some are beginning to look to other men and to look inward. They are the lucky ones.

Several years ago a man was referred to me by his physician for depression. His greeting and handshake were firm and confident, but his sadness was too intense to conceal. When his wife married him he was considered a "catch." Now she had divorced him after fifteen long years of marriage. He was in despair. He hated not living with his kids, knowing another divorced man was living in his former home, bringing his own kids there every other weekend. This man had wanted his marriage to work with all his heart, and he truly did not understand his wife's dissatisfaction. She claimed he was distant, unresponsive and unsupportive, and he believed that he must be all of those things or she would not have left him.

For a couple of years he worked inwardly—hard, searching work. He found that he was not all that bad and that it takes two to make a relationship succeed or fail, and that his wife had some problems, too. He also learned to relate in a more personal and more fatherly way to his children. Since that time he has remarried a divorced woman. He is less starry-eyed than he was the first time, and both are determined to build a relationship. He has a much clearer idea of what he wants from a relationship with a woman, what he will give and where his bottom lines are. He had to step back some from his career during this time to put energy into himself. Paradoxically, he found out that as he deepened and broadened himself, he enjoyed his profession in different ways, and, amazingly, new opportunities opened for him.

So far, I have observed how many social and cultural changes have affected men, the types of men that have resulted, and the substantial evidence of the underlying unhappiness of men. The spirit of masculinity has become withdrawn and defensive. Men, even while struggling, are generally still looking *outward*, particularly to women and the culture for their answers. A more hopeful sign is that a few men are beginning to look into their own psyches and to other men.

So far, our discussion has been empirical. Beginning with the next chapter, my argument will start with psycho-philosophical concepts and search for a model that provides a functional path to follow for masculine development in these confusing times.

2

SHOULD MANHOOD BE CONTINUED?

The idea that male energy could be good has come to be considered impossible. Yet all the great cultures have lived with images of this energy.

—Robert Bly[1]

Recent years have brought a growing emphasis on the concept of androgyny. Are men and women basically alike underneath it all? If they are, should we strive for an androgynous plateau after doing away with cultural sex roles? Is our common bond in humanity the place we should equally meet? Or do the differences in the masculine and feminine really complement and enhance one another? What about the joyful, tender, romantic moments? Will they be homogenized out of existence? Or have they already been lost as we have replaced the mystery of sex and love with the technology of sex and "how to" manuals for relationships? Or have they been lost as we have become involved in the polemics of sexual politics that mark the angry suspicion that one sex is somehow ahead of the other?

---

[1]Keith Thompson, "What Men Really Want: A New Age Interview with Robert Bly," in *New Age Magazine*, May 1982, p. 51.

Most writers and lecturers I have heard advocating androgyny have based their discussions on Plato's myth of the androgyne or hermaphrodite.[2] Plato developed his ideas from myths of primordial unity already ancient by his era. According to Plato human beings came originally in three types: man-man who sprang from the sun, woman-woman who sprang from the earth, and man-woman who sprang from the moon and partakes the nature of both earth and sun. Each unit was joined back to back, had four arms, four legs, two sets of genitals and a single head with faces front and back. Each being formed a rounded whole that could walk upright, or run cartwheel fashion, but they could never face each other. Their strength, vigor, and pride were great and they began attacking the gods. Zeus decided to split them down the middle to make them weaker. From this time forward each individual would feel incomplete and seek to return to this ancient state of wholeness by merging with another person. This story has two important implications in addition to the need to merge. It sets the stage both for heterosexuality and homosexuality, and the genders are of equal significance.

The myth of the androgyne implies a model of oneness that offers symbiotic comfort on the one hand, and the angst of separation on the other. This implication can be interpreted in many ways, and can be metaphorically connected to a host of psychological issues such as inflation, separation anxiety, and so forth. But most advocates of androgyny idealistically see a possibility for the reunification of these opposites that will result in a higher total consciousness. In fact, this view is usually masking a deep longing for an easy way out—a "return to paradise"—that ignores the importance of conscious awareness, discrimination, and the true value of opposites (three important points I will continue to discuss throughout this book). Indeed, analytical psychologists (analytical psychology is the name given to the psychology of C.

[2]Plato, *The Symposium*, translated by W. Hamilton (New York: Penguin, 1917).

EMASCULATION OF THE UNICORN / 17

G. Jung) consider the process of "separating the opposites" as the ego develops from the unconscious to be the origin of consciousness. This means that real life will never be a perfect unity and real people will always experience tension and conflicts from the fact of "opposites," such as good and evil, "I and thou," light and dark.

In one of the many Hindu myths of creation,[3] nothing exists except in the form of Brahma. Seeing that he is alone, Brahma is lonely and afraid. In his desire for company, he sees he is large enough to be more than one and splits himself into two pieces. These two halves became a husband and a wife. From this splitting we also came to experience ourselves as incomplete in the absence of the other. This story, however, has a slightly different twist from Plato's. Brahma fills his emptiness with his wife. They make love and create the people in the world; but when she realizes she had once been part of the husband who now makes love to her, she feels ashamed. Trying to escape his embrace, she turns into a series of animals. At each transformation, Brahma also turns into the male of the same animal and makes love to her. In this way all living things are created in pairs.

Here, as in our Judeo-Christian tradition, the feminine was originally contained in the masculine. Elsewhere, the concepts of masculine and feminine are often conceptualized according to the ancient Eastern principles or images of Yang and Yin. Everything in the world partakes of various portions of Yang and Yin including both men and women. The Yang/Yin principles are symbolic representations of masculine and feminine energies: the Yang principle is thought of as being the creative or generative element, the initiating energy, penetrating power, strength, impulsation, aggressiveness and arousal. It is assertive and outgoing. It is represented as heaven, sun, and spirit, and manifests itself in discipline, discrimination and separation. Yin, on the other hand, is repre-

---

[3]Sheldon Kopp, *Here I Am, Wasn't I* (New York: Bantam, 1986). See the discussion on creation on pages 30–36.

sented as receptive, yielding, withdrawing, cool, wet, dark, and containing. It is form-giving, connecting and collective—not spirit, but nature.

Eastern mystics tell us that they experience all things and events, including the Yin/Yang principles, as manifestations of a basic oneness. But at the same time they recognize the individuality of each thing and by no means suggest that all things are equal. They maintain that all differences and contrasts are relative within a universal unity. These mystics attempt to transcend purely intellectual concepts by developing an awareness of the relativity and polar relationship of opposites. If we focus our attention on one concept, we have also, by this very act, created its opposite. Lao Tzu says, "When all in the world understand beauty to be beautiful, then ugliness exists. . . ." Good and evil, pleasure and pain, life and death, and yes, even masculine and feminine, are not absolute experiences belonging to different categories, but simply two sides of the same reality and extreme parts of a larger whole. When examining the Eastern concepts, we must be careful to remember that they are never static. There is always a dynamic interplay between the two extremes. An overemphasis on one pole necessitates a need for bringing the opposite pole into prominence. The development of awareness emphasizes the notion of dynamic balance in the experiencing of the opposites. In nature the cycles of life circle continually. Only human beings have the capacity to create a temporary static plateau such as Western man has created by traditionally favoring the Yang over the Yin. Such a polarity of position (in terms of dynamic energy) invites a "backlash" from the opposite polar position as nature attempts to correct the imbalance.

Depth psychology has been profoundly influenced by the theory of opposites giving us a picture of the human being made up of entirely mutually opposite tendencies—intellect and feeling, introvert and extrovert, masculine and feminine, and the amoral drives of instincts and the conscious moral codes, to name a few examples. If we look around, we can see daily confirmations of these affiliations. Priests and ministers have affairs, respectable matrons shoplift, intellectuals make relationships a series of reasoned propositions, professors fall madly in love with young students, ideal marriages end in vicious divorces, and in the name of play men make games a competitive science. We can all remember from childhood when something was going to be done to us for "our own good" and we usually anticipated the result to entail suffering. This notion of opposites is one you will frequently encounter as you pursue this book.

Myths and stories almost as old as time (Oedipus, for example) inform us that fate strikes us through "not-knowing," the lack of self-awareness that the myth illustrates. Conscious awareness of life's cycles and forces is the only way to prevent us from being constantly thrown back and forth between polarities, compelling fate to punish us with tragedies. Conscious awareness is the indispensable condition for maintaining a dynamic balance between the opposites and transcending the tensions expressed in the different sides of human nature as well as the universe.

The beauty of the Eastern concepts of Yang and Yin is that they are not combative. They complement each other as opposites (retaining their own identities), reaching toward a universal harmony. The receptive completes the creative and the creative completes the receptive. Most importantly, both principles exist in men and women.

C. G. Jung, in his effort to examine the ongoing core of human problems, showed us that just as every man has recessive female chromosomes and hormones, he also has a group of psychological characteristics that make up a minority feminine element in his personality. A woman, likewise, has a psychological masculine minority component within her.[4] Jung uses the terms masculine and feminine to denote age-old principles much as the Eastern mystics did—not to describe cul-

---

[4]C. G. Jung, Collected Works, Vol. 9i, *Archetypes and the Collective Unconscious*, Bollingen Series, Vol XX, ¶. 512.

tural roles or stereotypes. Therefore, in normal development each man has a predominantly masculine personality with a complementary feminine component, and each woman has a predominantly feminine personality with a complementary masculine component. Men and women come in many varieties, however. His theory does not limit the roles and lifestyles of men and women nor how they may express themselves. The man's feminine side Jung called the *anima*, the woman's masculine side he called the *animus*.

Jung also continued using the term *eros* to describe what he conceived of as the feminine principle. *Eros* in the Jungian sense generally means personal relatedness, a keen interest in relationships and a prevailing attitude that works for conciliation and reconciliation. *Eros* evokes self-integration, subjectivity, and the concerns of individuals. *Eros* is rooted in the material universe and the earthy feminine qualities such as passivity and receptivity.

Contrasting with *eros* is the word *logos*, representing the masculine principle. *Logos* signifies power, meaning, deeds, and ideas. *Logos* stands for objectivity, structure, discrimination, and the abstract. *Logos* is also equated with the spiritual in the sense of the non-material. Jung emphasized that both *eros* and *logos* are equally necessary in human life and complement each other.

As I proceed I will try to deal with our individual differences without devaluing any of the components. We are accustomed to thinking otherwise, but differences in the sexes does not imply discrimination or roles. When we deny the differences, physical and psychological, we take a destructive path, because we are then denying essential components of our physical, sexual, and psychological identities. To deny the differences devalues the effects we have on each other and the need we all have for the confrontation of the other in order to help us find out most fully who we are, how we are different from and how we are like those closest to us. It also denies us the healing power of the other and our own capacity to be healers in the human arena of differences. My conclusion is the same as Jung's: as individuals we have dominant and complementary components, and like the Eastern mystics (and Jung as well), I see the masculine and feminine components as equal, of necessity complementing each other as universal forces. The gift of each enhances the other.

The masculine and feminine, *logos* and *eros*, grow hand in hand in healthy circumstances. Over and over as I have dealt with people in therapy, first one grows and then the other. They follow each other step by step as if endeavoring to maintain their balance. The masculine inspires the feminine and the feminine inspires the masculine.

Robert Bly notes that "the idea that any male energy when in authority could be good has come to be considered impossible."[5] Bly tells us the Greeks understood the nature of the positive male energy and termed it *Zeus-energy*. This energy includes intelligence, compassionate authority, health, physical authority, good will and leadership, and it represents positive power when utilized by the male in service of the community. He further states that all the great cultures since the Greeks have lived with images of this energy—except ours. This Zeus energy has been disintegrating in our culture.

The destruction of Zeus energy is reflected in comic strips such as "Dagwood," the male stereotype in cartoons as "Fred Flintstone," television situation comedies where the male appears childish and foolish and is saved or directed by his practical, intelligent (and managerial/matriarchal) wife. These insidious attacks combine with the absent or almost absent father and the aggressive stance of women to indoctrinate boys, starting at a very young age. For several generations our sons have tried to become men not only without connecting to the teachings and energies of older men, but also in the face of cultural denigration of the masculine. The absence of full-fledged masculine models and a cultural tradition of masculine development has abandoned boys to the conflicting influences of the media, marketing, and popular social causes

---

[5]Keith Thompson, "What Men Really Want," p. 51.

as these boys struggle to form male identities. Often boys are left with a deep sense of anger resulting from society's failure to meet their developmental needs. Boys trying to grow up have little understanding of their anger and how to deal with it. Sometimes they express it antisocially, but most often it is internalized and then projected onto women from a deep unconscious wound in their personality. We are so lost in our development that we not only need to learn about the masculine and the feminine, we need to relearn what masculinity really is.

The quest is now to discover how to renew manhood. From this renewal we can determine again how to define ourselves as men, how to become the individuals we already are in potential, and how to absorb and integrate the shocks we have endured—such as the changes in women.

3

FINDING THE MAN WITHIN

> True masculinity—not the macho type—is needed for men to be strong enough to meet the feminine in themselves. For this they must find their own masculine face—not a face defined by women.
>
> —Bud Harris

A young man came into my office as a participant in a therapy group. He explained that his wife decided to go back to school and then pursue a career—a modern situation. He proceeded:

> She didn't ask my opinion. She just told me it was time I did my share around the house, including cooking. So now I love to cook, I've had a few parties, asked people over, and cooked, so what's the problem? The problem is she's mad as hell and says I forced her out of the kitchen! What did I do wrong? I wish to God someone would clue us in on what men are supposed to do today.

Now, in the face of this very modern problem, please forgive me for not being able to resist going back to ancient times during the generation of S. Freud and dredging up his old saw of

"What do women want?" The naked truth is that this young man is still asking the same question. He's trying to be one of Andrew Samuels' good boys, doing what he is doing in order to please his wife. I certainly don't know what women want, but I am clear that this young man is on the wrong tack. Let us listen to another member of this group, speaking a few minutes later. This man is a little older, not so modern, a successful businessman who has had two heart attacks and complicated surgery. He says:

> All of my life somebody has been telling me how to act. Now we're getting all of this new stuff about feelings, sex-roles and other stuff. As far as I'm concerned, this just heaps my burden higher! I feel lost and I'm damn sick of it all—I want to be left just the hell alone!

As men, we are in a dangerous period of transformation because it is difficult to respect ourselves as we were and we have little idea of who or what to become. Our old support systems have crumbled and no new foundation stones are in sight. Where can we look for a renewal of masculinity which can also provide a few helpful answers for us? Well, this last man's frustrated statement, "just the hell alone," is not a bad place to begin our search.

Men must look inside themselves and then to other men to find some of these answers. The roots of masculinity and maleness are not out there in the minds of women, they are deep within our own psyches, where they have grown for centuries. Like all psychological experiences, they reside within our bodies as well, involving us totally, as I will explain later when discussing symbols and symptoms. They are found in basic human patterns of experience, development, renewal, and individuation. In our modern rush toward saving the world through rationality, we have learned to ignore the mythical pull of experience that once expressed and taught us these patterns. In our fashionable pursuit to debunk and reduce mythology, fairy tales and religion to children's stories, we have impoverished and deluded ourselves. In spite of our social ideologies we have reduced human life to a story without meaning. Our new ideal of a BMW, a hot tub, a deck, and a remodeled kitchen in every home, condo, or apartment simply makes life a hollow and demeaning story if we have no other purpose.

Formerly mankind created its culture by using myths, rituals, and fairy tales to give a sense of the mysteries of life and to connect people in society to those mysteries. In more primitive times, human beings lived these myths and tales. As we have "outgrown" these stories, they have continued to live, and they sneak right back into our lives in different forms. Ask our children. They know them—the old themes are there in comic books, cartoons, movies, and toys. Have you seen "He-Man," "Masters of the Universe," "Dungeons and Dragons," "Star Wars," "Star Trek" and many more? Many adults are captivated by movies, soap operas, books and plays, not realizing that the old themes are simply being recast over and over in different settings. Part of our hunger for these themes has been illustrated by the resurgence of books (three or four per year for the last ten years) on the Arthurian legends and the movies retelling these legends.

The mythological world lives right under our noses in what we like to think of as the "hard, adult" world of science and business. Thomas Peters and Robert Waterman, Jr. examine what makes our best companies successful in their book, *In Search of Excellence: Lessons from America's Best-Run Companies*.[1] They point out two important psychological factors: first, creative leadership (in the form Bly terms the "Zeus masculine") lives in these companies. Terms such as leadership, commitment, meaning, rituals, cultures, heroism, and intuition abound and underwrite the good of the company. In the second place, the value of mythology is clearly appreciated. In

---

[1]Thomas J. Peters and Robert H. Waterman, Jr., *In Search of Excellence: Lessons from America's Best-Run Companies* (New York: Warner, 1983), p. 75.

speaking of the creation of great companies such as IBM, Hewlett-Packard and the Bank of America, the founders and the creation take on roles of mythic proportions as stories, legends, and anecdotes about the founding and the founders are passed word-of-mouth through generations of employees. As Peters and Waterman say:

> . . . in an organizational sense, these stories, myths and legends appear to be very important, because they convey the organization's shared values, or culture.

> . . . if companies do not have strong notions of themselves, as reflected in their values, stories, myths and legends, people's only security comes from where they live on the organizational chart. Threaten that, and in the absence of some grander corporate purpose, you have threatened the closest thing they have to meaning in their business life.[2]

and

> We concluded that the Japanese were able to reorganize as seemingly ruthlessly as they did because security was always present: not security of position, for many were demoted or transferred to subsidiary companies, but security that had its roots in solid cultural ground and shared meaning.[3]

We may be more "primitive" than we think. We still need these myths and tales because, old and new, they serve the same basic purpose of connecting us with important values and patterns of living. If they can support a company as scientific, technological, and modern as IBM, surely we should be open to giving the ones that can affect our general culture a new look.

---

[2] *In Search of Excellence*, pp. 75, 77.
[3] *In Search of Excellence*, p. 77.

The old myths, religions, and fairy tales were in fact a boiling down of human experience into basic patterns of cultural behavior. These stories developed over the centuries, carrying powerful collective and personal meanings as they have been retold and refined by countless people. They are inspiration for much of our life, flowing from the countless acts of imagination that come together like a river whose waters touch all of us if we only let them. Themes such as death and renewal, principles of masculinity, femininity, heroes, fathers, mothers, wisdom, and evil have been repeated over the centuries. Many psychologists have written about myths and fairy tales. C. G. Jung, in studying the underlying structure of the human psyche, paid particular attention to myths and fairy tales. He considered fairy tales to be one of the purest expressions of basic psychological patterns, and he spoke of these patterns as archetypes.

In order to understand and appreciate these old tales, we must go beyond narrow reason and think in metaphor and symbol. The ambiance of these old myths and fairy tales may at first seem strange, but if we attend to them carefully and take them seriously, we begin to hear and understand them. Their meanings become thrilling and delightful. As we reduce our rationalism, we add another dimension to our perceptive processes. Symbolic meanings often need translating, but symbolic thinking becomes easier as we get used to it.

Several other authors have followed this process. Robert Johnson does an excellent job of exploring masculine psychology via the myth of Parsifal's search for the Holy Grail in his book *He*.[4] Robert Bly used the fairy tale of "Iron John" in an interview in *New Age* magazine titled "What Men Really Want" and later in his book *Iron John*. Both Johnson and Bly have greatly affected my thinking, my feeling, and my personal growth. I have picked a particular fairy tale for this book

---

[4]Robert Johnson, *He: Understanding Masculine Psychology* (New York: Harper, Perennial, 1984). He presents a very clear discussion of the psychological development of men and boys.

because I think it fits the situation I have defined and gives us some choices and directions. Another tale may suit you better, but whatever tale is chosen, developing a process of listening and examining is helpful.

In the tale presented here, "The Tinder Box," the authors note that this is Hans Christian Andersen's retelling of an old Scandinavian folktale that is similar to several other tales. I have purposefully selected Andersen's retelling of the tale because his personal problems with sensitivity, the masculine, and the feminine[5] are not unlike those in our culture. I have also examined the tale in contrast to earlier versions of it and will refer to them several times.

Individuation—Living Our Own Story

Each of us creates a story as we live. Our stories are unique, filled with our personal hurts, joys, triumphs, failures, and tragedies. Yet, all our stories combine to create a larger story, the story of mankind, that reflects human nature. Every one of us is a member of the human race and a participant in the larger story. As a participant, we all share, to a greater or lesser extent, in some measure of "human nature." Paradoxically, nature has also created each of us to be unique and identifiable one from the other. We have subtle biological differences, such as fingerprints. We also have separate identities developed through the unique combinations of our personal heredity, history, environment and personality characteristics that cause us to develop according to a unique pattern throughout our individual lives.

Respect for the uniqueness of the individual is one of the founding principles in the story of our society. Many psychologists have come to envision the goal of human development as becoming most fully ourselves. Jung called the process of

---

[5]Marie-Louise von Franz, *An Introduction to the Psychology of Fairy Tales* (Dallas, TX: *Spring*, 1978). See, for example, Dr. von Franz's discussion in the question-and-answer section of this book.

doing this the *individuation process*. I like the way Jung concep-
tualizes this process and will continue to use his terminology.
Jung believed that to become fully ourselves we had to
attempt to become wholly individual, and then live productively as an individual in relationships and in our culture.

The individuation process is the process of becoming an
"in-dividual" through self-realization and unfolds over our
entire lifespan. Self-realization results from the expansion of
conscious awareness and the continuous growth of consciousness. In the tenor of individuation, conscious awareness
includes the effort to know as much as possible about our
whole selves—including our instincts, bodies, emotions, and
conscious and unconscious minds. For our individuation
process to take place, our conscious personality must develop
and become a conduit for our self-realization. Another reason
I like the term individuation is because it goes beyond our
normal psychological descriptions of self-actualization, personality integration, and ego-consciousness (even though it
includes all of these), to include the whole person, and
reunites us with the community. Jung considered this process
a natural process and the goal of life. If we pursue this process
with diligence and self-honesty he thought that we would
perceive the pattern of our life, and through this perception
receive an impression of the center of our being that he termed
the Self.

With growing consciousness, we increase our capacity for
expressing the potential person we are meant to be. This
means that as our individuation process progresses, we
increase the capacity of our conscious personality to reflect
our total self. Of course, most of us never complete this
process, and in fact many of us never get very far at all. Most
of us find it difficult to fully separate or individuate from our
families, or from institutional and cultural influences. We
often remain trapped in the expectations and values of our
parents and follow the approved highways directed by our
society. If we are not careful we can end up living our lives in
patterns set by others. Yet, nature intends us to be unique and

different. We must search for the ways to become responsible for ourselves and to develop our autonomy and self-direction.

Let me give a simple illustration of this process. Every acorn inherently contains a pattern to become an oak tree. If all goes well, it falls to earth and grows into a tall tree. In a simple way we can say this acorn has individuated, it has followed and fulfilled its pattern of growth. As the oak needs soil, water, sunlight and other things to grow, we need other people, society, and culture. As the growing acorn must root in the earth we must root in the natural parts of ourselves.

Some acorns fall in difficult places to grow and become gnarled and twisted, some become sick, some die and some are cut down or burned up. The same is true for us as we struggle to grow, and if we survive we may have many scars. Some of these scars are psychological. They are the result of the traumas and complexes of childhood and adolescence that wound, gnarl, and twist us. Many psychology books are devoted to the healing and overcoming of these scars.

If the oak tree grows tall, it must break through the earth and reach toward the sky. During our individuation process, once we are beginning to root, we must follow a similar analogy. We must break through the crust of a layer of societal norms which have a certain social value, but no absolute validity, and can hinder our growth if we unconsciously identify with them.

One big difference between us and oak trees is that we have something called "consciousness," and as I have pointed out, it is the conduit of our self-realization. Consciousness is defined as having an awareness of one's own existence and environment. Implicit in this awareness is an ability to observe ourselves and make decisions as well as a capacity for discernment, judgment, evaluation, and choice. We can reflect on our past and plan our future. We can produce culture, art, poetry; we can study philosophy and religion—all having little to do with our material survival. To compound this amazing ability, we can also experience and be aware of emotions, use them also to make decisions, and, most mysteriously of all, to experience love. With consciousness we develop a sense of "I-entity."[6] To simplify his discussion of the personality, Jung used the term "ego" to describe this "I-entity," the center or focal point of our consciousness, the part of ourselves with which we are consciously identified.

Allow me to mention once again that the Self is the name given to the total personality. This Self includes the unique pattern, the potential person who is within each of us and seeks throughout our lifetime to be recognized and expressed through the ego.

All of this complex psychological language is only a tool to help us find our story—to unravel it from our tangled histories and the pressure of our lives—and then to live it as fully as we can. To live it with meaning. To live it with a sense of honesty and destiny that is unique and our own. And, finally, to live it knowingly as part of the greater story of us all.

If we think about it, this process will make sense. A feeling of personal security develops as we realize it is not necessary to struggle to be like someone else or to meet another's ideals. We stand on our surest ground by learning to be our own selves. As we feel more secure and complete within ourselves, it becomes natural to seek the ways we resemble the human "family" and how we can relate, belong, and contribute without again losing ourselves.

The psychological Self, the container of the personality and personal blueprint for growth, orchestrates the individuation process as we move through the complex spiritual and psychological problems of living. Metaphorically speaking, the Self directs the stage upon which the characters in a fairy tale act. The main character in the tale usually represents the ego and the transformations it undergoes. The other characters, people and animals, represent different parts of our personality in different stages of development. The Self and the

---

[6]"I-entity" is a term coined by M. Scott Peck in his book *The Different Drum: Community Making and Peace* (New York: Simon & Schuster, 1987). Peck uses this term to describe the ego as the center of consciousness and conscious identity.

universal patterns we live connect the personality to the deeper river that flows through all human experience.

A Comment on Modern Learning

One of the most exciting things about studying fairy tales is that we begin to get back in touch with the wisdom of age-old human experience. For example, in primitive cultures, when a boy went through the initiation ceremonies to become a man he was led through them by a *ritual elder*, not by his father. It was the job of the ritual elder to teach the boy the history, wisdom, laws, and religion of the tribe and to instruct him in sexuality, which he usually did through myths and stories.

In our modern world both men and women have lost touch with this important human asset, the wisdom of experience. We have neither the time, place, nor patience to listen to our elders. We have lost our connection to them and what they have learned from living. Our communications have become rapid, concise, and we have to (or we think we have to) digest an extraordinary amount of material. Managers and businessmen are up to their necks in plans, reports, and printouts. No wonder they want everything written to them on one page or less. When we are not swamped with business, we are reading books and listening to tapes, cramming ourselves with content—the ways to do everything from being a one-minute manager to how to communicate with one's teenager. We are looking for more people to tell us what to do and how to do it on every level of our lives. Peters and Waterman[7] tell us that the best companies have managers who have an intuitive grasp of the company based on hands-on experience. Their experience and knowledge are based on getting out and around in the life of the company, based on acting, trying, failing, succeeding—based on living their profession, not just thinking it.

---

[7] Peters and Waterman, *In Search of Excellence*, general discussion throughout the book.

We trap ourselves in the same paradox when we tell someone to "be spontaneous." Spontaneity is impossible to schedule, plan, or command. We learn enormous amounts of data and information but have concentrated so heavily on learning that we have forgotten that only the process of living can teach us how to effectively make use of what we know— in other words, how to convert this knowledge to the wisdom of living. Listening to these old stories lets us become re-acquainted with this process. Once again we encouner the basic patterns of timeless human experience, that Jung labeled archetypical images in analytical psychology.

Let us begin retracing our steps toward ancient learning by reading the following fairy tale and trying to discover the meaning in this story for us.

PART II

THE FAIRY TALE:
AN ELEMENTAL
BLUEPRINT FOR
DEVELOPING
MASCULINITY

4

THE FAIRY TALE

"Fyrtoiet" ["The Tinder Box"][1] was one of the first fairy tales Hans Christian Andersen wrote. It appeared in a cheap sixty-four-page booklet, *Eventyr, Fortalte for Børn* [Tales told for Children], published in Copenhagen, 8 May 1835. Andersen was 29 when he wrote the tale and embarrassingly short of money, so it is easy to see why the story appealed to him. It was, in fact, a retelling of a Scandinavian folktale, known in Denmark as "Aanden i Lyset" ["The Spirit in the Candle"], which Andersen had loved in his childhood, but which was not then well known. In the traditional story, a soldier obtains riches by fetching a candle from a sleeping troll at the request of an old woman. He refuses to hand over the candle, lights it, and finds that this summons an iron man to his service, who enables him, since this is his desire, to have meetings with a beautiful princess. The soldier is found out in much the same way as Andersen's soldier; is condemned to be burned at the stake; and is saved only at the last moment by his supernatural henchman, whom he manages to summon by obtaining permission to light his pipe.

Comparison with "Aladdin and His Wonderful Lamp" need not be resisted, particularly when it is remembered that

---

[1]"The Tinder Box" has been reproduced from *The Classic Fairy Tales* edited by Iona and Peter Opie (London and New York: Oxford University Press, 1974).

The Arabian Nights was the favorite reading of Hans Christian Andersen's childhood. The tale of Aladdin is, like "The Tinder Box," a tale of a mortal being made use of by a supernatural, on the promise of rich reward; and several of the incidents have much similarity. The magician knows he cannot himself go into the hole wherein lies the lamp, and inveigles Aladdin to enter it for him. Within the cavern, Aladdin finds three halls, much as the soldier finds three chambers—which, incidentally, do not feature in the folktale "Aanden i Lyset." Aladdin's discovery of the lamp, his enriching himself with the treasure he finds, and his refusal to hand over the lamp to the magician, are all actions paralleled by the soldier. (If indignation was allowed to be expressed on behalf of witches and wicked magicians, here, surely, are deserving cases, for both old crone and the magician offered their helpers generous rewards.) Finally, each of these slightly disreputable heroes wins himself a beautiful princess with the aid of his stolen luminant.

The Tinder Box[2]

Once upon a time, a soldier came marching along on the highway. He had his knapsack upon his back, and his sword by his side; for he came from the wars, and was going home. Presently an old witch met him; she was a loathsome-looking creature; for her underlip hung down over her chin.

"Good evening, soldier!" said she. "What a fine sword you've got, and what a large knapsack! You look truly like a brave soldier; and therefore you shall have as much money as you can wish for!"

"Thank ye, old witch!" replied the soldier.

"D'ye see the great tree yonder?" asked she, pointing to a stout oak that stood by the wayside. "That tree is quite hollow; and if you climb up to the top, you will see a hole in the

---

[2]This text is the first translation of "Fyrtoiet," which was made by Charles Boner, and included in *A Danish Story-Book*, 1846.

trunk through which you can slide down and get to the very bottom of the tree. I'll tie a rope around your body, that I may be able to pull you up again when you call."

"And what have I to do with down in the tree?" asked the soldier.

"To fetch money, to be sure! What else do you think!" continued the witch. "But you must know, that when you have got to the bottom of the oak, you'll find yourself in a large hall, lighted by a hundred lamps.[3] There you will see three doors, all of which you can open, for the key is in every one of them. If you enter the first door, you'll come into a chamber, in the middle of which, on the floor, a great money-chest stands, but which is guarded by a dog with eyes as large as tea-cups; but that you need not mind. I'll give you my coloured apron; you must spread it out on the floor, and then you may bodily lay hold of the dog and put him on it; after which you can take out of the chest as many halfpence as you please. But if you want silver, you must go into the second chamber. However, here sits a dog upon the chest, with a pair of eyes as large as mill-wheels; but that you need not mind: put the dog on the apron, and take as much silver as you please. But if you would rather have gold, you must go into the third chamber, and you can take as much as you can carry. But the dog that guards this money-chest has eyes as large as the Round Tower[4] at Copenhagen. That's a dog for you! But you need not mind him: put him on my apron, and take as many gold pieces out of the chest as you please; the dog won't do you any harm."

"That wouldn't be amiss!" said the soldier. "But what am I to give you, old beldame? For 'tis not very likely you would send me down the hollow tree for nothing!"

"No," said the witch, "I don't ask a farthing! You must only bring up with you the tinder-box that my grandmother forgot the last time she was down there."

---

[3]In my following discussion of the tale I will refer to these lamps as candles, as they were in the earlier versions of the tale.

[4]The Observatory: so called on account of its round form (translator's note).

"Well, give me the rope," said the soldier. "I'll try!"

"Here it is," said the witch; "and here too is my coloured apron."

The soldier now climbed up to the top of the oak, slipped through the hole in the trunk, and stood suddenly in the great hall, which was lighted, exactly as the old witch had told him, by a hundred lamps.

As soon as he had looked round him a little, he found also the three doors, and immediately opened the first. There really sat the dog with eyes as large as tea-cups, and stared at him.

"Ho, ho, my dog!" said the soldier. "Good fellow!" And he spread the witch's apron on the floor, and set the dog upon it. He now opened the money-chest, filled all his pockets with copper halfpence, shut it again, put the staring dog on the cover, and went, with his apron, into the second chamber. Good heavens! There sat the dog with eyes as big as millwheels.

"You should not look at me so fixedly," said he to the dog that was keeping watch; "that weakens the eyes!" He then set the animal on the apron; but when he saw the quantity of silver coin, he threw away the coppers and filled all his pockets and his knapsack with the bright silver. Afterwards he went to the third chamber. Well, that was enough to disgust anybody! The dog really had eyes as large as the Round Tower, and they rolled in his head like turning-wheels.

"Good evening," said the soldier, putting his hand to his cap and saluting in true military style; for such a monster he had never met before. However, after he had looked at him for some moments, he thought it was enough; so he spread out the apron, lifted the enormous dog off the cover, and opened the money-chest.

What heaps of gold he saw! He could have bought all Copenhagen, all the sugar-plums, all the games of soldiers, all the whips and rocking-horses in Europe, with the money! At the first sight of such rich treasure, the soldier threw away all the silver with which he had laden, and stuffed his pockets, knapsack, cap, and boots, so full of gold pieces that he could but just move with the weight. Now he had money in abundance. The tremendous dog was put on the cover again, the door of the chamber shut, and the soldier called up the tree.

"Hallo, old hag! Now, then, pull me up again!"

"Have you got the tinder-box?" said the witch in reply.

"I'll be hanged, if I hadn't nearly forgotten it!" said the soldier. He then put the tinder-box in his pocket; the witch drew him up out of the tree; and he soon was standing again on the highway with all his treasure.

"What do you want with the tinder-box?" asked the soldier.

"That's nothing to you," answered the old hag. "You've got money in plenty; so give me the tinder-box."

"No!" said the soldier. "Tell me directly what you'll do with the tinder-box, or I'll cut your head off with my sword!"

"No," cried the witch. "I won't."

And the soldier instantly drew his sword and chopped her head from her body; so there was an end of her! He then tied up his money in her apron, put the bundle over his shoulder and the tinder-box in his pocket, and trudged off to the next town.

It was a large city; and he went to the first hotel, asked for the best apartments, and ordered the most delicate things for dinner; for he was now a moneyed man.

The waiters, it is true, thought his boots rather strange-looking for so grand a gentleman; but they were of another opinion next morning, after he had been out shopping; for they now had the most elegant boots to clean, and the finest clothing to brush. The soldier had become quite a dandy; he talked of the curiosities of the town, and was told about the King and the beautiful Princess.

"How can I see her?" asked the soldier.

"She is not to be seen," was the answer; "for she lives in a large brazen palace surrounded by many towers and high walls. Only the King visits his daughter; because it has been foretold that the Princess will marry a common soldier, and the King won't hear of such a thing."

"I'd give the world to see the Princess," thought the soldier to himself; but as to getting a permission, it was of no use thinking of such a thing.

Meanwhile he led a merry life; went often to the play, drove about in the royal park, and gave a good deal to the poor. It was praiseworthy of him to be charitable; but he knew well enough by experiences what a poor fellow feels who has not got a penny. He was, moreover, a rich man, had handsome clothes, and many friends, who told him every day that he was an excellent creature, a perfect gentleman; and all this the soldier liked to hear. But as he was always taking from his money and never received any, he had at last but two-pence-halfpenny left. So he was obliged to leave the handsome lodgings he had lived in till now, and to take a small garret, to clean his own boots, and darn and mend his clothes himself when they wanted it. None of his old friends visited him any more; for they could not, of course, go up so many pairs of stairs for his sake.

It was quite dark in his room, and he had not even money enough to buy a candle. Suddenly he remembered that, in the tinder-box which he fetched up from the bottom of the hollow oak, there were a few matches [sic]. He therefore took it, and began to strike a light; but as soon as the sparks flew about, the door of his room was thrown open, and the dog with eyes as large as tea-cups walked in, and said, "What do you please to command?"

"Well done!" cried the soldier, astonished; "that's a capital tinder-box, if I can get all I want with so little trouble! Well, then, my friend," said he to the dog with the staring eyes, "I am in want of money, get me some!" Crack! the dog had vanished, and crack! there he was again standing before the soldier, holding a purse filled with copper coin between his teeth.

Now he perfectly understood how to employ the tinder-box: if he struck with the flint and steel once, then the dog with the copper money appeared; if twice, the one with the silver coin; and if three times, then came the dog that guarded the chest of gold. After this discovery, he returned immediately to his former handsome lodgings; his numerous friends came to him again, and testified their sincere affection and attachment.

"Well," thought the soldier one day to himself, " 'tis very strange that no one may see the beautiful Princess! They say she is a great beauty; but what good will that do her, if she is always to stay shut up in the brazen castle with the numerous towers! I wonder if it really be impossible to see her! Where's my tinder-box? I should like to know if it's only money that he can procure." He struck the flint, and the well-known dog with saucer-eyes stood before him.

"It is midnight, it is true," said he, "but I should like so much to see the Princess only for a moment!"

In a moment the dog was out of the room, and before the soldier thought it possible, he saw him return with the princess, who sat asleep on the dog's back, and was so indescribably beautiful that anybody who saw her would know directly she was a Princess. The soldier could not help it; happen what might, he must give the Princess a kiss, and so he did.

Then the dog ran back again to the palace with the lovely Princess. The next morning at breakfast she told her parents of the curious dream she had had; that she had been riding on a dog, and that a soldier had given her a kiss.

"A very pretty affair indeed!" said the Queen. So now it was agreed that, next night, one of the ladies of the court should watch at the bedside of the Princess, to see into the matter of the dream.

That night the soldier felt a strange longing to see the beautiful Princess in the brazen castle. The dog was therefore despatched, who took her again on his back and ran off with her. But the cunning old lady quickly put on a pair of good walking-boots, and ran after the dog so fast, that she caught sight of him just as he was going into the house where the soldier lived. "Ah, ah!" thought she; "all's right now! I know where he is gone to"; and she made a cross on the street-door with a piece of chalk. Then she went back to the palace, and lay down to sleep. The dog, too, came back with the Princess; and when he remarked that there was a cross on the house where the soldier lived, he made crosses on all the street-doors in town: which was very clever of the animal, for now the lady would not be able to find the right door again.

Early next morning came the King and Queen, the old lady, and all the high officers of the crown, to ascertain where the Princess had gone to in the night.

"Here's the house!" exclaimed the King, when he saw the first door that had a cross on it.

"No, it must be here, my dear," said the Queen, perceiving the next house with a white cross.

The Queen, however, was an exceedingly clever woman. She knew something more than merely how to sit in a carriage with an air; and therefore she soon found out a way to come on the traces of the dog. She took a whole piece of silk, cut it in two with a pair of golden scissors, and with the pieces made a bag. This bag she had filled with the most finely sifted flour, and tied it with her own hands round the Princess's neck. When this was done, she took her golden scissors and cut a small hole in the bag, just large enough to let the flour run slowly out when the Princess moved.

The dog came again in the night, took the Princess on his back, and ran off with her to the soldier, who wanted so much only to look at her, and who would have given any thing to be a Prince, so that he might marry the Princess.

But the dog did not observe that his track from the palace to the soldier's house was marked with the flour that had run out of the bag. On the following morning, the King and the Queen now saw where their daughter had been; and had the soldier arrested and put into prison.

There sat the poor soldier, and it was so dark too in his cell; besides, the gaoler told him that he was to be hanged on the morrow. That was indeed no very pleasant news for the soldier; and, more unfortunate than all, he had left his tinder-box at the hotel. When day broke he could see out of his little prison window how the people were streaming from the town to see the execution; he heard the drums beat, and saw the soldiers marching to the spot where the scaffold was erected. Among the crowd was a little apprentice, who was in such a hurry that he lost one of his shoes just as he was running by the prison.

"Hallo, my little man!" cried the soldier to the boy: "You need not be in such a hurry; for nothing can be done till I come! If you will run to the inn, at the sign of the Golden Angel, and fetch me a tinder-box that I left behind in my room, I'll give you a groat for your trouble;—but you must make all the haste you can!"

The boy wanted very much to get the groat; so off he ran to the Golden Angel, found the tinder-box as described in the soldier's room, and brought it to him to his grated window. Now let us see what happened.

Outside the town a high gallows had been erected, which was surrounded by a quantity of soldiers, and thousands of people occupied the large field. The King and Queen sat on a splendid throne that had been erected for them, opposite the judges and the councillors.

The soldier was already on the highest step of the ladder, and the executioner was just about to put the rope round his neck, when he implored that they would grant him, poor sinner that he was, one last wish. He had, he said, a great longing to smoke a pipe of tobacco, and as this was the last act of grace he should ask for in this world, he hoped they would not refuse him.

But the King would not accede to it:[5] so the soldier took out his flint and steel, and struck one, two, three times; when presently all three enchanted dogs stood before him; the one with the saucer-eyes, as well as the other two with eyes like a mill-wheel, or the Round Tower at Copenhagen.

---

[5]The text is here incorrectly translated. In the original, the old soldier remarked that before being executed a prisoner always had the right to ask one harmless favor; and the king did not like to say no.

"Help me out of my difficulty!" called the soldier to the dogs. "Don't let them hang me!" Immediately the three frightful dogs fell on the judge and the councillors, seized one by the leg, another by the nose, and tossed them up in the air, so that in tumbling down they were dashed to pieces.

"We are not graciously pleased—" cried the King; but the dogs cared little for that, and took King and Queen, one after the other, and tossed them like the rest in the air. Then the soldiers grew frightened; and the people called out, "Good soldier, you shall be our King, and you shall have the beautiful Princess for a wife!"

Then the soldier seated himself in the King's carriage, and all three dogs danced in front of it, and shouted "Hurrah!" The boys in the street whistled, and the soldiers presented arms.

Now the Princess was liberated from the brazen castle, and was made Queen, which she liked very much. The wedding festivities lasted eight days, and the dogs seated themselves at table, and stared with their great eyes.

The Tale Begins

Now we can begin to examine the tale for symbolic and psychological meanings and the messages for manhood. As the tale begins, we find a soldier marching along the highway going home from the wars. He has his sword and his knapsack. We note in this simple beginning that this tale, like most fairy tales, does not happen in a particular time or place. Often tales indicate this universal quality by opening with "once upon a time." When this form of opening is authentic, it is one of the first indications to mythologists that the tale is one connected to timeless human experience. The tale begins with a male as the central character, thus giving us the additional clue that this is a tale dealing with some portion of the masculine individuation process.

Now in olden times the highway was not a common road. It was a special road under the protection of the king, so it was presumed to be safe. This king in fairy tales represents a number of things, as we shall see later. He stands for the father, the status quo, and conventional as well as cultural values. Thus we could say the soldier is following the conventional safe road into manhood. A parallel to this pattern is reflected in my own life and the lives of some of my contemporaries. As I mentioned earlier, when I finished high school in the 50s, I followed the advice of my father and high school counselors and attended a good college in order to have a secure future and to be assured of the ability to support a family. I followed the conventional road of my time expecting to have a successful career, a house in the suburbs and to live happily and productively. The culture always seems to offer security to those who choose to follow its direction. The highway here suggests an orientation toward life that is traditional in form.

The soldier is an interesting figure as the beginning character in the tale. He is not a prince, a child, or a fool. Nothing is special about him or his birth. He is not even an officer, a knight, or a hero. He is ordinary and in this vein represents all men, our basic masculinity, and the potential contained in this masculinity. We shall see this potential develop as the tale proceeds. In general the soldier is a protector and defender of the culture and its values. Psychologically he does this soldiering in an unconscious manner, following the orders of officers and kings.

As a psychological figure in the story, the soldier represents the "ego" of Western man and the "I" experiencing the story. As the soldier's journey unfolds, so will a path illustrating growth and individuation.

The fact that the soldier is a grown man in this story is an important feature. The issue of a boy becoming a man in our culture is a serious problem (our culture has lost its ritual elders and rites of passage for young men), but it is a different problem from the one dealt with in this story. Men are going to have to solve some of the problems of manhood before we can again figure out how to bring boys into it. The fact that the soldier is already a man shows that he has an identity and is capable of performing the basic business of living. He is capable of carrying out his identity in a sustained way and of carrying out life's functions with a certain amount of courage and effectiveness. Psychologically speaking, he has developed some ego strength. This strength is necessary for a man to confront and integrate both his own inner life and the outer world, but it does not mean he is psychologically a fully developed man. His possession of a sword and knapsack symbolizes these strengths. He has what he needs to be self-sufficient at this point.

In the process of developing ego identity as young adults, we all go through a process, beginning in early childhood, of selecting certain portions of our personality that become our preferred way of dealing with the world. These are usually based on the norms of society and are reinforced by our parents and social institutions as we grow up. During this process other qualities that could have been ego, but did not fit the perceived norms, are rejected and repressed into the shadow or dark (unconscious) side of the personality. A simple illustration may help clarify this process of selection.

Bobby and Susy, two toddlers, are playing together. Susy reaches over and snatches a toy out of Bobby's hand. Bobby responds by smacking her. As he smacks her, his mother walks in, sees him hit Susy, and Susy dramatically starts crying. Bobby's mother grabs him, perhaps shakes him a little, scolds him and sends him to his room to think about what a *bad* boy he has been. In his room, Bobby feels discriminated against, isolated, and unhappy. He knows or imagines that mother is now out there comforting Susy. If this sort of thing happens often enough, it will affect the development of Bobby's personality. He learns to repress his spontaneous, angry, and self-defensive behavior, and seeks approval by appearing to be a "nice" boy. Please don't misunderstand my point and think I mean Bobby should grow up smacking people. I am oversimplifying in order to illustrate my point.

Furthermore, Bobby may learn to become passive-aggressive in expressing his anger, keeping his anger unconscious, while "accidentally" bumping into Susy, or breaking something of hers. Bobby may also learn to be sneaky, reaching over and giving Susy a big pinch when mother isn't looking. If Bobby continues developing in this way, he will form one type of what psychologists call a *negative mother complex* as part of his personality. Under the influence of that complex, Bobby will become anxious and self-critical whenever he acts in a spontaneous, angry way and especially when he acts this way with other people, notably women. Bobby's feelings of hurt, anger, rejection and fear are now trapped and living in his unconscious, attaching themselves to each new similar situation, growing larger with each one, until they have an irrational life of their own. The irrational feelings can overwhelm what is otherwise a sensible perspective whenever Bobby unconsciously senses himself in a situation in some vague or distant way reminiscent of the situations that began this whole chain of events.

Under the influence of this complex, Bobby will be passive in conflicts, always trying to please, denying his own feelings to the point he loses touch with them. He will try to find the soft way through life's problems. At the same time, Bobby will build up a reservoir of unconscious anger or in a few cases he may rebel and develop a compensating personality style of belligerence and aggression. You can quickly see how such a complex will affect adult Bobby in relationships, social and work situations. In Jungian psychodynamic terms, Bobby has taken this spontaneous, self-protective energy (that he could have learned to use consciously through the ego as assertiveness, for example, rather than aggression) and repressed it into the unconscious shadow side of his personality. He has adapted by developing an ego position of appearing good and expressing this position in his relationships through his persona (his public face, which I will discuss more fully later).

Of course, reality is much more complicated and the process of selecting personality characteristics is influenced by many people and institutions—fathers, coaches, teachers, friends, relatives, peers, schools, churches, and so on. Mother complexes can take many forms. An opposite form could occur if Bobby's mother thinks he is Mr. Wonderful, can do no wrong, and showers him with praise, admiration, and affection. When he is very young and cute, it is easy for him to elicit these responses. In fact, though, Bobby is now symbiotically fulfilling a psychological need of his mother and will learn as he grows older that he must please her "ideal" in order to keep her favors coming. In this case, Bobby develops a *positive mother complex*, but he still must seek acceptance and love through behaving in a certain way to get approval and special treatment and, in the process, he denies a true part of his personality.

Obviously, to get along in a complicated world we must make choices as to how we will behave. We begin making these choices long before our consciousness is very developed. Naturally, we tend to do what works for us at the time. With maturity the key is to develop enough conscious awareness about ourselves to keep the patterns that are useful to us in expressing our personalities and to discard what is false, destructive, or outdated. The more conscious we become, the better we can discriminate what is honestly in tune with our own individuality and individuation process. Developing consciousness in this manner is difficult and complicated.

Theoretically, other parts of the personality, such as the feminine side, are rarely well-developed in young adulthood. The absence of any other characters in the beginning of the tale reflects psychological repression or a lack of development of these other parts. Please note that being what we call a "soft" male—not having a fully developed masculine identity or having a confused masculine identity—does not mean that the feminine side of a young man has been developed, no matter how sensitive he may appear.

A Look at the Method of Understanding Fairy Tales

If you compare the original tale with what I have been saying, the following points emerge. You can see in the original that the storyteller brings us only the essential ingredients of the tale. These are the ideas that have stood the test of time and represent what is essential for us to learn. The storyteller does not tell us anything about the experiences that go on in the tale. In a novel, for example, we have to reconstruct what the author describes in our mind. In a movie we have simply to follow the author's and the director's construction. In a fairy tale, the storyteller leaves it to us to construct what the experiences are like. We have to use our own imagination, and this is one of the most important parts of the process. Nourishment of the imagination helps us amplify the experiences of the images in the story and connect the message to our personal lives in a way that helps us understand ourselves and our culture.

If we do research in books of symbols, literature, art history and in other stories, we come up with amplifications like the following:

• There is one soldier. The number one is not considered a number by symbolists. It rarely appears, but where it does, it often alludes to the paradisiacal state of unity which preceded good and evil. It may also stand for the masculine principle.

• Soldier traditionally stands for bravery, devotion to a cause, lower rank, and defender of the culture and its principles.

Intuitively we may add that as one soldier, he is alone on this journey on the traditional path (as I am alone, I am one person), apparently secure. But we can see that symbolically he is in a state of oneness, a paradisiacal state, from which we can conclude he is about to confront change and transformation.

This approach to understanding the tale is somewhat classical and academic, but it adds an important depth to some of the symbolic meanings. This academic approach can be tedious at times, so I will try to integrate it with a more personal one.

The second approach is the process of personally and culturally questioning the meaning of the experiences in the tale. I will do this primarily on the cultural level, citing some cases at times to give individual examples. We can take this process forward individually by asking ourselves such questions as the following: How do I soldier in life? Where do I soldier the most? How does this attitude affect me and those around me? How do men in America soldier symbolically? What are your answers to these questions? Sooner or later I am going to address these questions, but the value for you lies in your building your own picture and developing your own point of view versus mine and society's.

These amplifications associate another dimension with the soldier. This dimension reflects a personal/cultural state of mind, one that many consider dominant in American men. Do we still put on armor to venture into the world? American men seem to keep on marching even when they are depressed, unhappily telling themselves repeatedly that they are "fine" and numbing themselves until something burns out, often their sexual potency or their heart. Soldiering is doing the right thing, the expected thing, the sensible thing, the supportive thing. We soldier without thinking, unconsciously, going with the crowd, following the prevailing winds and attitudes of our families and culture. Sometimes from laziness or fear, but often never realizing we have the opportunity to think for ourselves and dare to be out of step with the stereotypes. We delude ourselves into thinking we are happy if we can fulfill a stereotype successfully. Occasionally, fits of temper, sexuality (affairs), or mid-life crazies burst out as our repressed sides—our shadow and feminine sides—cry out for recognition. But to most "normal" people, the important thing is to control these outbursts and get back to soldiering.

In the 1950s, men armored themselves (emotionally, psychologically, and often in muscular rigidity) to go out and fight the daily battle in the business world. They had difficulty taking the armor off in order to relate to those close to them and even realizing that they were armored. The new male, the soft man, the Peter Pan, the pseudo-liberated man, has simply changed or enlarged the parade ground on which he marches. He has added the marching ground of personal relationships, not out of ignorance like the 1950s man, but out of defensiveness. He marches on, trying to produce multiple orgasms, splitting household duties, sharing careers and so forth, to please women, still not looking inside the armor to his own depths and needs. He still thinks he can be happy if there are women in his life and the women are happy, or if he can have sex and keep the woman outside the armor, avoiding the dangers of emotional entanglement.

But is a soldier always a soldier and nothing else? My personal experience and that of those I work with have taught me that regardless of age, soldiering can be a good *precondition for change* if we can heed the call to transformation. Too often a man's "call" today comes in the guise of divorce, acting-out kids or illness. The next chapter shows how the soldier in our story receives this call.

You can see, as we integrate the classical and the personal methods of exploring the symbolic meanings based on the essentials of the tale, our position has changed. We have changed from listeners to those who, in truth, are telling the story to ourselves. I hope you add your ideas to mine and discard mine when they do not agree with yours.

5

THE
WITCH APPEARS

As we return to the tale, the soldier is still walking along the traditional highway—the highway of life. Presently an old witch meets him. She is a loathsome-looking creature, but she greets him with flattery, telling him he will have as much money as he could wish for if he follows her instructions.

Everyone knows that fairy tales are full of witches. Young and old, we are enthralled by them. Witches persist in our imaginations, wonderful figures, full of secret knowledge, powerful magic, hidden ambitions and cackling revenge. In stories old and new, whether she is old and ugly or young and seductive, she beguiles us with a fascination for evil and the dark mysterious side of life. But why does this witch turn up now with such a shocking appearance?

Psychologically, the years of childhood are considered to be the years when individuals slowly become aware of the world and themselves. As we get older and more consciousness develops, we begin to build our egos and inner strength and adapt to the world. This process involves a number of painful shocks as we realize our separateness, and the imperfection of the world. These shocks are necessary as the catalyzing agent in our conscious development. The appearance of the witch represents one of these shocks coming our way in adulthood. She is like the serpent in Eden and will challenge the soldier's conscious orientation toward life. Her dark and ugly appearance actually represents a call to higher consciousness, as the appearance of something dark and ugly usually does in fairy tales. If the soldier accepts the proposal, accepts the call, he will find that he has to divert energy from his life's journey. When he does, he will find the treasure of self-realization through some form of the ugly feminine. But that is getting ahead of ourselves.

What are these calls like, and what does it mean to have a call to higher consciousness? The form of these calls depends on our personal psychological development. Jung roughly divided this development into two stages. The first stage is in early adulthood when the young man finishes the ego development that began in childhood. During this stage, his energy is directed outward toward establishing his identity through action and achievement. In the second stage he begins to redirect his energy inward, reclaiming the parts of his personality that were lost in the first stage and developing a deeper, fuller orientation toward life. Traditionally, changing into the second stage correlated roughly with reaching middle age. Although that timing often fits, our culture has become more complicated, and it is simpler to say mid-life in our psychological development.

Psychological mid-life is the time when we begin to turn inward to a more mature and spiritual orientation as we sense the ending of our physical life. This is the time, for example, when a Native American began the transition from brave to "grandfather," becoming one of the wise old men of the tribe. Our current so-called "mid-life crisis" often represents just as important a call, but in reality is often a call to achieve the personal identity we failed to clearly develop in adolescence. In fact, this is a call echoed in the physical and psychological symptoms men have that I will discuss throughout this book. This call, if a man has the courage to truly answer it, demands that he look back and ask, "At what point did I betray my own existence and begin turning my energy against myself?"

Some men get to psychological mid-life at a young age, and some men never get there. Most of us continue going through both stages in a spiraling manner with the first stage decreasing and the second increasing. These calls to a higher or deeper consciousness are the shocks or opportunities we get to help us along in these stages.

Some of these calls in both stages of life are normal, and we naturally seem to run into them. Getting married, having a child, choosing a career and getting the first big job are examples of these. Other examples seem more cruel and often unfair: the loss of a job, a loved one, divorce, or the illness of someone we love. Some calls are more inner-oriented, such as overcoming handicaps from childhood or dealing with depression. Most of us experience a great deal of emotional intensity in childhood that culminates in late adolescence when many are interested in spiritual and cultural values. In the pressures of everyday adult life we tend to repress these concerns, and they may become lost in the rush into early adulthood. This loss may become a smouldering wound which flares up later.

The calls in the second half of life may also come in external ways such as divorce, an acting-out child, loss of a job, or the illness or death of a loved one. However, there is another situation familiar to most therapists. It begins with small ailments such as headaches, anxiety attacks, fatigue at work and increased moodiness. If these are not attended to, they may escalate into alcoholism, obesity, use of tranquilizers, sexual difficulties, heart attacks and changes in jobs and spouses. Something has happened to shake our values in the old systems. The therapist then finds a successful man sitting in front of him who seems to have everything a man in the conventional world would want, but who is miserable. His life lacks meaning; he cannot figure out what his wife wants from him, or he cannot control his teenager, and everything he does seems to make matters worse.

When these events come along, we have a choice. We can listen to them or shut them out. We can choose to ignore them and go right on soldiering down the highway, being a good lawyer, doctor, businessman, minister, college professor—a typical 20th-century male. But the Self I discussed earlier (our whole personality including our inborn urge to grow) may not stand for this kind of stagnation. This Self is determined to create psychological growth and will continue to repeat certain calls and escalate predicaments and ailments until they get renewed attention. Of course, we have additional options: we can stiffen and rigidify our attitudes, cling to the highway and perhaps even become a pillar in the community—in effect a pillar of the past. Becoming fundamentalist in religious attitude works well for some. Many men today seem sophisticated enough to realize something important is going on, but are frightened of confronting it. They try to placate it by following the latest trends in health and psychology. They do everything from jogging to attending the newest pop psychology workshop that comes along. Most of us can tell the difference between the jogger who enjoys his health and body, and the one who is running away from himself as fast as he can.

Too many men and women come to therapy, marriage, or family counseling wanting a quick solution to get everyone back on the highway without having to take a deep look at themselves. They come into our offices appearing sincere, caring, and hurting. But if it seems they might have to do some painful digging into their own depths, then they look for another therapist. They want a therapist who can give them a "prescription." They are looking for a cop-out. They want to be able to say, "I did what I was supposed to do—I asked an expert," and now he is to blame. Often, these people end up saying, "I went to three (or more) marriage counselors and still got divorced," or, "I spent a fortune on that psychologist and Johnny still got kicked out of school and now all he does is sit around over at his mother's smoking dope." The problem is John senior, because usually "good" John wants to find a soft way through this mess. He wants to find a way that avoids confrontation and is guilt-free. Good John especially wants to avoid how his chicken-hearted approach to life has contributed to the situation. The fact is that these symptoms/calls require deeply committed personal responses.

The witch is one of the common threads running throughout a man's developing life. We have to meet her at least twice in life, though not necessarily in the same form.

In our fairy tale, the soldier immediately takes up the witch's offer. This action is natural, the way nature intends us to act. *We should answer the call.* It will certainly involve suffering and changes, but we all face these things whether we like it or not. Psychologically, once the witch appears and the soldier accepts her offer, the stage is set for action and growth.

The Witch

Symbols are so fundamentally human that their existence is virtually self-evident. It has been said that to be human is to symbolize, as is evidenced by centuries of art, literature, philosophy, and religion. In psychology, symbols have a profound meaning, but we have slipped into giving them easy meanings as repressed material. We must be careful not to be too simplistic when we search for symbolic meanings. Symbolic figures must help us increase our self-understanding or synthesize what we know into new meanings. If they do not, then we have just played an entertaining game, a "Trivial Pursuit of the Mind." Being good at this game may make us feel more in control, but does not really help us live more honestly and effectively. Many *insight* oriented therapists fall into this trap. These therapists generate a never-ending stream of insights into their clients' personalities and then consider these clients "resistant" because they do not change. These therapists flourish in public mental health clinics and hospitals because they always sound like they know what they're talking about. The meaning of the witch in our tale must go beyond the elementary significance she may represent—our fear of mother, or our own bad feelings about our mother that we have repressed. The image of the witch invites a closer examination than the few sentences I wrote about her in the previous section.

The witch's positive aspect is that she challenges us to greater consciousness. Why this paradox, the ugly old witch challenging us to grow as men? What is her meaning as part of our personality?

If we look back far enough into history, we find that the term witch originally meant wise old woman. She was the descendant of priestesses in the service of the great goddess. Marion Zimmer Bradley tells an interesting story of the recession of the great goddess (the chthonic feminine) in *The Mists of Avalon*[1] as the masculine/Christian/logos principle developed in the time of King Arthur.

Please forgive me for I must once again take time out to vent some of my frustration about modern learning techniques. Our modus operandi for using words is to become increasingly reductive, supposedly seeking simplicity and clarity (with the exception of those who write instructions for assembling any kind of toy or household machinery). There are some dangers in this reductive process. We often are reductive to relieve anxiety or because we are lazy. Reducing experience to words enables us to avoid many perplexing subjective issues. Moreover, once we have reduced our experience to words, we seem to feel we have some control over the situation. We also think we should be able to quickly read and understand everything in one shot—the "USA Today" approach to learning. This approach ignores the fact that life is complicated and that if we attempt to truly write about it, then the writing is complicated, and we must be willing to *study* it if we want to understand what is being said (philosophers and theologians have always struggled with this fact). In the wake of these attitudes toward word usage we find ourselves thinking in reductive, simplistic and cliched ways. For example, the term "repressed into the unconscious" has become so common that most people who use the term, including many psychologists, have no awareness of the elaborate theoretical nature of this expression and its implications.

---

[1]Marion Zimmer Bradley, *The Mists of Avalon* (New York: Ballantine, 1982).

Now that I have said all of the above, please note that preceding this discussion I used the word *chthonic*. I like this word and will continue to use it because I think it gives a special flavor to characteristics that have become buried in our unconscious due to the development of our culture and our personal and collective adjustments to societal norms. This word *chthonic* expands rather than reduces the meaning of repression. The chthonic feminine consists of feminine characteristics that are primitive, pagan, earthy, and instinctual— characteristics that are banished under the earth into the underground of the unconscious with the ascendance of rational Western thought.

Now back to our search for the meaning of the witch where I left off with Marion Zimmer Bradley. She tells a beautiful story illustrating the recession of the chthonic feminine into the mists of Avalon (the unconscious) in the face of the developing masculine/Christian/logos principle personified by King Arthur and his reign (the Western version of Yang). As these masculine principles developed, the witch became very different. She has become the opposite of the motherly figure who always feeds us and gives herself ceaselessly to others. The witch does not feed others; she feeds on them, especially living by devouring children or stealing a man's masculinity. She is the opposite of the life principle. Her energy flows inward not outward, down to feed the dark recesses of a woman's psyche or a man's anima. In our case, we will be talking about the man's anima, his own feminine side.

Whenever we're soldiering along as men, the witch is liable to pop up. She comes in response to our having a conscious attitude that is too masculine in some way. In other words, we are unconsciously pursuing a course that has too much Yang. We are out of balance. The witch may be reflected by a real woman in our life. It may be a wife, or lover, or even a secretary, or a woman co-worker who starts acting witchy. I once asked a woman who was in marital therapy why she was acting like such a witch to her husband. She replied with tears springing to her eyes, "I hate it! I don't know any way to get him to express a feeling!" This husband insisted on being so detached and objective (also protecting his image of "good" and "mature") that he had lost touch with the feelings that make us human. She was becoming witchy, an inhuman extreme, in an unconscious attempt to contact him emotionally. This explanation is for men. The women I know already understand this situation very well.

The witch can catch us in another way, too. We can become so caught up in our own moodiness or depression, that we are bewitched out of our masculine ability to discriminate and to act. These situations represent ways our feminine side compensates by turning on us when our attitudes are too one-sided. Still another witch all men have to deal with is the psychological image of mother.

The soft-man, the Peter Pan and the pseudo-liberated man have not dealt with this image successfully, and such men get little help from our culture and other men. When Jung speaks of the anima, he considers her the "archetype of living,"[2] meaning she conveys to man his joy of living, his creativity and much of his vital activity. The anima embodies the experience and manifestation of all that is feminine in a man, and is a bridge or spiritual guide into the depths of his personality. This may include such tendencies in our personality as vague feelings, moods, intuitions, receptivity, romantic love, and feelings for nature. She, the anima, is a deep psychological figure that in her positive form can inspire us and in her negative form can destroy us. This part of our personality develops in four or five stages throughout our lifetime.

Mother, with all her attributes, is the first image of the feminine we get. If the boy has trouble differentiating from that image, whether it is good or bad, it eventually turns into a psychological complex, a mother-complex, a witch that affects both how he relates to himself and to real women.

---

[2] C. G. Jung, Collected Works, Vol. 9i, *Archetypes and the Collective Unconscious*, Bollingen Series, Vol. XX, ¶. 66.

Earlier, I discussed how men can develop either a positive or a negative mother complex using the example of Bobby and Susy. This example illustrated the development of a *personal* mother complex. Now I would like to explore another kind of mother complex, the *cultural* mother complex. Men can experience either the personal, the cultural, or both. At this point it is easy to see how confusing this situation is, and you can imagine how one complex can compound the other. In fact, the cultural mother complex can have a strong influence on the development of a man's personality just as the patriarchy has affected women's development. The cultural mother complex results from adopting societal attitudes and behaviors. Andrew Samuels' description of today's men behaving in nourishing ways to please women reflects this cultural mother complex.[3]

Understanding how the culture fosters this complex in different ways is important if we want to understand our development. The loss of touch between boys and men and the loss of initiation rites into manhood are crucial. If boys are primarily raised by women for the first twelve to fifteen years of their lives, being taught to please and obey women, how can they possibly avoid a mother complex? They are mama's boys. Momism is also fostered by the patriarchal attitude men and the culture (including many women) have had toward women. It works like this: women in an unconscious way have carried the narrow, patriarchal sanction as men projected their own capacities for feelings and values onto women in an idealistic fashion. The American man has tended to be passive with his woman, placating her with everything from furs to appliances—material things. He dodged true relationship with his wife, preferring work or "the boys," at the same time attempting to get her to manage and mother him. Both sexes collaborated in the process. It makes sense for a

---

[3] Andrew Samuels, editor, *The Father: Contemporary Jungian Perspectives* (London: Free Association, 1985), p. 6.

woman to want power, even if surreptitious, if the possibilities for relationship are closed or limited.

In real women, the feminine can also turn negative and let the masculine side take over. In this case the negative mother complex can come forth in the woman and be veiled by her masculine side. She becomes aggressive and demanding. Interestingly, she usurps the patriarchal form, but with no true spirit or meaning. All too often, many single mothers are led into an emotional war with their adolescent sons because the mother's masculinity is the only adult masculinity in the home, and it occurs in this negative form because the mothers are desperate. They are trying to mother and father their sons, and no true masculinity can arise in this family setting. The boy sees any aggressive, demanding tendencies not balanced by the masculine or feminine spirit as severely threatening his own growing identity, and he fights back with everything he has, even threatening violence. He will go to almost any acting-out extreme in this situation. If the mother tries to balance this fight with her feminine side, switching suddenly from being aggressive and demanding to being concerned and nurturing, he thinks she is crazy or that she does not know what she wants or is trying to keep him a child. The only hope I see for a woman caught in this dilemma is to send the boy to live with his dad, or to get the help of a good male therapist who understands this process. A lover or new husband can rarely handle this problem.

Two other problems develop in men who are living to please women. They fail to develop their own feminine sides and miss the fullness these sides can bring to life. Even worse is the unconscious backlash this sets up in men's psyches. Men who are serving women in a shallow and manipulative way hate the fact that they are being emasculated on a subliminal level, and build up a reservoir of unconscious rage against women. Women often sense this underlying rage. Even though they know and appreciate that he has been so "good" and so "supportive," they have a vague sense of uneasiness, waiting for the other shoe to drop. These women are subliminally aware that their men have put on their supportive behavior like a suit of clothes, to protect themselves and to impress others. One of these days this behavior will wear out and anger or retribution may come bursting through.

To be truly supportive means listening and responding with warmth and understanding, and not offering solutions until they are invited. But you must not do this in the role of a comforting "mother" or "father" to your wife or girlfriend (or to other adult friends). You must keep an eye on your own position and function in this situation, maintaining the integrity of your own personality, and dealing honestly with your own emotions. In other words, be supportive in the context of a fully human interaction, where the other person knows and meets the human being inside of you, and not just the one-dimensional role of a pseudo-parent or -therapist. There is more to come on relating with depth, authenticity, and feeling in the second half of this book.

We may view all mother complexes as either negative or positive. The first develops out of fear, and the second develops out of need. The negative mother complex is an image a man carries of the critical mother. She can show up to puncture his balloon when he is most successful, and she can show up when he is feeling down to make him feel worse. As much as he tries to serve and appease, he is never good enough for her, and when he is successful, he feels like an impostor deep down inside. This image often feeds on the notion that men are basically flawed and have gotten the world into an awful mess. This mother-image is commonly characterized as devouring and castrating. The man who lives in the power of this image has a need to serve that makes him over-cautious, holds him back from adventure, and opposes his romantic notions. A man possessed by these emotions also feels guilty and unlovable. Sadly, he has a hard time relating to women because he is afraid of them, afraid they will all turn into negative mothers.

In the positive mother complex we see the other extreme. The man with this complex has been so close to mother and loves her so much that he is afraid if he gets too close, he will get swallowed up, so he keeps a distance. Often, as an adult, he is lazy and self-centered in relationships. The need or the enjoyment of being loved and cared for can seduce him out of his masculinity. As you can imagine, he also has trouble relating to women. Men stuck in this complex may try to manipulate women to mother them emotionally and then act out, almost like adolescent boys, to gain distance in the relationship. For example, such a man may surprise his wife by buying a new car he had not discussed with her and that was not in the budget.

Interestingly enough, however, in my experience a man with a positive mother complex is the one most potentially capable of developing a very deep and intimate relationship with a woman. Women often intuit this but, unfortunately, until the man deals with this problem, the closer she tries to get, the more frightened he becomes.

As a boy grows up, emotional and spiritual growth is deeply affected by his relationship to his mother. She is the first feminine figure in his life and his experience of her imprints how he will form his own feminine side and ultimately relate to women. He will get his deepest ideas of what is desirable as feminine from his mother. The way she relates to his masculinity will affect the way he grows into manhood. A mother who does not like or trust men can alienate her son from his masculine identity. A quiet, long-suffering mother may well produce a quiet, long-suffering son. A mother who is too good can cause a son to put women on a pedestal.

Joseph Campbell illustrates what happens when men try to live the ideals of their personal and the collective mother, and how this process leaves women hungry for love and intimacy:

> We remain fixated to the unexorcised images of our infancy, hence disinclined to the necessary passages of adulthood. In the United States there is even a pathos of inverted emphasis: the goal is not to grow old, but to remain young; not to mature away from

Mother, but to cleave to her. And so, while husbands are worshipping at their boyhood shrines, being the lawyers, merchants or masterminds their parents wanted them to be, their wives even after 14 years of marriage and two fine children produced and raised are still on the search for love. . . .[4]

Naturally, boys must separate from their mothers as they develop from childhood onward. Today, most boys do not make the separation from mother and the transition into manhood in a healthy way. In effect, if the personal mother complex doesn't get them, then the cultural mother complex does. With our loss of rituals and initiations into manhood, our absent fathers, and our general lack of understanding of what masculinity is, the boy is sure to meet the witch. The witch now has three different forms: 1) the cultural mother complex; 2) the negative personal mother complex; and 3) the positive personal mother complex. By adulthood the last two have become images in our personality and may or may not reflect the totality of our real mother.

---

[4]Joseph Campbell, *The Hero with a Thousand Faces* (Princeton, NJ: Princeton University Press, 1973), p. 11.

6

JOURNEY
INTO THE EARTH

As we move further into the fairy tale, we are in the portion richest in ancient symbolism. This part is the most complex symbolically and the most difficult to grasp, partly because these rich ancient symbols are metaphorically connected to our deepest psychic structures and processes. The modern mind has difficulty grasping both the symbols and the processes because, at first, it is difficult to connect them to our immediate experience of living. But if you follow closely, I think you will begin to understand and enjoy them by the end of this chapter as their powerful connections reveal themselves.

In the story, the witch has offered the soldier a bargain that will give him all the money he wants—something every adult would like. He is to climb down into the earth through an oak tree while still attached to her with a rope. There he will find himself in a large hall lighted by a hundred candles. In the hall he will see three doors, each with a key in it; through each door he will find a chest of money. The first room will contain money made of copper, the second of silver, and the third of gold. Each chest will be guarded by a dog. The first dog has eyes as big as teacups. The second dog has eyes as large as mill-wheels, and the third dog has eyes as large as the Round Tower at Copenhagen. In order to protect himself from the dogs, the soldier must in each case place the witch's apron on the floor next to the chest and put the dog on it. The soldier may then take as much of the money as he wants.

Not fully trusting the witch, he asks what is in it for her. She replies "not a cent." All she wants is a tinder box her grandmother left the last time she was down there.

Of course, the soldier goes from room to room following her instructions, filling and then emptying his pockets and knapsack until he fills them finally with gold in the last room. Then in his excitement over the money, he almost forgets the tinder box.

Let us pause to examine the symbols one at a time, to see what each means in our journey as men and to find common themes in them.

The Rope

For this experience the soldier needs to remain tied to the witch. Likewise, as we have our first experiences of real masculinity, the primitive, instinctual masculine, we are still bound to the mother. This happens twice in our lives for sure, and if we are not careful, this bondage can continue indefinitely. The first experience is in early adolescence and the second in early adulthood, usually around the time of a first job or marriage. The beginning change of adolescent boys from the passivity of childhood to the activity of young adulthood is easy to see: they launch into this transition by the use of resistance and defiance. Wise adults know adolescents need to struggle, but they also need firm limits. Such limits contain them because they have not gained control of their budding masculinity and do not know how to direct it. Mothers of boys this age are familiar with the scornful replies their concern and helpful comments elicit. The adolescent has to destroy the myth of a happy, nurturing family in order to gain his identity. Paradoxically, during this process he must actually maintain the same myth in order to have the strength to separate without feeling abandoned and lost in the earth.

The second stage, in early adulthood, is also a transition period, but one with fewer violent emotional swings. This transition leads to a more active and independent stage: for example, young men finishing college or training and getting jobs, finishing tours in the armed services and getting out on their own, or getting married and having their lives turn from being relatively carefree to rather serious.

Being tied—the rope!—to the nurturing environment of the past is helpful in both these stages. On a personal note, when I was away at college and working, I felt adult and independent, but part of me held onto the security of knowing I still had a room at home and a family for holidays. I'm sure many of you felt the same.

The Oak Tree and the Earth

The soldier is on his way, even though he does not realize it. Now we can say that the soldier is beginning to represent the figure of a hero, an image that has deep significance for us. Every ordinary man has to muster a heroic part of his personality to undertake the journey in this tale and in his own life. Fortunately or unfortunately, depending on your perspective, we usually begin this journey naively, with little conscious awareness of what we are doing. The soldier is not aware this is a journey, especially one that will affect his whole life. He just thinks it sounds like a good deal. A lot of us feel this way when we are approaching manhood/adulthood. One clue that the soldier is equipped to be a hero is his sword. We also know that he has the potential to become the future king if he follows his fate. Remember that psychologically he represents the "I-entity," the ego part of all of us journeying on our road to development.

One of the oldest and most primitive rites of passage known is an individual crawling through a hollow tree or log. The journey from one end to the other constitutes the rite of passage. And whenever we make these journeys, or transitions, we hope to come out the other end with stronger possibilities in our personality.

What of the tree? The image of the tree firmly implanted in the nourishing earth, rising into the air, extending its branches, blooming and receding throughout the seasons, has always stirred our imagination. We have many references to trees in our everyday language—"sturdy as a tree," "solid as an oak," and so on. In psychology we know that our inner vision of a tree often represents how we are experiencing our lives. The draw-a-tree exercise is one of the most common projective diagnostic techniques used by psychologists. It is particularly good with children who have not yet learned to build the protective walls we hide behind. This useful diagnostic technique is based on the timeless symbolism trees have for us.

Passing through the tree is a symbol of rebirth. Eric Neumann tells us that the motherhood of the tree represents not only nourishment, but also comprises generation, the bringing into being of many masculine characteristics.[1] The sun is born from the tree goddess; Adonis was born from a tree. Osiris, the ancient Egyptian god, was a tree god. The tree also represents life. It shades and shelters many living things and often feeds them. Trees replenish the very air we breathe, and as we look to the future we are beginning to become alarmed at our loss of them. People living in our cities long for trees and plant and pot them in every little space they can. Their atmosphere is nourishing to us in every sense of the word. Druids worshipped them, and Greek mythology is full of sacred groves.

Trees also represent death. Many primitive people buried their dead in trees. Until recent times we buried our dead in coffins made of trees. In my heart I would rather be buried in a pine box in the mountain forests of my home state than in the steel and concrete boxes in current use. The gallows tree is another old symbol, certainly familiar in our history of the South and West.

The tree traditionally is a religious symbol as well, beginning with the tree of knowledge in the Garden of Eden and extending to Christ hanging on the cross, the tree of death. Here is one of the contradictory notions coming from the nature of

---

[1]Eric Neumann, *The Great Mother: An Analysis of the Archetype* (Princeton, NJ: Princeton University Press, 1955), pp. 48–53.

the tree. Christ on the cross represents the fruit of suffering and the promise of resurrection and rebirth, much as the tree moves from summer to autumn to winter and then to spring. The tree rooted in the depths is a symbol of destiny and new life.

The tree is also a masculine phallic symbol: the switch, the limb, perhaps even the serpent living in its branches may also have the same potential. But Neumann[2] adds that in the character of the tree the male is "contained," retaining his dependency on the Great Mother, the feminine earth-womb character. Think of this the next time you comment on how strong or sturdy a man is, and wonder where the great goddess touched him, or still holds him in her power.

As we see the soldier passing through the tree, into the earth and returning, we may feel that we already have a good sense of the symbolic meaning of the earth based on our discussion of the tree. Most of us have heard that many primitive cultures, including that of Native Americans, referred to the *earth* as *mother*, and the *sky* as *father*. However, not every culture took this view. In Egypt it was the opposite. Geb (the earth principle) is masculine, and Nut (the sky principle) is feminine. To say the earth represents the Great Mother nourishing us all or the basic feminine principle is too simple a definition for our story. Most importantly, in my opinion, the *earth* also represents the metaphor of our *deep inner-selves* that can either nourish or overwhelm us, and about which we have well-grounded ambivalence. This is the earth of Adam, the container of human nature, and all the potentials of life that have been and can be.

From this history the tree becomes a symbol of the individuation process. The soldier passing through it confirms for us that he is beginning his personal journey of self-realization. The tree also represents the growth and development of the psyche as distinguished from the instincts, which are usually represented by animals.

When our story began, we saw the soldier was alone and we can surmise that the missing part in this tale is the femi-

---

[2]*The Great Mother*, pp. 48–53.

nine—not just women or mom, but the feminine within oneself. A man or a culture losing touch with the innate feminine
element usually implies a too rational, too ordered or too
organized attitude. Our culture fits this description. You may
disagree and say our culture seems to be coming apart at the
seams and we are on the verge of possible chaos. You could go
further and assert that emotional chaos, alienation and confusion have risen alarmingly in the last thirty years. I would
agree with you! But I would say this is the result of our too
rational, too scientific, too technological approach toward
dealing with life's problems. This is the eruption of the
shadow side of our too one-sided approach, the other pole
drawing the pendulum back. Don't forget the French age of
reason was followed by the chaos of the French revolution.

Naturally, the soldier's journey will then begin in the
earth. But he finds there not the feminine needed to fulfill
his potential, but his own instinctual animal nature,
renewed energy and light all contained in the traditions of
the past as reflected by the great hall (as discussed in the
next section).

This symbolism may begin to sound a little bizarre, but if
we come out of the tale for a minute and look around in our
world, we see plenty of evidence of similar journeys. In popular psychology books, such as Eric Erikson's *The Life Cycle
Completed*, Gail Sheehy's *Passages*, and Daniel Levinson's *The
Seasons of a Man's Life*, we see men going through life transition points that have been collectively ignored or misunder-
stood. If we read the more personally oriented biographies of
great men, we find that Sigmund Freud, Carl Jung, Winston
Churchill, Anwar Sadat, and many others went through periods of deep inner journeys.

In the Earth

Once through the tree, the soldier finds himself in the great
hall with one hundred candles. Imagine the great halls of
ancient times—massive wooden beams, walls of stone and

wood, perhaps covered with ancient shields and weapons; imposing rooms decorated with tapestries, animal skins, and furs. Such was the great hall of the king of Denmark where the half-human monster Grendel called forth the ancient hero Beowulf to battle. Grendel's defeat and death caused his terrible mother monster to arise from the depth of the sea, devouring men and calling Beowulf to heroic battle once again. Such was the hall where Odysseus was finally united in symbolic wholeness with his wife Penelope after his many years of travels and adventures. And, of course, we remember the hall of King Arthur in Camelot, where Merlin created the great round table with the *Siege Perilous*, a symbol of chivalry, heroism, and wholeness that still lives in our imagination, films, and stories. From this hall began the search for the *Holy Grail* illustrating the best in masculinity: man's aspiration to be more than he is, to unite with the feminine and find a higher spirituality that assures renewal. Great halls— scenes of feasts, glory, and tragedy—the habitat of kings, queens, heroes, beautiful princesses, knaves, fools, monsters, and wizards. It's a wonderful symbol for the powers, mysteries, and dangers of the unconscious. Hardly could the soldier imagine what a miraculous place he had inadvertently entered.

The hall is brightly lit, not by roaring fires and flaming torches, but by candles. A collection of flickering candles represents the delicate light and flame of individuals united into the wholeness of "one hundred," just as the individual (the one) is the carrier of life and consciousness, and unites with others (the many) into the symbol of everything (the "one hundred"). We can also interpret how everything is always related to the life of the one, just as Brahma, the original male/female one couple, and this one couple populated the world illustrating an elemental pattern in creation myths. Think of the inner world of each of us as a "state" or, as mythology often conceived it, as a kingdom. We hope to realize and live our own unity in relation to others as we fulfill our lives. United states.

Fire changed human history, being the first great separator of humankind from the guilt-free natural world. In this perspective, firelight is often thought of as the light of consciousness that set humanity on its way to civilization. Candles have lit many places in the history of the human mind and spirit. Candles represent the personal prayers of the people as they flicker in great spiritual halls or in tiny, humble chapels. Candles lit the rooms in castles, cathedrals, and humble huts alike. The light of consciousness often shines and is brought together in the halls of elegant and sacred places, in great universities; but just as often it seems as only one small light in the humble darkness of a peasant hut as we are one small light in the darkness of the universe. Here, the one hundred candles in the great hall under the earth may be interpreted as the collected wisdom of the inner world, not our brilliant individualistic flame, but the wisdom of generations lost beneath the earth in the unconscious, as we are always seeming to lose touch with the meaning of our cultural history.

In the midst of the great halls of kings, men, and heroes, we need the soft light of candles. Not so long ago I knelt in a church and lit a tiny candle for a child I loved who had died on my birthday. I am not a member of that church, but she was, and so I felt drawn there. As I meditated on the small flame of that candle, I thought of the small flame her life had been. A gentle little flame, but a flame that warmly lit the lives of all around her. She was different from us, born with many birth defects—a body that just would not work. She grasped life with eagerness, openness, and love, through a lifetime filled with torment. She wasn't a pillar of fire doing great works, but a candle, glowing, enlightening, and touching the hearts of those around her. That is candlelight. It glows in our spiritual halls, representing the passage of life on birthday cakes or romantically warming lovers with the flame of the heart that lights the way to many inner riches.

Together, the hall and the candles may be seen as standing for the process of becoming an individual, as well as the earthy instinctive wisdom available to us. These notions are deep within ourselves, and deep within the cultural traditions of our past.

Both of these areas of inner potential are difficult to connect with, even though they are part of us. As modern men, our orientation is primarily rational and extroverted. Based on this, we have a deep cultural reluctance to look within. We are generally pulled between two poles within our culture and within ourselves. One pole is represented by the man of action, who prefers physical action, and who tends to be suspicious of psychology and the inner life. The other extreme is represented by the man who lives by his mind. He may live on many levels—from corporate management to the university—and prizes development of the mind and the capacity to think, often devoting much of his life to study and reflection. Development of his intelligence, understanding and insight are his goals. This man, like the man of action, has a great deal of trouble getting *into* the inner journey. He wants the journey to be linear and logical and has difficulty dealing with the ambiguities and paradoxes of his own inner world. He wants the journey to be philosophical and cerebral. He is skeptical of those of us who grope around in such areas as feelings, the feminine, and the body (other than to make it a healthy machine). Men of action and men of rationality do not understand men who are lost in their feelings and feminine sides.

The shallow traditions of our apparently young culture offer us few images of masculine diversity. To whom in our history do we look back: the soldier, the cowboy, the frontiersman, our statesmanlike founding fathers? Past these, our roots come from a conglomeration of cultures. In spite of that, our American culture, including the masculine, cries out for a connection with earthly wisdom. The special place of the farmer in our hearts illustrates this need. For years we have protected him with legislation. Even though farming is now big business, scientific and mechanized, the farmer still maintains his grip on our collective heart, as shown in the movies *Places in the Heart, The River*, and *Country*. Here the farmer is still the independent person struggling for survival with nature on the one hand and the vast impersonal forces of government and business on the other. The farmer is an image of independence and connectedness to nature we are loathe to give up.

Two tasks have emerged for us. The first is accepting the validity of the inner journey, an expansion of consciousness that enables us to look inside ourselves to discover the basic patterns of life and to encounter our inner world of feelings, thoughts, instincts and symbolic imagery. By pursuing this journey, we attempt to follow nature's striving to bring life to the fullest fruition within ourselves. The goal of this journey, called the individuation process, is to be able to live more independently and authentically in relation to ourselves, others, and the culture.

The second task is finding an *inner* tradition that is deep enough to help us in our modern experience. I hope to show the validity of the inner journey to help connect us to an essential depth perspective as we travel in and around this old tale.

Three Doors

We find now that we run into several sets of the number three—three doors, three keys, three dogs, and three chests of money. All are connected to the feminine by being *in* the earth and having characteristics of the feminine, though the number three itself is considered a masculine model symbolically. It is a number representing potential and movement through time. When connected with the feminine in man, it means something inferior that is pushed into the shadow side of the unconscious. Simply stated, the chthonic masculine has been forced into the unconscious in our culture. You might say "boys will be boys," but "men can't be men" any longer. We have been enculturated to believe this essential masculinity is an undesirable trait. Note the frustration and helplessness a man feels when confronted with an angry woman. Why can't he be just as angry? Why can't he react naturally and spontaneously? Because good boys and nice men don't do that. If rationality does not work, he has to be careful not to be brutal, and often the best thing to do seems to be to leave, withdraw, or placate her. But, paradoxically, withdrawing and placating in the face of a woman's instincts and irrationality can be even more infuriating. She is left with the feeling nobody is home inside his skin. However, three is also considered the number of the creative masculine and the emergence of action out of passivity, and thus we also have hope and the opening of opportunity.

Doors, too, suggest thresholds and movement. Each door with the key in it offers accessibility and movement from one state of being to another. Throughout life we frequently have a sensation of doors opening and closing to us, opportunities gained and lost. Doors also represent the feminine, leading into the world, birth, and eventually out of the world, death. The doors represent the opening of new passages in the individuation process. Each threshold we cross in the process of individuation means that our personality reorganizes in ways more closely attuned to its basic patterns. We become more clearly and essentially who we are, in spite of enculturation and early childhood influences. We need a way appropriate to our own development, but not in defiance of the world. Often, we must go back to our origins. The journey does not necessarily need a long psychoanalysis or attempts to correct what went wrong in our childhood, though this process is helpful to many. We need to try to understand the basic patterns of who we are—the true foundation of our personhood. Gaining this understanding is hard and deeply involved in our personal history.

Many of the men I have worked with began this change with their wives saying to them: "Look at all the good things you have; you're successful, you have a good job, our income is good. We have a good family, we live well and enjoy weekends and vacations. Why can't you just be happy?" The men do not know how to answer. Those who changed their careers as an answer found earlier interests essential to them that had been buried in their rush and struggle to gain adulthood on the collective highway. Every one of these men became even more successful in their new endeavors.

The Treasure Within

Money represents far more than just a useful intermediate commodity that facilitates human transactions and relationships. A compulsion for money arises directly from the wounded or neglected feeling side of life including inner values and outer relationships. Men trapped in hardened attitudes unconsciously try to compensate the dryness of their lives with materialism and achievement. Almost every day we can look in the newspaper and see examples of the runaway greed in our society (in business, politics, sports, trashy exposes, and even in religion), illustrating the loss of values and meaning in our lives.

Traditionally, money means security, freedom, power, independence, happiness, potency, crime, and more. The difficulty we often have in dealing with it is that a grain of truth is in each meaning, often just enough to confuse and mislead us. The history of money reflects a value system which even now is used to judge many areas of men's self-worth. In the 1950s, corporate managers were supposed to be motivated first by money, second by power, and third by prestige. Many women found earning money in the 1970s to be a reinforcement of their individuality. For our purposes, we need to look again at the basic, older symbolic meanings.

All of the monies in this story are metal. This metal symbolizes life energy in solidified form. The symbolism of money has a hierarchical value. In the alchemical tradition, metals may be grouped progressively: the base metals represent the basic instincts of the body, and gold represents the culminating point of the progression. The first chest is filled with copper, the metal for common people. Copper was associated with Aphrodite and Venus, the goddesses of love. The second chest was filled with silver. Silver symbolizes purity, innocence, and a clear conscience. Silver also represents spirituality and fidelity, as well as the dark side (the tarnished side) of these virtues, deceit, and betrayal. Judas, as we know, was paid thirty pieces of silver. Gold is the highest metal, standing for the sun in man. In gold is a mixture of the divine spirit and the human spirit. In psychology, gold equals self-knowledge, particularly of those parts of us that have been lost or buried. Since the metal was in the form of coins, it was apparently once above the ground and used by man. Now it is buried, cut off from the world of men. Each of the different coins may represent stages in masculine development. First is ordinary life, love, work, marriage, and reproduction. As we progress higher into silver, we become more spiritually oriented but also suffer the ambivalence this brings us. True spirituality robs us of our simple religion. Many of the older initiations into manhood included the spiritual dimension of becoming a man, orienting the initiate toward a deeper perception of himself.

Gold is the perfect metal and will not tarnish. Gold brings some of the strength and wisdom of living into our experience. Gold also is the zest for life. No matter how much we jog, exercise, and diet (all good things in their own way), I am convinced that health and longevity are governed by our zest for living and how deeply rooted it is in our psyche.

The soldier in our story is impoverished. He has no money, no deep self-knowledge and no deep instinctual energy. He must gain the money to come into his own. He will also see that he must learn how to use it, how to direct it. Most of us have difficulty directing our energy. We are often torn so many ways that we are convinced we just do not have enough of it. Too many men seem to live like the soft-man—a life never bursting with zest and enthusiasm. The soldier, of course, finally takes only the gold. But later in the tale when he has squandered the gold, he regains all three sources to help him proceed. We need the common; we need love and fertility, just as much as we need the divine and human spirit.

The money is connected to the feminine by being contained in chests. As you can probably guess, money has an interesting connection to the mother. Money took its name from Rome's great mother goddess Juno Moneta (Juno the admonisher) whose Capitoline temple included the Roman mint.[3] The attendant spirit of Juno was Cupid, corresponding to the Greek god Eros, who was both the child and companion of Aphrodite. Originally, cupidity meant eros or erotic desire, and in our times its meaning has evolved to greed for money. The intertwining of the two meanings of cupidity is easily noticed in our nighttime television soap operas.

The Dogs

A strange collection of dogs guards the treasure. Dogs and animals in general represent the complementary instinctual side of our nature in fairy tales. Initially in this tale, they are threatening, but later they become helpful companions to the soldier. It is important not to devalue the symbols of our instinctive nature. We need them; they connect us to our surroundings and to life's process. Here they guard the treasure. Later we shall see that the soldier needs them to accomplish all of his transitions but one.

We think of dogs as man's best friend, faithful and helpful as they are in our story. But dogs are also ambivalent figures symbolically. They may be mad, depraved, vicious, scavengers, or fierce. So we need to respect and deal with them in the proper manner. The soldier does this first by following the witch's instructions and then by luck until he learns for himself. Dogs were also depicted at the feet of women on ancient tombs, denoting faithfulness and affection. They are related to the jackal, the symbol for the Egyptian devouring mother. The great goddess of birth was given dog sacrifices.

---

[3]Barbara Walker, *The Woman's Encyclopedia of Myths and Secrets* (San Francisco: HarperCollins, 1983), p. 667.

These dogs have the most unusual eyes I have ever run across. The eyes are unusual in proportion to the value of the money they guard. Dogs are often thought to have abnormal perception because they can see in the dark. In folklore they can see ghosts, fairies, spirits, and the angel of death. All of the eyes are wheel-shaped and share the basic symbolism of the circle—a state of union with nature. The idea that they are spinning may represent the turning of wheels of fate, progress, and transcendence. Practically, the eyes mean we have a certain responsibility. The dogs guarding the treasure indicate that as we develop consciousness and self-knowledge the instincts must accompany with their corresponding viewpoint or perception at each level. The eye is also a traditional symbol for consciousness, a window to the soul. The final dog has eyes like a tower, an observatory. As our development reaches the final stage, we must have a standpoint that allows us to be seen and gives us an objective perspective on what is going on around us.

We need the chthonic masculine to get along with men, culture, and the masculine side of women. The animal power and the aggression that comes with the chthonic masculine, however, needs to be consciously controlled. This control implies using the utmost vigilance to be sure our power does not break out unconsciously. To become a man in the fullest sense is to have this capacity but also to be the master of it. If we are overcome by instincts, rage, and violence, then our masculinity is not fully developed. We have been so thoroughly taught that anger and aggression are bad that we attempt to suppress them. Then we either become helpless, turn it against ourselves in addictions such as overwork, overeating, alcohol, exercise; or it turns to illness, or explodes in a rage that can damage us and those we love in painful ways. The answer is to use anger consciously and appropriately—a process that can only be learned after the development of a well-grounded personal identity.

In the soldier's first experience of his instincts, he needs to place the dog on the witch's apron, ideally within the context of a nurturing environment. The apron is a symbol of the domestic feminine. We easily see this first experience in the struggling anger and sulkiness of adolescent boys. As difficult as the process is for parents, boys needs to act angry and sulky in order to separate from the parents. But, more importantly, they need to learn they have power and how to use and control it before they try it in the world.

A danger is involved in this process. The soldier cannot keep using the apron. He must return the dog to its position and later contact him in another way. Becoming a man also means putting aside our cowardice and longing to be protected by the mother. Many of the women I have worked with have become very frustrated with the male need to be mothered.

In this regard, the apron can also be considered a cover for sexuality. Many men have not picked this apron up and returned it to the witch yet. These men become dependent on sex to symbolize relationship and a feeling of nurturance. Often, it seems an addiction. The sex act itself is the symbol and such men may need sex every day or several times a day. They make statements like, "It is so easy for her and only takes a few minutes. If she loves me, what is the problem?" The problem is that the women eventually begin to feel like machines, not lovers, and then perceive that these men have a problem. If nurturance and relationships depend only on sex, then men will become bewitched out of their instinctual masculine energy. These men are caught in an awful paradox. They need sex to feel loved, and they fear sex because it threatens their defenses against those repressed feelings about the mother. Men must solve this addiction and paradox before they can truly experience intimacy, nurturance, and a feeling of relationship (things that often normally come with sex).

Most people know the story about the seduction of Samson and his subsequent loss of strength. People don't know that knights were only allowed to spend a short time in the castles with their wives and lovers before they had to leave because it was feared that they would lose their desire to quest after too much time. One way that modern men have tried to avoid this conflict is to develop the stylized playboy or recreational approach to sex. At first this sex appears to be fully instinctual, but in reality it is not. This approach to sexuality robs the instincts of their rich connectedness to the earth, and thereby to the spirit and to our deeper selves. In both of the above cases, sexuality loses its meaning for us, and our body lets us know through impotence or premature ejaculation, driving us to compulsive sex that never fulfills, or to painful withdrawal from the field. Women cannot save us from this predicament. We have tried to get them to save us, and many have tried to help or enjoyed the power it gave them. But, we have to be able to save and develop ourselves in order to be able to relate to women. More about this subject will unfold as the story progresses.

The Tinder Box

The final image in this part of the tale is that of the tinder box. The box was left by the witch's grandmother, and in her we have the lineage of the negative mother. The tinder box kept flint and steel dry for fire-starting. Dryness is also a masculine characteristic, one the feminine symbol of the box is designed to protect. Laurens Van Der Post tells the Bushman tale that it was Mantis, their spirit of wholeness in life, who brought fire to the earth. The Bushmen called him "Old Tinder Box."[4]

This symbol brings to mind the story of Pandora, Greek mythology's tale of the first woman on Earth. Angry because Prometheus stole the Olympian fire, Zeus created Pandora as an instrument of vengeance, an evil being whom all men would desire. Pandora brought with her to Earth a box which Zeus had warned her never to open. Eventually her curiosity

---

[4]Laurens Van Der Post, *The Heart of the Hunter: A Journey into the Mind and Spirit of the Bushmen* (New York: Penguin, 1965), p.166.

overcame her and she lifted the lid for one quick look, and all the miseries of men flew out into the world. She slammed the lid of the box shut, and in so doing retained our most basic virtue—hope.

Flint represents fire; striking it draws forth the fire which resides in the stone. The stone is an ancient religious and alchemical symbol of the individuation process. The stone traditionally signified the inner spiritual man and showed that spirituality must integrate the everyday physical side of nature. Steel is the conquering spirit (the soaring, aggressive, challenging, eagle spirit) bringing forth the fire from the flint. Striking the spark illustrates the spiritual principal of giving birth to each individual.

We have difficulty imagining what fire meant to primitive people. In our times it is either energy or it is destructive, but to the primitive it was much more than that. It was the only light in the dark; it provided safety against the danger of the night; it provided the warmth of life against the cold. To keep the fire or maintain the living coals when a tribe moved was often a sacred and honored job. Terms like "keeper of the flame," and "I seek the flame," are still in modern use. Fire is our greatest image of living awareness, the light of consciousness in man. This was the gift to man, stolen from the gods, for which both Mantis and Prometheus had to suffer.

In myths and tales fire represents emotions and passions which can either burn or spread light. Passion compels us to sacrifice too cerebral an attitude, and enables us to realize the spirit. As our soldier progresses through each stage of development in the tale, he will have to call forth passion and light until they enable the final scene. In alchemy, fire indicates one's participation in the work and is equated with the passion one gives to the different stages of growth.

Tom Peters and Nancy Austin pick up this theme—fire, passion and participation—illustrating their functions in corporate life in their book *A Passion for Excellence*, the follow-up book to *In Search for Excellence* which Peters co-authored with

Robert Waterman. This is their answer to how to practice excellence in whatever stage one is in.

Fire is also transformation and purification. It burns away the impurities. "He has been tested by fire." The fire of emotions in women and often in ourselves scares us to death. But without the fire of emotions, no development takes place, and no higher consciousness can be reached. For this reason God says, "But, because you are lukewarm, neither hot nor cold, I will spit you out of my mouth" (Rev. 3:16).[5] If someone is dispassionate about life and does not suffer—if one has neither the fire of despair nor hatred nor conflict nor love nor annoyance nor anything of that kind, then that person has little growth and little life.

So, fire, whether it represents the negative conflict, hatred, jealousy, or any other affect, speeds up the maturation process and is a type of "judge" that clarifies things. People who have fire may run into trouble and may suffer despair from the destructive effects of emotional outbursts, but at the same time, if that fire is extinguished, all is lost.

We can have too much or too little fire or not enough. Learning consciously when to strike the sparks is important and, based on an instinctual awareness. I will illustrate this timing in the next chapter.

Masculine and Feminine

As we have examined each symbol, I have carefully tried to point out that each has a connection to some part of both the masculine and feminine principles. Every symbol that is masculine also has its connection to the feminine. Every symbol that helps (or stands for) the masculine identity has some connection to the mother. For centuries these symbols have reflected both the masculine and the feminine principles on different levels. The deeper we go in one, the closer we are to the other, which can enhance or destroy us. The gold is in the

---

[5]I use the New English Bible for any biblical quotations.

earth. Symbolically, we see an illustration that the masculine and feminine constantly combine and interact like the Yang and the Yin, growing together and enhancing each other's progress if we hold them in consciousness—in perspective— viewing them from the tower.

7

KILLING THE WITCH

The witch has now pulled the soldier back up through the tree. He has the gold and the tinder box. He asks the witch what she will do with the tinder box, and she refuses to tell him, even after he threatens her. So he simply cuts off her head, and that is the end of her. This turn of events is startling. What ingratitude! She has made an honest, straightforward bargain with him which he accepted, one that made him rich. Then he casually chops off her head. Often in tales and folklore a pact is made between the devil, or the devil's representative, and a human. Paradoxically, the darker figure is often straightforward in these contracts, and this behavior forces us to reconsider our moralistic sympathies.

This situation reflects the problem of evil as seen by nature. Nature deals with reality, not morality. Please do not think I do not believe in evil. I do, and I think at times we must take a clear moral stand against it. However, we must stand against evil not only with strength, but with great humility, not righteousness. Nature will teach us repeatedly that we are unable to see the evil in the good, and the good in the evil in our lives. Evil incitements in fairy tales are usually opportunities to increase consciousness.

How does the soldier handle this paradox? First he reacts with instinctive wisdom. He questions her, and when she refuses to dialogue or relate to him, he immediately cuts off her head. He uses the sword, which now takes a shift in symbolic meaning. Previously he had used it unconsciously in the service of the community. Now he converts it to his personal use. At this point, the sword becomes one of the most powerful masculine symbols, one of focused consciousness and masculine discrimination. A man must make a conscious decision to end his relation to the mother and accept his aloneness in order to engage the life energy (the gold) stored deep within him. Remember, the tale is dealing with psychic reality, not morality. Psychologically, when the soldier kills the witch, he ceases being a soldier and becomes what is often called a hero in fairy tales. Killing the witch paves the way for the soldier's transformation to a king.

Robert Bly parallels our discussion in his interpretation of the fairy tale "Iron John."[1] He suggests that psychological man passes through a phase when he is in all essentials dominated by the feminine principle. Man needs to reinstate the masculine principle through rediscovering "Iron John," the instinctual masculine. Iron John becomes a guiding rule of life and source of energy. To get to Iron John, the boy has to steal the key to his cage from under his mother's pillow. Robert Bly describes Iron John as the ancient, hairy, instinctive, primitive, and sexual male that dwells at the bottom of the psyche. Men have been out of touch with him for so long in our culture, that he is more frightening to us than our inner feminine, which is frightening enough.

> . . . the deep nourishing and spiritually radiant energy in the male lies not in the feminine side, but in the deep masculine. Not the shallow masculine, the snowmobile masculine, but the deep masculine, the instinctive one who's underwater and who has been there we don't know how long.[2]

---

[1] Keith Thompson, "What Men Really Want: A New Age Interview with Robert Bly," in *New Age Magazine* (May, 1982), p. 36.
[2] "What Men Really Want," p. 34.

Bly continues, pointing out that once a man takes this step, he is moving against the cultural image of men today. He is moving away from pleasing mother and the search for being good. Of course he has to steal the key, because mother knows he will quit being a good little boy and become independent of her approval.

Robert Bly's discussion is particularly interesting because in early versions of "The Tinder Box," the soldier received riches for bringing back a candle. In this task he was helped by an iron man. Both the iron man and the dogs symbolize the deep instinctual masculine. Perhaps the dogs represent a regression of this masculinity to an even deeper level than we realize.

Let me reiterate Bly's statement about the shallow masculine. Please *do not* misinterpret my discussion of the deep, instinctual masculine, Iron John, in a *shallow* way, supposing that real men behave like cave men. What we are really talking about is the *natural* man in each of us. We have lost touch with the natural depth and integrity of nature. Keep in mind that nature knows certain limits, not just excesses. Animals compete and fight for food and territory, but only for as much as they need. It takes civilized man with his existential anxiety to get into greed, endless competition, and useless killing. Furthermore, the natural man in us will always respond to a woman, maybe not in the way she wants, but she will know someone is home in our skin she can contact.

Let me repeat: to get in touch with Iron John does not mean we give up our intelligence and consciousness and regress to the stone age. It means to integrate our deep instinctual, masculine selves into our self-awareness to deepen and strengthen our lives—to add human depth to our robot-like rational selves. Then people know there is someone alive within our skin, and we are part of nature rather than separate from it. This natural man in us must be lived in a 20th-century manner.

Jim was struggling with this very issue when he had the following experience. Jim is educated, well known in his field, and works for a large religious organization. The president of his particular institution resigned, and Jim was given the thankless job of chairing the committee to find a new president. Meanwhile, an ambitious colleague was appointed the acting president. As the committee was nearing its final selection, it became apparent that the ambitious colleague was not in the running. This colleague was embittered and fired off a blistering letter to the executive board accusing Jim of many unethical behaviors. He went even further by making this letter public and sending copies to all staff members. This letter amounted to character assassination, serious enough to affect Jim's professional relationships and future.

Jim had worked long and hard on this committee and had tried to be meticulous in his conduct. This letter left him feeling hurt, betrayed, and bewildered as to how he should respond. High-minded friends advised him not to stoop to the same tactics in response. Intelligent friends advised him that others would see through such a shallow attack. Cautious friends suggested this man was a powerful adversary. Even if Jim won this time, this fellow would be sure to get him back, as he had demonstrated more than once with others. Kind, well-meaning friends counseled that this was a religious community and, for the sake of the community, Jim should go and talk with his colleague, try to understand his bitterness and reconcile with him. In the midst of his dilemma, Jim had this dream:

> I was playing in a football game. There was a large stadium filled with people. I ran with the ball and was tackled. As I was getting up someone hit me late, viciously, from behind. I jumped up to find a referee, the coach, or even the owner of the team, to tell them what happened.

Jim asked me what I thought about this dream. I responded by asking him what his immediate reaction to such a hit would have been back when he was playing ball. Jim said without hesitation that he would have jumped up and spiked the ball right in the guy's face. Neither of us had to say any more.

This dream is not telling Jim to go punch his colleague in the nose. But the natural man, the instinctual man, is saying, when unfairly hit do not run around looking for institutional mother support (unless it is a police matter). Take responsibility for responding—jump up and respond in a clear, forceful, emotional manner. The natural instinct will strike the spark if we let it.

Jim agreed with this response, but he did not stop at this point. He sat down and used his intelligence, years of experience, and political acumen to develop a strategy for confronting this man quickly, forcefully, and publicly, in a board meeting. He struck the spark and responded in a 20th-century manner. In fact, this confrontation ended with his colleague rescinding the letter and reconciling with Jim. Jim learned something about the importance of his instinctual masculinity—even when operating in modern sophisticated institutions of learning and spirituality.

Now let us return to the fairy tale. By killing the witch and bringing up the gold, the soldier has committed himself to the principle of consciousness as a way of life. He must leave the safe, conventional highway, and begin the journey of self-knowledge. He claims his masculine power as his own and refuses to let it remain in the service of the mother image—personal or cultural. As we shall see in the next chapter, he now has this new energy but does not know what to do with it.

Stages of Development

This stage of development sounds like one all men have to go through. But I cannot stand calling it that! "A stage" is too reductionistic, a trick our culture has learned to play on us to keep us on the highway. Superficial theorists devalue every major transition in our lives and irreverently destroy their meaning by diagramming them into stages. We, as a culture, have lost the art of living and do not know it. We have lost the sense of life's deeper meaning and how to connect to it. We are desperate for a path, so we try to categorize, label, and compartmentalize everything we do, especially in psychology and social science. We even rob death of its power and mystery by reducing the emotional processes around it for all involved to a series of "stages of grief."

Killing the witch is not a stage! It is a transformation! It is the major point of transition in a man's life. His entire future is tied to it no matter what his age. It is a point of psychological rebirth, a time of suffering the death of the child and a release of the need for nurturance from the mother. The man now is alone, a feeling not to be discounted or denied, but to be fully understood, because it is the basis for true relationships in the future. The man will never be the same again. To call this a stage is our ridiculous way of robbing this process of its meaning.

This time calls for the deep masculine nature and great courage. All of the great myths and tales of the hero slaying the beast or dragon are about this particular transition, for it is the hero in the man that makes him male.

Therefore, this passage was marked by solemn ceremonies and initiation rites emphasizing wholeness, nature, aloneness, the depths within, and spirituality. In our country Native Americans acknowledged both the transition and the spirituality in a young man's vision quest. The young man would sit alone in the wilderness within a circle of stones. Here he would overcome personal discomfort until he had a vision of his totem animal or an animal for him to be named after, one that exemplified his true nature.

This event, calling for the most heroic effort in a man's life, has become virtually unknown in our culture. We have lost the entire notion of death and rebirth, even though Christmas and Easter, Hanukkah and Passover, winter and spring pass us by every year. On every level of life, death is the forerunner of life renewed. No birth comes without a prior death. The acorn dies for the emergence of the oak. The maiden in the woman dies at the birth of a baby. In the life of the spirit, immortality comes only through death.

The real sadness is that a man's deep masculinity supports his heroic attitude; it really *prevents* violence in the world, rather than causing it. Remember, the feminine can only appropriately save us once, when she is our mother and pulls us back up from the earth. After that, we are on our own; we have to be able to relate to the feminine in ourselves and to the feminine in the outer world. The repressed, rejected, and "unrelated to" feminine in men turns on them, goes crazy, and causes the vanity of driven ambition and major wars.

The personal mother in our century is required to walk a narrow line between being considered either overprotective and controlling, or abandoning. In fact, her current position is inhuman as we have placed too much responsibility on her. The support and critically needed intervention of the culture, men, and fathers are also needed, and requires men who have reached self-responsible and culturally responsible adulthood. (This problem is specifically addressed in chapter 16.)

In spite of missing this transition to a truly self-responsible masculine adulthood, we have developed a dangerous appearance of wholeness. Men's semblance of being more sensitive and receptive is often deceptive, as I pointed out in chapter 1. Research supports this view:

> Given the recent struggle to loosen traditional definitions of masculinity and femininity, we might assume that there would be differences in the intimate relations of men who are twenty-five and those who are fifty. And although younger men are likely to be more openly concerned with these issues, all the research evidence—my own as well as others'—suggests that integrating that concern into their behavior has been met with difficulties.[3]

Marion Woodman points out:

---

[3]Lillian B. Rubin, *Intimate Strangers: Men and Women Together* (New York: Harper-Collins, 1983), p. 83.

The "mother's son" for example, so vulnerable to feeling guilty that he is not "better" or "more manly" or "more capable," thinks automatically of pleasing the women in his life. He may believe this is how he feels, but it is not a true feeling. It is thinking contaminated by the mother complex. It is sheer sentimentality, a plea to be loved, and, whether it is answered or not breeds resentment because it puts all the power in the hands of a woman.[4]

The Hero

The image of the hero has been with us from the beginning of time, and first started man on his journey out of the animal kingdom. The drive that has fueled our efforts to harness and overcome nature, to understand her secrets and utilize her energy, comes from our drive to be heroic. Even in our books and movies we acknowledge the heroic aspects of the achievements of science and technology. The most heroic struggle of all has been the fight for consciousness. In recent years, we have become increasingly aware that our hold on consciousness is a lot more tenuous than we once suspected. The stress and calamities of the world can threaten us very quickly. In our tale, the journey of the soldier/hero is also a story of the quest for consciousness. Our culture and modern education have turned their backs on heroes in almost every field except science, technology, and medicine. But in our tale we find a new sphere for the hero, the inner world in each of us, the achieving of our personal conscious identity (ego), our will, and a depth of self-knowledge. To remain an individual who stands for his values in a mass culture, to meet the feminine, to father children in a committed way, to deal with changing roles—all of these things require an inner heroic attitude.

The hero in myths and tales can once again become a model for developing an attitude of living that may serve as a

---

[4]Marion Woodman, *The Pregnant Virgin* (Toronto: Inner City, 1985), p.156.

guide as we struggle on our way. He also reminds us of all the possible transformations and possibilities in life. What kind of men want to seek the Holy Grail? The Grail, according to many mythologists, is the inner image of the feminine. The heroes went out—the knights—not the king, not the priests, nor the farmers. To relate to the feminine in themselves and in the outer world, men today need a heroic attitude supported by their deep masculine nature.

The soft-men, the pseudo-liberated men, and many others, have not yet developed the heroic attitude needed to slay the witch. When we do not pass through this transition, we end up feeling like this man when faced with intimacy and relationship:

> . . . I actually feel scared at times like that. "What are you afraid of?" I asked. He stared out the window for a bit, then with some agitation said: "Damned if I know. It's like a kid in a way—scared I'll say or do the wrong thing and wind up in trouble, so better to just hole up and keep quiet."[5]

A Cultural Wound

Our fathers, those who were men in the 1930s and 1940s, were severely wounded by the Depression. The war was enough to respark some masculine spirit, but was not sufficient to heal that Depression wound. Being helpless to provide and care for those you love is devastating to the masculine spirit. Many poor and minority men still experience this frustration, and this bitterness is the root of much of the anger between men and women in these classes. Those Depression-wounded men laid the foundation for our cultural mother, looked to her for security, and developed a symbiotic binding to her. They created banks that were guaranteed by the government, large corporations with all-encompassing fringe benefits, and a wel-

---

[5]Lillian B. Rubin, *Intimate Strangers*, p. 80.

fare society that would take care of the old, the sick, and the infirm. None of these things are bad in themselves, but symbiosis comes with a price. The witch will have her due. She will stunt our individual growth and in so doing sap the creativity, the will, and the sense of responsibility from us.

Peters and Waterman, in *In Search of Excellence*, pointed out that this situation does not have to be the case.[6] Corporate cultures can foster the best creative masculine values. But most of us need more. At some point we have to decide what we need to do to kill the witch. Some men do not have to leave the corporate or institutional world. For others it is the only way. I have known a number of men who come into therapy in their early or middle thirties. Their complaints fall into two categories: 1) impotence, marital difficulties, or feelings of boredom; and 2) slight depression, for although they are successful at work, it is no longer challenging and exciting. Like the man in mid-life I discussed earlier, they are moving well along life's highway, but suddenly they discover it is not enough. They become puzzled and afraid, not knowing how to restore what they lack.

Often these men have been to a therapist before. Too often, therapists today try to fix the problem—sex therapy, marital counseling, changing negative thoughts, and so on. Many counselors and therapists have side-stepped into a shallow process of shaping people up to get them adjusted and back on the highway. If we get a man or a woman back to normal and through the immediate crisis, we think we have done a good job. But the meaning behind the feelings, the symptoms and the crisis are more important. The real quest is to go into the depths, discover the meaning, and bring it out into the living world. Most counselors and therapists would readily admit that the discouragement of creativity, individuality,

---

[6]T. J. Peters and R. H. Waterman, Jr., *In Search of Excellence: Lessons from America's Best-Run Companies* (New York: Warner, 1983). See especially chapter 12, "Simultaneous Loose-Tight Properties."

and natural rebellion is no service to the culture or the client. But their problem-solving rather than problem-amplifying approach to healing belies their beliefs. Problem amplifying deepens and broadens the issue in order to more fully understand it—to avoid psychological bandaiding.

Most of the men I have worked with felt they were meant for better things. They had general ideas of success, but only vague ideas of their own needs that they wanted to fulfill with "success." Most of these men went through a period of frustration when they realized no easy answers came forth. Some were already on the verge of change psychologically and did so quickly. Others had to work long and hard, searching out their inner selves. Most had to make a change of career or job, or at least a change to another company. The outer change symbolized the inner change. The main reflection of the inner change within all of them was the brightness in their eyes and the vibrancy of their presence. Even if they continued the same job and had the same family, a change was noticeable. The difference is a sense of aliveness and strength that was missing before. If you look closely enough, more maturity is evident, more humanity (though it is not expressed as caretaking softness), and more passion for life.

Not surprisingly, some went through divorces. The men changed from who they were, and not all the wives liked the change. What surprised me was that many of the women who fought the change the hardest (or who most resented the changes they would have to make), ultimately became ardent supporters of the process. The wives changed their attitudes when the men could reach into their inner depths, could communicate what it meant for them in terms of deep feelings and inner processes, and could resolve to pursue this course for the sake of their own lives. I respect this ability to understand men's personal vision and their poignant need for life if they believe in it enough to take a stand for it and communicate it in feeling terms. Most women are also more receptive once the men quit blaming women for their problems!

Father

The father should have a fundamental role in helping the son separate from the mother. Our tale has no father or wise man helping the soldier, and in fact there are no parents for him at all. This lack tells us that he is dealing more with parental images and the culture in the parental roles than with real parents. The story has no direct image of the father, only the king as the cultural father image. This pattern fits our culture, because fathers are in a confused state today in our country.

Traditionally in myth, folklore, and psychology, the father stands for law, order, authority, and the world outside the home. His responsibility is to teach the children to respect and obey the culture's form, and to competently take their place in the world. A prime function of the father is interceding between the son and the mother/mother-image, so that the son can develop and fulfill his own masculine image and move out into the world. From my perspective as a clinician, I think this intercession rarely happens in our families, which is unfortunate.

The absent father, though a cliche, is more of a problem than ever. Whether due to divorce, animosity between the parents, investment in career, or emotional withdrawal and defensiveness, the result is almost the same. If the father desires to be a child himself, we have an even more serious problem. Now we have the new, more nurturing male father, but he is also confused as to masculine values and how they compare and conflict with feminine values. Often these men have a frightening inability to intercede between the child and a mother who is behaving like a father out of her masculine side.

While not new, this phenomenon has become more widespread and difficult to deal with. Women have reached into themselves, often into their masculine sides, and found their heroic personality. Unfortunately, this side cannot always be left at the office and finds its way into the home and plays the father role, wielding authority over children and husband alike. Dad is on the run and often comes off like Dagwood, a good natured bumbler. In more modern marriages the children may run to dad for nurturance when they hurt. Certainly these dads are not interceding to help their sons leave mother to create a vibrant masculine identity for themselves.

As a child therapist I have become convinced that nothing is more frightening to a child than frustrated, angry grownups. In spite of all we used to hear about presenting a united front, both parents need to be able to intercede when the other parent is going too far. Or when the other parent isn't going far enough.

Children need a feeling of stability and control. They are *little* and need to feel their parents' support and protection. To children, parents are *big*. Over-responsive, angry, hysterical parents terrify children. Unresponsive parents also terrify children. Feeling small and that no one cares leaves us feeling alone and frightened. Children need to see real emotions in their parents as well, or they cannot grow up with an understanding of how real people function. But, parents must strike a balance and remember that being a parent is an important responsibility. Listen to your inner voice of instinctual wisdom. We have developed the habit of listening to so many experts we have lost touch with *common sense*.

The dominant father type, though reduced in number, is still around. His way is the only way! The son isn't taught to risk, create, explore his own ideas or form his own opinions. Only the father is allowed to express himself, and he usually expresses anger. If his son tries to be different, this father feels betrayed and he then concentrates on punishing every small mistake his son makes. Often, this punishment is verbal—bullying and humiliating the son. The father ties his son to his orientation to life through emotional force, and therefore holds the son's developing masculinity captive. This type of relationship is less likely today due directly to the women's movement. But a son in this position is in just as much trouble as one who is a mother's son.

A final danger posed by absent fathers is the potential for the mother to become the son's companion. This situation happens more easily today. Many women are pursuing what used to be exclusively masculine interests. They are interesting, educated, and liberated. When fathers are not there for whatever reason, making the son a companion is an easy trap to fall into. Women have difficulty working, pursuing careers, and raising children all at once. Often doing all of this and maintaining a fulfilling relationship with a mature man (if they are divorced) is impossible. A companionship relationship with a son can arise at an early age almost without being noticed. At first, many sons will find this connection flattering and pleasurable, but it can lead to great pain and struggle in the son's individuation. I have seen a number of such mothers who could not understand why, all of a sudden, their sons were angry and seemed to hate them so much.

A woman without a husband will naturally tend to transfer what she would have expected of him—that he be a hero or a companion, for instance—onto the son. Unconsciously, she hopes he will fulfill what his father did not. Often tired and lonely, such a woman can easily become vulnerable to the "companionship trap" with their sons as they unconsciously seek friendship and intimacy. But the development of her son's identity depends on the destruction of this symbiotic relationship.

8

THE TALE CONTINUES

Having killed the witch, the soldier is ready to pursue his journey. He has been into the depths of his personality and has claimed some of the gold coins (life energy)—and the tinder box—for himself. Psychologically, he has freed his masculinity and male energy from the mother complex. In normal development every young man has to leave his mother this way. This process is often painful and seems a betrayal to both mother and son. This transition does not mean rejecting the mother. It means cutting the "tie that binds" to enable the young man to return and then relate to his mother as the human person she really is. In a culture like ours that has lost the process of transition, and in addition has a cultural mother complex, the issue of separation becomes much more complicated. The separation, if it occurs, may be a lasting tear. The real mother and the son's unconscious image of mother become confused and intertwined. He may end up always being loyal to her as mother, losing his chance to relate to her and appreciate her as an individual adult. Even worse, he may spend his life in an unconscious war with her that even her death does little to heal, for at this point the real mother is not a participant in the struggle. The struggle has shifted from the outer world to the inner world of the son's own unconscious personality. Jung sums this up:

> The mother apparently possesses the libido of the son (the treasure she guards so jealously), and this is in fact true so long as the son remains unconscious of himself. In psychological terms this means the "treasure hard to attain" lies hidden in the mother image, i.e., the unconscious.[1]

The soldier instinctively keeps the tinder box though he does not realize its value. It provides access to the unconscious, the source of inner strength and creativity. He doesn't know how to use it except in the ordinary way. Psychologically, this means he must not dissipate the inner spark or the heat of inner fire by letting it be unconsciously acted out or projected onto others. Ironically, the soldier has the possession of the inner fire, has it contained, but has no conscious idea of its strength and potential. Many men feel this way; even successful men, ignorant of their own fire, feel like imposters in their success. They know how to control and contain their fire, but not how to unleash it in a creative or initiating flame.

Whenever we go through a major passage, we emerge with more clarity about who we are and have a stronger foundation for our personality. As a result, we live on a new level of consciousness, never being able to return to our previous level. The soldier's journey reflects this new level as he proceeds to a new city instead of going home. The city holds many new outer levels, as all cities do. The new level of consciousness gained in evolving from soldier to hero fosters the appearance of new characters in the tale. Each passage we go through introduces us to new tasks in life, to the possibility of making new portions of our personality conscious, and to the opportunity of understanding and integrating them.

---

[1] C. G. Jung, Collected Works, Vol. 5, *Symbols of Transformation*, Bollingen Series, Vol. XX, ¶ 569.

The Merry Life

Much like the businessman who needed a career or job change to reflect his inner changes, the soldier also makes some changes. He invests in a fine place to live, fine new clothes, lives a merry life and shares generously with his friends. He was generous because he knew well enough what it meant to be penniless.

Both the businessman and the soldier have changed their external circumstances to fit the change in their internal situations. We are now talking about the two worlds of our personality, the inner and the outer. Often, one of these worlds reflects the other. When living through terrible outer events, discriminating between the two worlds is very helpful. If the situation is extreme, distancing or disconnecting our inner selves from the outer events can save our lives. But in everyday life these two worlds generally complement each other so that in effect, if we are conscious, we live in both worlds as if they are really one. This is integration. In fact, we need this consciousness to maintain our balance of living. Some people live so involved in their thoughts or emotions that they cannot function practically in the world. Some also live their outer roles so completely that they lack depth and genuineness in their lives. Jung developed a theoretical model for helping maintain balance in this complex life task.

Earlier in my discussions of Jung's theories, I mentioned the ego as the center of our conscious personality and "I-entity." The ego is essential if we are to comprehend the world and find our way in life. The ego is the part of our inner world necessary to help us connect and adapt to both worlds. Theoretically, if all were ideal, it would orient us toward outer reality on the one hand, and toward our inner subjective reality on the other. In our ideal model, the ego should be able to perceive and adapt in both worlds, distinguish the concrete from the subjective in both, decide when it is not in our best interest to adapt, and then to take a personal stand. This may sound somewhat difficult and complicated to you. Actually, it is much more difficult and complicated in real life. The inner and outer worlds do not fit any neat theoretical models. The outer world is full of strife and events we cannot control or predict, and the inner world is often largely unknown and filled with unconscious complexes and defenses based on our personal history. Moreover, these complexes, the unresolved results of the incidents that gnarled and twisted our growth, not only affect the way we perceive both worlds, but also how we respond to inner and outer events.

We have developed some additional psychological functions to help us in the complicated task of dealing with the inner and outer worlds. One of these is the *persona*, often referred to as a public face or "mask." The term "mask" suggests that the persona is a facade and not the essential nature of the person. The essential nature of the individual remains behind the impression given when viewed from the outside. The persona is partially a calculated public face one assumes, plus various other elements, including such things as our personal propensities, early training, and others' expectations of us.

As our I-entity develops, we choose various roles and integrate them more or less into a dominant I-entity, or personal identity. When the persona roles fit well, they truly reflect our abilities and authentic selves, and facilitate normal social interaction. A healthy I-entity tries to adopt different persona roles according to the needs of a particular situation. However, one can have some of the following problems in this area.

Society seems to have a life of its own and wishes us to adapt to that life. Society tries to imprint its personality on us, through its instruments (parents, teachers, and other representatives of social institutions) in order to have us mesh smoothly into the social sense of order and enhance the society's existence. The criteria for societal standards, however, are always measured and distorted as they are passed through the perception of the personalities and institutions attempting to implement them. Thus, we are constantly pressured to conform to a model that may be changing and occasionally nonsensical. While growing up, we must adapt to the society around us. Growing up under the constant influence and pressure of society can reduce us to living a provisional life, one suited for the time but never connected to a personal sense of meaning, authenticity, or fulfillment. In such a case, we may become or achieve something impressive and indeed valuable, but that has nothing to do with fulfilling our personal destiny. Because some adaptation is necessary, we are left with a never-ending quest to find and become our authentic selves and still live in society. We are left with the task of constantly maintaining the tension between living in our society and also being "ourselves."

Here is where the persona can serve us in the healthiest way—by maintaining an interface between our societal selves and our authentic selves—and going a step further to help us realize and express ourselves as authentically as possible in society. Therefore, we must be aware of both our societal role and our sociocultural norms. We must not blindly adhere to them or allow them to create our identity. Too often, we begin to lose ourselves when we are forced to still that small childhood voice that tells us perhaps it is not us, but the world that is at fault when we begin to feel alienated.

The persona is an important aspect of our I-entity (ego) and our entire personality. It is a personal tool that can help us function effectively in the culture as we attempt to fulfill our societal roles as well as ourselves. The persona can also help protect our private, sensitive, personal, and intimate selves from the battering of a turbulent outer world. While not a definition of our personality, a healthy persona should help us express important parts of ourselves in a way that integrates them with the outer world.

The persona is usually represented symbolically by such things as clothes and, at times, our furnishings and surroundings. The change in the soldier as he takes his new energy into the world is reflected in his new persona, his new clothes, and his new living quarters. We have all heard such old sayings as, "You can't tell a book by its cover," "The habit doesn't make the monk," and "Clothes don't make the man." But if you have read anything about dressing for success, positive mental attitudes and management politics, you know that to some extent clothes do make the man. Consider the meaning of uniforms—football, Army, Navy, doormen, or even gray pinstriped business suits. They all say something about the wearer's group, function, status, and frequently give a clue as to how the wearer feels about himself.

Problems begin for us when the persona is either "consciously" constructed to be only a mask, or "unconsciously" deteriorates into a mere mask, no longer fulfilling its purpose. Then it either conceals a void or, worse, falsifies the essential nature of the individual.

If we totally identify with our persona, we have no life as an individual, and end up living values that are based on the expectations of others. The healthy persona is a compromise between the expectations of others and our individuality. If we are too identified with a successful persona, we may lose touch with our inner life and values, inviting the hubris and retribution the Greeks told so many stories about. We may also end up alienated from both reality and the people in our lives. If our persona is rigid and defensive, we are likely never to fully engage in life and relationships, "hiding our candle under a bushel." However, having no persona leaves us sensitive and confused, vulnerable, and we feel exposed in every social situation, making life and work a very painful process.

The soldier has in fact become quite a dandy with his money. Often after a major passage or change, we rush out with enthusiasm (perhaps a little inflated) and energy only to end up feeling down after a while. The soldier follows this course.

The Princess

The soldier hears of the princess. She is unavailable. The king has her locked away, and allows no one to visit her except himself. As one of the players on the stage of our personality, the princess in the tale is the man's feminine side, the anima.

You may recall how I described the anima. She represents "the archetype of life" for the man. A man "animated" is full of life, and to be without her is to be lifeless, to be unconnected to the realm of nature and feelings.

If we look at the anima in our developing psychological model along with the ego and the persona, we can get a sense of her psychological function. The persona is a mediator between the ego and the outer world while the anima is a mediator between the ego and the inner world. This means the anima is complementary to the persona and has a compensatory relationship to it. Put another way, if a man over-identifies with an outer role, or becomes identified in an unbalanced way with his intellect and neglects the balance of his interior life, then he loses his relationship with his inner woman. When this happens she will torment him with emotions, irritations, lack of self-control, moods, and depressions. Looking at this situation metaphorically, we can surmise that his inner woman is trying to bring him back from his identification with a role. She wants him to get out of his provisional life and create a fuller sense of reality based on his own essential nature. In short, she is jealous and wants him back in relationship with himself. She causes his moods, so to speak, by her angry and bitchy behavior. In fact, his inner woman is behaving a lot like a real woman does when her husband is too rational, too distant, and not in touch with his emotions— when she can't contact the man within his skin.

The further a man gets away from his feminine side, the more unconscious and threatening she (the anima) will become. If he learns to relate to her, she will give him warmth and strength. Conversely, if a man lets his inner woman run his life, his public face will not be very effective. He may be lost in fantasies and seem to live in a dreamy state, rarely bringing his creative potential to fruition. Many middle-aged men who have over-identified with their rational thinking side find themselves discovering an underlying sense of depression that has been inside for years (especially if they have been soldiering for twenty years). I will devote another chapter to a fuller explanation of the meaning of the feminine side and what it holds for us as we live our lives as men.

The appearance of the princess has important implications in this tale. The first is personal for the soldier. By freeing himself from the mother, he is now ready for the second stage in the development of his feminine side. His feminine side is no longer under the mother's influence. If a grown man has not made this transition, his own feminine side will behave very much as his wife might if she has to constantly take second place to his mother. She will be angry and depressed, and conflict will constantly drain his energy. The next stage for the soldier is growth into romance and sexuality, leading to his potential for relationship. Of course, these stages are not as cut and dried as they sound. They follow this course of development over the long run. In the short run, we often spiral from one to the other and back. For example, one can easily conclude from our discussion that I think many American men fall in love and marry before they settle their mother complexes. Then, of course, they have a double problem, and having true adult relationships with women is very difficult.

My experience indicates many men with a cultural mother complex actually seem to "mother" their wives sexually. They approach their wives with timidity, attend to every sexual need of their wives, utilize all sorts of foreplay, all the latest techniques of clitoral stimulation and rarely can be accused of being sexually selfish. Then they come to therapy wondering why their wives are losing interest in sex and they are having problems with impotence. Spontaneous passion, lust, romance, anger, and humor are all lost in this scenario. This "mothering" attitude can turn "good" sex (most of these men evaluate their techniques and sexual experiences by the latest articles in women's magazines) into boring sex—and nothing is more boring than boring sex. The sex has become boring, the wife has lost interest, and his body is rebelling because this complex of being a good boy is preventing the authentic, natural person from taking part in one of our most intimate relationships.

If a man's instinctual side is buried and his feminine side is in prison, he cannot have a real relationship because he is not a real person. He must become a real person before he can honestly relate, and this is not easy in a marriage that has its own history of hurts, hopes, disappointments, and misunderstanding. These marriages are based on a false impression of who the partners are, and sadly may end once they have done the work to allow the real people to emerge. It is just as sad, however, to see someone's self-realization thwarted because of the fear of divorce, the fear of being alone, or the fear of facing parents, friends, and children and saying, "I made a mistake."

The imprisonment of the princess has both personal and cultural implications. On both levels a conscious attitude prevails that has a contemptuous outlook on feelings, relationships, nature (including human nature, the source of our vitality), and feminine consciousness. Psychologically speaking, feminine consciousness is more unfocused and instinctual; it reflects an attitude of acceptance and unity, or a wholeness of life, and a readiness for relationship. It is the opposite of a man's focused consciousness (logos), but this does not make it either chaotic or unconscious: it is simply a different way of perceiving and evaluating.

The psychological perspective on masculine and feminine consciousness goes something like the following. All consciousness involves images. We cannot think without images. All images involve figure and ground. One kind of person focuses on the figures. Another focuses on the ground and the patterns of relationship in the figures. In short, we have the emphasis of masculine consciousness focusing on the figures (a discriminating perspective), the emphasis of feminine consciousness on the ground and relationships (a unitive perspective), and human consciousness including both.

Analytical thinking, a derivative of masculine consciousness, is founded on attention; that is, to carefully focus consciousness sharply on a defined area. This focusing is like using the mind as a spotlight, focusing on the world a piece at a time, classifying and organizing the pieces as you go along. When coupled with language, this process gives us a model of the world that appears easier to understand than the world itself. Initially, focused consciousness had tremendous advantages for mankind and guided us into civilization, modern science and technology. This mode of consciousness led us even further as we recognized the demonstrable efficiency of rational thought and the reasoned course of action.

This process of consciousness has now surpassed the limits of creative masculinity. It has now become patriarchal in the negative sense—rigid, self-defensive and overbearing, like the old king. Now we realize this narrow focus ignores the connecting nuances and subtleties that comprise reality. Often, these subtleties may defy quantification and appear subjective or even nonexistent when someone tries to focus the spotlight on them alone. Many businessmen trying to rely on quantification, forecasting, and computer models have learned the hard way that numbers are not enough. They are having to rediscover that intuition may handle some situations better than reason and numbers. Complicated events, often moving so fast words cannot keep up with them, as well as subjective factors, call for intuitive understanding. Then we must shift toward what Peters and Waterman call "hands-on experience" or living knowledge as the basis for decision making. In brief, this is a return to making decisions by a wholistic perception of the overall picture, including the unitive patterns of relationship of the figures and the figures and the ground.

Feminine consciousness gives us an "ecology" of perception or consciousness when combined with masculine consciousness. This "feminine" perception is an area we are struggling to relearn as we attempt to deal with our modern problems in the science of ecology (the natural system that is our life support system) and relationships. We need to regain our balance and develop human consciousness with a deeper sense of the ground involved from this new perspective.

The deeper ecological grounding of consciousness demands we examine our behavior from an ever-increasing moral and ethical perspective. In the area of morals and ethics we are in deep trouble. Morals and ethics in practice are founded on wisdom. As we have pursued rationality and the measured course of action so vigorously, the neglect of wisdom has gone so far that most of our leaders, teachers, and intellectuals do not have the faintest idea what this term could mean.

We need to relearn and reintegrate into a more balanced consciousness the feminine consciousness that we have lost. Then we must realize the increasing ethical and moral sense of responsibility demanded by the modern age, and ground this once again in the wisdom of human nature.

In our tale, the king—the paternalistic principle—has imprisoned the princess and is keeping her for his own use. This imprisonment prevents her from fulfilling her destiny and bringing renewal to the realm. As long as she is imprisoned, new life cannot flow out into the world. One way men have imprisoned the inner woman is by projecting irrational feelings and often intuition onto women. In this way, men identify only with focused consciousness and repudiate all else. In extreme cases, and in a cultural sense, everything that can be called irrational is projected onto women, and described as women's characteristics. We have educated our children implicitly and culturally to these values, and it is a shame that some women, in searching for their freedom, have merely joined the worship of focused consciousness. Their anger and envy have remolded them in the unbalanced male image. Although women should have this option available to them, it might help if they realized that focused consciousness is the very foundation of the patriarchal principle in our culture, and that they give up their own feminine strength and wisdom if they subscribe too much to the same principles that men do. The queen in the tale represents the old matriarchal principle that gains its power by supporting the patriarchy.

Imprisoning the princess in a brazen palace means that we have imprisoned her in an idealistic or enchanted state. Men often project their own feminine side onto a woman and then idealize her. If she does not meet this ideal and insists on being human and earthy, the man ends up very disturbed and may come to loathe her. From this dualism comes the so-called Madonna-whore complex. The split is illustrated by the statement a father of teenage boys and girls once made to me. "It's really a problem having teenagers. You try to teach your son to get all he can and your daughter not to let anyone touch her." For us to have the flow of life, the princess must ultimately be freed from her father and brought down from the upper isolated world to the world of life and humanity.

The Imprisoned Princess

For a man to free his own imprisoned inner princess, he must have some idea as to how to find this part of himself. A good place to begin is by looking at the different ways life in the outer world mirrors and reflects the hidden potentials and the unknown parts of ourselves. Psychologists call these reflections projections.

Projection is an unconscious process used to attribute our difficult emotions, unacceptable motives, and unknown characteristics to others. Often projections defend us from anxiety, provide us with emotional isolation, and protect us from the pain of disappointments and frustrations. The unknown aspects of ourselves expressed in projections reflect characteristics that we experience as "other," perhaps even strange, to our ordinary modes of consciousness. Because of their alienation from our habituated and conditioned points of view, projections are a treasure chest of our unknown qualities and potentials. Sometimes they include dangers as well. Dangers exist when we depend on (or live too much in) projections. That is when we live too much in fantasies and insist on remaining unconscious. In such instances, we cannot determine our true nature, or the nature of reality, or we come crashing down to earth when reality finally appears. Men tend naturally to project the image of what is "other" to themselves symbolically in the form of a woman—the being with the "other" anatomy. In projections and fantasies, the images of women can frequently be understood or experienced as representatives of alternate forms of perception, behavior, emotions, and different value systems. In this sense the inner woman can lead a man to his own potential for healing, growth, and a deeper sense of his own self. Because projections are unconscious, we must learn to discover them through clues offered by behavior and emotions. When we encounter our own projections, they usually affect us forcefully. They excite and attract our attention, forcing us to direct our focus toward them as they attract or repel us. Every time we feel a little rush of infatuation, every time we have a fantasy, an image from our inner world is entangled with it, and it represents a little piece (or perhaps a big piece) of our unknown selves waiting to enrich our lives.

If a man has a tragic love affair—or one that is all-consuming like Dante and Beatrice—he has usually projected his entire feminine self onto a woman. Such a projection is impossible to live; it must end in tragedy because there is little chance of having a more conscious and personal relationship. In more down-to-earth cases, you and I, we find such situations as these:

He is _____ and is attracted to her	because she is _____.
quiet and shy	outgoing and vivacious.
intelligent and rational	spontaneous and adventuresome.
working for a large company	managing her own business.
restrained and cynical	bubbly and enthusiastic.
controlled and orderly	chaotic and hysterical.

In our marriages and relationships with women we find that projections may inspire the initial attraction, and in actuality may provide the seeds for mutual understanding if they are withdrawn and we encounter the *real* other person. If we marry based on these projected attractions and attempt to maintain them, we usually find that they deteriorate and rigidify. Then the very attributes that originally attracted us begin driving us crazy with each other, unless we can find a way to reclaim and develop the projected part of ourselves. It is easy to see how these simple examples complement each other and you can probably think of many more. The important point is to spot the characteristics of women *you* become infatuated with, and see if you can imagine these characteristics as potentials in yourself. Incidentally, you may have noticed they may not all appear positive. If we like to think we are rational, controlled, and orderly, we do not like to believe the hysterical rages of our partner might reflect a deep need for development in our personality as well as hers.

Thinking about projections is helpful for self-understanding. But written exploration is much better than just thinking about them. A good start is to make a list of the following: women you are most comfortable with, with whom you are most uncomfortable, women you fall or fell in love with, women you cannot stand, women you find sexually exciting, women you find very repulsive, plus any other categories you would like to add. For each of the persons or groups listed, see if you can delineate the traits and qualities they have that cause you to feel as you do about them. Then see if you can write about the ways you may possess these same qualities and how they may be affecting your life.

Fantasies, dreams, and infatuations often reflect (in either a direct or a compensatory manner) traits and characteristics that are missing in our personalities. The examples I mentioned are compensatory. The loss of these attributes is generally due either to lack of development or, even more seriously, to wounds to our personality early in life. If they are lost due to wounding, they are pushed deep into our unconscious, far from conscious awareness and control, and are then reflected in the images of fantasies and dreams. Due to this repression, for example, the images and rituals in men's sexual fantasies are charged with unconscious meanings.

Ed had the same type of sexual fantasies for over thirty years. He fantasized himself as an adolescent boy having sex with older women. Ed had been close to his mother when he was small, but she had run away just before he entered puberty. He had never felt his mother's confirmation of his masculinity, her pride in him as a young man. At a deep level Ed also felt that if he had been more lovable she would not have left. Real or fantasized, approving or disapproving, mother makes a powerful impression on our young feminine side. The women in Ed's fantasies comforted, confirmed, and loved him until he could deal with himself in a manner compassionate enough to enable him to face his anger, hurt, and loss. Only after this self-confrontation could Ed begin relating to real women without the ghost of his mother's abandonment haunting the relationship. As you read this, you can easily see the images and the message for Ed in his fantasies, but when we are living our own experiences, the messages are not often this easy to see. The amazing thing to me is how Ed's mind was operating in a compensatory manner to heal and comfort him as well as to give him some idea of what his problem was.

In dreams, whatever is going on is particularly independent from consciousness. In fantasies, on the other hand, the events take place on the level of imagination, a meeting place for both the conscious and the unconscious. Here both sides meet on a common field creating a special life experience that combines the elements of both areas. Strong infatuations generally arouse a strong and active fantasy life. Sexual fantasies bring images from our unconscious to conscious involvement in a vigorous mental and instinctual way. Dreams are a bit more independent in their meanings. The unconscious has its own agenda in dreams and is concerned with compensating our attitudes and pursuing our individuation process in its own way.[2] Often we are not as closely affiliated with the per-

---

[2] If you are interested in dreams, two good books to begin with are Robert Johnson's *Inner Work* (San Francisco: HarperCollins, 1986) and Eugene Gendlin's *Let Your Body Interpret Your Dreams* (Wilmette, IL: Chiron Pub., 1986).

sons and the emotions dreams invoke as we are with those in our fantasies, even though the meaning of dreams may be just as profound.

Attacking our fantasies with "focused" consciousness is not the way to understand them or any other symbolic material from the unconscious. The material in fantasies should be approached in a relaxed, friendly manner. We are trying to listen to another, more colorful, metaphorical language that can disappear or become distorted under the concentrated spotlight of rationality. This language reflects the nuances and subtleties of our personalities. Remember, however, that what we learn from the unconscious must be joined with our conscious knowledge to form a deeper understanding of ourselves and a new level of consciousness. Fantasies are rarely meant to be acted out, and the unconscious is not an "oracle" telling us how to live. With the right attitude, the psychological process of contacting, listening to, and understanding dreams and fantasies is essentially the same. As in understanding most psychological processes, the first major step is to take the process seriously, to pay attention to it, to look for the meaning of the feelings evoked by the images.

Feelings and emotions have a meaning behind them. Emotions are the clues to the psychological meaning implicit in our fantasies. Usually there are two sets of emotions in respect to our sexual fantasies. There are the emotions we experience within the fantasy, and the emotions we have when we observe the fantasy. These emotions do not just happen. There is a special situation in our life or history, or a special attitude, thought or experience, that a particular image has activated to cause these emotions. Finding out what this image has activated is a key in our process of self-understanding. Looking for the meanings of the people, images, and rituals is practically the same association process that I have been using to explore this fairy tale. As with projections, written explorations are also helpful. The simple observation of how rich and colorful these fantasies are can tell us a lot about our potential for experiencing life, as well as indicating our state of mind. Often, a good place to start is with the image or activity that is the most puzzling.

Ed, who fantasized about having sex with older women, felt loved in these situations. During a moment of personal sexual magic, his perception of women changed, as his psyche made an effort to heal the conflict that began with his primitive experience of his mother and the hurt caused by her abandonment. He felt comforted. In reality, Ed is a forceful, successful executive. Once he learned enough self-compassion to be okay with his inner woman—and this was a big step— he found he must go one step further. He needed to learn how to let a woman love and comfort him physically, and even how to risk asking her to do this. Ed also needed to learn how to choose women capable of loving him this way, not all the time, but when he needed it. We all need to be loved this way sometimes. We need to let our vulnerability show and have it loved and nurtured. If we need this kind of love all of the time, we are back to dealing with a more serious problem— the witch. Incidentally, Ed still enjoys his old fantasies at times when he is under stress and pressure.

Next, it's important to figure out how to bring what we have learned into the world of our living experience. Of course, fantasies are also safe playgrounds where we control not only the actors, but also time and space. Even when unexamined, fantasies enrich our experience and add happiness and fun to our lives. Likewise, fantasies can be safe areas for escape in times of stress, tension and self-doubt, nurturing us through difficult times. Fantasies can also be testing grounds for experimenting and for relaxing the rigid defenses of masculinity and responsibility. But fantasies have a dangerous side as well. They can seduce us out of real life and the suffering necessary to work out real relationships, they can keep us from discovering who we really are. Looking at the rituals, women, and situations in our lives can frequently lead us back to our hidden selves and the subliminal aspect of living.

Every experience includes a host of little experiences. Men's sexual fantasies accompanying masturbation usually include rituals, as well as people, props, and scenery. Rituals or ritualistic scenes are often included in the fantasy, and ritualistic behavior is often performed with masturbation. Beginning as boys, there is a ritualistic defiance of parental control and a ritual assertion of developing manhood in masturbation. Think for a minute. It is against the rules of propriety, if nothing else. It is the male generative act. It is a great deal of fun and also invites wonderful spasms of guilt. Boys are bonded in this forbidden area. Whoever heard of girls having a "circle jerk"? Boys often joke about masturbating. They are also careful to ritualistically keep it a private matter, even when practiced jointly, away from the eyes of adult authorities. In adulthood, the rituals often become complex as I will discuss shortly. But one common factor in adulthood is that they usually ensure privacy and an intense focus on oneself. In some instances, masturbation can be considered an intense, concentrated form of introversion and may even reflect a man's need for time alone and a need to pay attention to himself. Other questions we can ask are: What do we like to consistently visualize? What do we like to read? What is it we like to do over and over that we find stimulating?

Rituals within fantasies are also important. Rituals of time, place, persons, and activities can give us rich information. Who are we in them? Are we the same every time? What are we doing? Or even more important, who is she, the woman (or women) in our fantasies, and how do we relate to her? Over and over again, is she a whore? Do we always please her or does she always please us? Do we look at her with contempt? Could it be, for instance, a reflection of how we view our own primitive sexuality, or our own feeling and natural selves? Do we rape her night after night, or day after day? Do we rape our own sensitivity by soldiering and being dogmatically rational and objective? Is the magic of fantasy the only place we can experience our primitive selves? My questions represent only a few ideas and what these rituals and fantasies meant to a few men. Each of us is unique, and the images mean something different according to our own history and experience. But we all share in a culture that has fostered the soldiering approach to life, a cultural mother complex, the locking away of our feminine, feeling, creative and natural selves in some way.

Bob was an engineer in his early 30s. He masturbated, ritually concealing himself, compulsively, once a day for years. Then it began to increase to twice a day, three times a day, often consecutively. His wife felt angry and neglected. Bob rarely enjoyed having sex or making love with her. It took a long time to realize what this compulsion meant in his life. The pressure and desire to masturbate had gradually increased over the years. His fantasies were rich and colorful, filled with life. Finally, we got a clue by noticing he was often a painter making love with his model. Bob had wanted to be a painter, and had cut off that part of himself with an early marriage, taking on the responsibility of husband, father, and young professional. He had imprisoned his muse. He wrestled with the idea of what he should do. Should he chuck it all and go back to change careers? But he enjoyed being an engineer and a father. What Bob discovered was that he must answer his muse as an avocation. Not as just a hobby, mind you, but as a serious commitment that took time, devotion, and dedication. This commitment allowed him to express his creative energy in a needed way that fulfilled him. It took him away from his wife and family, demanding introversion and time alone. However, his masturbation decreased dramatically and became fun rather than a compulsion. Once again, Bob found he could enjoy making love with his wife. He could enjoy having her meet him in reality, as he had once enjoyed having his model do in his fantasies. He could relate to her and his children honestly as a more satisfied person. They all felt more satisfied, although he didn't meet his former ideal of what he thought constituted a fully involved, sensitive husband and father.

In our fantasies we find the images and imprints (often as opposites) of the women we have lived with and loved, the women we have feared and avoided, the women we have worshipped and revered, and often the deep primitive woman that we have desired in so many ways (from Eve, to Madonna, to whore). Often, we may see the ideal lover—or the ideal state—that represents a deep inner longing. From these images we can learn the characteristics of our own inner woman, and find out some of the things we may need from real women in the world. Long therapy and a lot of trust are necessary for a man to share his sexual fantasies and rituals. I usually begin the process of exploration simply by asking what are the images in the fantasies and what feelings do they evoke. Exploring the images in writing is also helpful and requires courage and privacy.

When the issue of sexual fantasies finally comes up, a deep struggle is going on to unite love, joy, and personal acceptance with the instinctual side of masculinity. Early in life, boys learn to hide sex from the anxious eyes of mothers. As boys mature into men, they are often left with a deep impression that nice girls, like mom, must think sex not nice at some deep inner level. As these feelings become part of us, we continue fragmenting ourselves, horribly splitting mind and body, love and the instincts. One of the most common elements in men's sexual fantasies is a woman who gives him permission to do what he wants and then enjoys the experience with abandon. This fragmentation is the early fear of mother incorporated into a personal inner inhibition, unconscious, that affects our relationships with all the women in our lives, and makes us wish *they* would free us from our fears.

As our culture has rigidified, men and often women have forced more and more of our needs for understanding, tenderness, touching, sensuality, nurturance, and love into the arena of sex. As a result, our sexual fantasies have come to represent much broader and deeper needs than just sexual union. A man who has spent years "soldiering" may fantasize a woman in control of him (or bondage or humiliation), to compensate his rigidity or his need to give up responsibility and be nurtured. Bondage in fantasy (or reality) can be the other side of masculine separateness and strength that has become too rigid. I have run across a surprising number of men whose masturbatory rituals include semi-hanging themselves and partial asphyxiation. In every case I have known, the man had an inhibition about releasing his own phallic power in the world and in his relationships with women—that is, to be who he is and to ask for what he wants in a natural way. Men who have large collections of pictures of breasts often cannot face their needs for nurturance (and therefore try to objectify them) because of the witch's continuing hold on their lives and their own inability to love. These are only a few samples of how men have fragmented themselves.

Women and one's relation to them in fantasy often show symbolically the unlived sensitivity in men, the unlived physical and instinctual sides of their lives, and their need to be able to love someone physically. Most men fantasize pleasing their partners, frequently in a gentle and thoughtful way. The myth that men are interested in "one thing" and women are interested in "meaningful relationships" still lives on, even as incidents of male impotence become epidemic. I have met few men, either personally or professionally, who either enjoy or fantasize about living the impersonal sex life of a healthy rabbit.

Men need to love. Men need to be loved. Men need to be inspired. We need these things from real flesh-and-blood women, and we need to learn how to get this nurturance from our own inner feminine selves as well. The rituals and women in our fantasies can be a helpful guide in the search for wholeness and fulfillment. Often the soft men who appear sensitive and like to touch women are themselves starving for a woman's touch; they need strong, living enthusiasm and want to be desired with passion—a deep, physical passion, not the shallow arousal of orgasmic techniques illustrated in the sex manuals our culture seems so intent on promoting as a substitute for love. Of course, such a response from a woman would scare these men to death, for it takes a man deeply rooted in his own earth strength to accept physical love from a truly earthy woman. The deep passion from inner and outer women can constellate a deep passion for life and living that "animates" our lives. Men, by and large, have imprisoned this passionate inner woman in the brazen castles of movies, pornography, dreams, machines, and fantasies.

The King

Earlier I referred to the king as the father principle, representing the status quo and whatever is conventional. Now I would like to expand that discussion. In depth psychology, the king often represents the Self, that is, the *total* of the personality. In myths and folklore the king usually stands for the dominant male cultural attitude in the realm of the personality. So we see, as with other figures, the king is a symbol on two levels, the cultural and the individual. In many tales, including this one, the king is old and must be overthrown. This symbolic action is needed to bring a renewal of consciousness to the culture and the individual.

The old king brings on his overthrow by becoming rigid, too one-sided, and resisting renewal. In a cultural sense, this situation represents a collective neurosis. By keeping the princess imprisoned, the king in our fairy tale is preventing her marriage, keeping out a prince who would eventually become the new king representing new consciousness. The princess becoming queen would represent the evolution of the feminine, and renewal would be continued through her having children. Because renewal is being blocked and the positive form of the feminine is being denied, the future holds no promise and the stage is set for a breakdown.

We modern men have developed an egocentric position just as the king did. Our ego has identified too much with the outer world and its goals. The goal of the ego is then to protect itself and its own ambitions and values. It has become a psychic institution with its own "Peter Principle." The deeper we are in this state, the more difficult our process of self-realization becomes. The life that results from this egocentricity is increasingly rigid, uncreative and resistant to any kind of change. The

Self, as it orchestrates the process of self-realization, in contrast, is creative and unpredictable. As a result, we have a conflict that leaves us anxious, threatened, and defensive.

The experience of individuation is going to involve suffering because the death of the old king, the egocentric attitude, is necessary. Often the right instinctive behavior is the best way to approach this problem, and that is how the soldier responds, summoning the instincts and shadow from deep in the earth by striking a spark.

Paradoxically, the more life energy you have, the more serious your breakdown may be—and this breakdown is good! (That is, if you can find the meaning in it.)

Many men put aside dreams of using their artistic talents, of starting their own business, or of pursuing their own interests, to keep on soldiering, doing the practical and accepted thing—being good boys and often becoming quite successful. But part of them becomes increasingly rigid and imprisoned. They become pitiful old men if they do not first have a heart attack that kills them. They become fragile and helpless, badgering their wives, and forcing the world to finally mother them as their reward.

I know the story of one man who was in management for thirty years. At about age 50, he was manager of a great insurance company's district office. He was a good father and faithful husband. For years he had dreamed of building sailboats. One day, to everyone's surprise, he had a nervous breakdown, and had to be put in a mental hospital.

Paradoxically his breakdown reflected a strong sense of Self and a life force that would not allow him to continue living in a manner that split him from himself. Through this experience, and with the help of a therapist whose interest went beyond getting him back to "normal" (soldiering along the collective highway), he underwent a true transformation. When he came out of the hospital he began building sailboats. Of course his story was more complex than this short vignette, but my point is that his "breakdown" led to transformation and a life more congruent with his own nature.

It is difficult for us to understand, and often even more difficult for the women in our lives to grasp, that a man's dream requires a man's commitment. Hobbies, Sunday school classes, volunteer work and so-on will not fill the need presented by a dream. Nor will working on it part-time or on Saturday afternoons fill the need, unless this is a building time that will later lead the dream into the real world.

Most of us develop some kind of symptoms if we need them. Several kinds have been discussed earlier. These symptoms are often a call letting us know the old king is going to have to die if we are going to fully live.

A King's Dreams—Vision and Commitment

In primitive cultures, the cycles of a man's life were clearly marked by rituals and ceremonies. As a result, both the man and his community recognized and accepted the new or renewed status in his life. Native American men, for instance, went through the cycles of being boy, brave, mature man, and, finally, "grandfather" or wise old man. Each transition was evidenced by rituals and ceremonies. To become a man, the boy had to go through an initiation that was often very formal. In the hunter-warrior tribes, this initiation included the quest for a vision that would give the young man a sense of his adult identity and the pattern that his life could fulfill. Frequently, when one of these men felt out of harmony with himself and the world, he would again seek a new vision to help him return to his path or to find a new direction. As a brave, there were many honors he could earn, and groups that he could belong to, that would signify his growing status, his value to the community, and also help solidify his maturing identity. Such a life cycle is also illustrated by the different stages of "kingship" in fairy tales. As I have mentioned before, the king represents both the ruling principles (or attitudes) in the individual's mind and the prevailing attitudes in a culture.

The beginning of the cycle in fairy tales is represented by the potential king in some form. He may be a prince, a common man in some mode, such as the soldier in this fairy tale, or even a dumling. But whatever his form, he represents the promise of renewal, creativity, and generativity that will bring new life and energy to the kingdom. Next, the king matures and, as he does so, he embodies the principles of life and living. He provides order and justice by his living example, and thus prevents the kingdom from fragmenting. He fulfills the promise of his youth. The final phase of kingship, and frequently the most common in fairy tales like this one, is that of the old king. The old king may be wise and generous. He may be sick and dying. But, most often, he has become negative, rigid, and defensive in some way, like the king in this fairy tale. This king represents a concretization of cultural masculine values resulting in the exclusion of creativity and new life energy.

Often when we realize something is terribly wrong with our lives, our personalities are being ruled by an old king. We then get physical and emotional ailments, overworking, attempting self-medication (for example, drinking, overeating, extramarital affairs, and so forth) in an attempt to avoid facing the realities of our personal needs and unhappiness.

Daniel Levinson,[3] in his studies of men's lives, concludes that as adolescent boys evolve into young adulthood, they construct a "dream" which will order the seasons of their lives and steer the course of their destinies. This dream is a vague sense of themselves in the adult world and includes imagined possibilities that generate excitement and vitality. The young man's developmental task is to give the dream greater definition and to live it out. I call this dream the prince's vision, which in turn becomes the vision of the young king and is lived out, defined, and modified by the mature king. Levinson's study is concerned with the generation of American men immediately preceding the generation that I am discussing, which includes the difficulties of the soft male, the Peter Pan, the manipulating man, and the pseudo-liberated man. In this

[3]Daniel J. Levinson, *The Seasons of a Man's Life* (New York: Ballantine, 1978), p. 91.

earlier generation, individual achievement, primarily in occupations, seems to dominate a man's life journey toward his destiny.

As men recognize the possibility of becoming more balanced in their approach to life (see Part III of this book) and focus more on individuation and reclaiming disowned parts of themselves, relationships and spirituality will claim as important a part of their visions as achievement does. Continuous self-renewal will also become more important, as will a constant openness to challenging our perspectives on life. This continuous self-renewal means to become a prince again and again, with new visions and new potentials. It also means becoming a prince again in our own country—that is, to become increasingly congruent with our true inner selves. We have become so alienated from ourselves that our own country may seem strange at first, often frightening and foreign. We are lucky if we had a brief vision of it somewhere during adolescence that will help us realize it is the homeland of ourselves and is a place within our own psyche and body.

Men who have remained under the mother complex have either failed to develop a prince's vision to structure their way into adult manhood, or they have developed a false vision constructed to appear in a certain way to please others. Even if they appear strong, men who are trapped in dependency have trouble developing the attributes of commitment.

Commitment entails courage, discipline, service, and duty. Courage is a virtue in commitment—the courage to live ascetically, not dominated by needs of comfort, and to stand pain, often emotional, while remaining focused on a personal vision. Picasso, for example, had a radical ability, and the courage to focus on his art—to serve this vision. His commitment also reflected duty, because his vision—while very personal—was also an expression of his view of the story of humanity, and a reflection of his duty to his art and therefore his own individuation process as part of that story. His work, his efforts, were in service to these aspects of his life's process. Note that courage here implies service to a vision, and not bravery in the service of dominating others. It's a longer lasting kind of courage.

A man who is trapped in the poverty of infantile dependency, needing to please for acceptance, affirmation, or love, is doomed in relationships. He is trapped between his needs and an underlying rage, and has little energy available to love others. He is either overinvolved in manipulating and pleasing in his relationships, or he is underinvolved, because he cannot allow himself to participate emotionally as an autonomous adult. He certainly cannot move in and out of emotional relationships in a manner that reflects both commitment to a vision and the importance of relationships.

More than anything else, a man's true vision of either his life or a particular quest will activate his desire to live. One meaning of commitment is to say "yes" to the vision and to allow one's self to be urged on and carried by the desire that enables us to wholeheartedly embrace our cause or destiny. In fact, to say "yes" to the desire and to obey it causes it to become a demand to live. In the long run the only way to find out the truth of a vision is to live it, risking failure and loss, for then we find out the most important truths about ourselves. In the final analysis, what we do and what we live determines who we are—not what we say or think we are, but what we do.

A vision that structures our life is a psychospiritual reality. Such a vision, if it is true, helps lead us to our true identity. If the vision is not true, as in the discussion in the previous section, it will lead us to a crisis in our identity. Often during initiation rites, Native Americans would take on a new or special name to reflect their new identity and to acknowledge that while still ordinary, the very purpose of their existence had changed. A man's worldview is changed by his vision, and his life takes on a new or different meaning.

When in adulthood we pursue a vision that is alienating us from ourselves, we may have difficulty being open to a new vision until we are at the end of our rope. If we are in the process of compulsively avoiding ourselves, we may find that even after we apply our best thinking, both sides of the war within come out even, and we stand to lose something important no matter what we do. At this point it is best to stop fighting with life. We must pause and attempt to regain contact with the inner voice of our nature and become receptive to our own renewal process. During this process we must be very careful to remember that practicality is the greatest enemy of any vision.

Native Americans did not think a man was losing his grip on things in times of personal crisis. A man's ability and manhood were taken for granted because they had been proven in his manhood initiation rites and in his experience. So, instead of becoming anxious and insecure, or obsessive-compulsive about work, or impotent with his woman, he would seek his inner voice in the receptive darkness of a sweat lodge. He tried to find out why his inner world was incongruent with his outer world and sought a vision that would unfold the possibility of reconciling these worlds if he fulfilled its promise. Then he could make a new beginning.

Two kinds of visions empower the individual and the culture. The first is an inner vision of who we really are and who we can be. This vision helps us recognize and stay on our personal thread throughout our lives. The second vision is more explicit as to fulfilling outer potential in the culture. Both, however, demand a man's commitment. Both call for duty, service, focus, and courage, supported by the deep strength (the instinctual strength) of the masculine.

I will give examples of both. The well-known story of Ray Kroc, the founder of McDonald's fast food chain, is a legend that illustrates a vision of outer potential in the culture. And please note, this vision came late in life to Ray Kroc—in his 50s. His vision was strong and simple and he adhered to it vigorously. Everyone knows Ray Kroc was successful. But this did not mean that he lived "happily ever after." Life continues to be a struggle. Having a vision helps give meaning and purpose to life, but it is not a panacea for life's difficulties.

The story of the man in management who left his job to build sailboats is a story illustrating how a man expressed his inner vision of who he was by a change in occupation. This story also empowers the culture as it impacts everyone who hears it. The legendary Cherokee Chief Sequoyah combined both visions as he invented the Cherokee alphabet. He withdrew into a cabin for over a year, working by torchlight in seclusion, leaving all the farmwork to his wife until his vision was realized. Then he brought this vision back into the world with great effect. Nowhere in a history book is it said he was less a man for not continuing to "soldier"; in fact, leaving the soldiering to others facilitated his getting into the history books as a great man.

In the healthy process of renewal we learn to listen to our inner voice of authority and often change with less drama, but never without some conflict and separation from old ways. The renewal of visions is as different as people are different. Such renewals do not always mean drastic changes. They may often mean a revitalization and a recommitment to a vision we lost sight of in the turmoil of daily living.

The Queen

The king, as we've seen, represents the patriarchal masculine that has become too rigid. In our culture this principle has become too one-sided in rationality, extroversion, and thinking, the dominant masculine principles. The queen supports the king even though he imprisons the princess. The queen, then, as the dominant feminine principle in the realm/person, has lost her instinctive reactions and has come to symbolize the matriarchy that supports the patriarchy. Being from the south, I am reminded of the cliché of the "steel magnolia"— the woman who has the "iron fist in the velvet glove." She is the managerial wife who acknowledges the male as the man of the house but subtly runs the life of everyone in the family.

The queen is not healthy in this tale, so she must perish. If the queen were healthy, she would add warmth, compassion and wisdom to the king, and if he did not accept her in a healthy manner, she would bring retribution to him. Her retribution is the revenge of nature, a natural consequence to a wrong attitude which may not in itself be immoral or illegal. For example, a man who leads a driven life long enough will find that his body gives him certain disorders.

The witch shows up in her second form as the queen. The queen stands for the cultural mother-image and one of the collective parental images that we must separate from to be finally independent. If we are to become independent, we must separate from our parents, both familial and cultural, not necessarily physically but psychologically.

Darkness

As the soldier was living merrily, he always took from his money but never replaced it. When we lose our path we exhaust our physical and emotional capital. Finally he was forced to leave his fancy lodgings; his clothes became old and worn, and his friends faded away. He rented a small room and was in the dark because he could not afford a candle.

What has happened to the soldier? Essentially two things. He has taken his first burst of masculine energy and spent it. In the process, he overidentified with his persona and therefore did nothing to renew the energy he found deep within. Now he is in the dark, perhaps depressed, certainly lonely and isolated. In order to renew himself, he will have to get back in touch with the dogs, his instinctual and shadow sides, and maintain them as companions. When becoming sophisticated, someone special or superior, even if generous, we must be careful not to lose our connection to our earthy side that holds the key to renewal. His loneliness shows his need to renew his relationship with these inner companions.

Charging into adulthood full of hopes, dreams, and energy and then having a small burnout happens naturally to a young man. He must then reassess himself and his ambitions to learn more about who he is and what his real strengths are. He then moves from young adulthood into adulthood. The men I previously discussed who were in their late 20s and early 30s were at this point. This transition point is new. The soft-man, the Peter Pan, and those who have not yet left mother do not reach this transition.

Some men charge so strongly into adulthood that they miss this transition. Their momentum carries them right past it. They are likely to have a more severe mid-life adjustment as their personality attempts to balance itself. One of the major lessons we have to learn by mid-life is that our energy is limited, and we must use it carefully and renew it.

A man must also learn that life is filled with conflict and struggle. Obligations and desires constantly conflict. On the opening page of *The Road Less Traveled*, Scott Peck maintains:

> Life is difficult. This is a great truth. . . . Most do not fully see the truth that life is difficult. Instead they moan more or less incessantly, noisily or subtly, about the enormity of their problem, their burdens, and their difficulties as if life were generally easy, as if life should be easy.[4]

Our culture seems to foster the belief that we have the right to live happily ever after. Even when going to therapy, people still expect this unrealistic state. I have had clients get so furious at the first page of Peck's book they would not read the rest of it. Many seem to hope they can get centered and flow mellowly down the center of the river of life. Often we can accept on a "head level" that life is difficult, but not in our emotional depths. We have such a media history of "happily ever aftering," or of "having it all," in the 80s vernacular, that deep down we hope for, long for, and even expect such a fate. This mother complex, our longing for the great mother, says if we can just get the right wife, lover, job or whatever, or be a good enough boy, we will be rewarded by a return to paradise.

---

[4]M. Scott Peck, *The Road Less Traveled* (New York: Simon & Schuster, 1978), p. 1.

Even psychology and new age consciousness carries on the myth of living happily ever after. If we can find the right psychological balance or the right cosmic harmony we can return to paradise. Jung once told Laurens Van Der Post, with a laugh, that he "could not imagine a fate more awful, a fate worse than death, than a life lived in perfect balance and harmony."[5]

Individuation does not work this way. A man finds that he must continually be able to go back into the depths, to his deep masculine energy to renew himself and to fully understand what he wants, what his deep needs are, and to insist they are heard. Through the emotions sparked as he takes out the tinder box and strikes flint and steel, he can develop his true feeling capacity and free his feminine side from her prison.

---

[5]Laurens Van Der Post, *Jung and the Story of Our Time* (New York: Viking Penguin, 1976), p. 76.

9

RENEWAL

As the soldier sat in the dark, he remembered the tinder box. He took it and began to strike a light. With one strike the dog guarding the copper coins appeared. He immediately sent the dog to replenish his supply of money. With his new money he moved back to his handsome lodgings. He had learned how to use the tinder box and could now summon all three dogs as he wanted them.

Psychologically, the soldier has learned how to relate to his instincts and emotions. He has learned to summon and direct them when his energy needs renewing; he can focus them to serve him. Just as we have three dogs and three types of money, we also have three basic masculine issues connected to the instinctual side of men—power, emotions, and the self-knowledge resulting from the realization of the instinctual self. In this respect I mean the *psychic* instincts of man which integrate our biological selves with our psychological selves in order that we may experience life as an organic whole. For example, as man has an instinct to survive, he also has an instinct to carry his survival further, and is driven to become more himself and to express himself in some manner.

Modern man has lost touch with these natural instincts (the bedrock of our personalities) and their resulting emotions (the energy) that connect us to the natural values of life and nature. Man is left paralyzed, looking for experts to tell him right and wrong on the one hand (polls for politicians, the field of bioethics for medicine, etc.—relief from individual responsibility), and the soulless pursuit of greed and materialism on the other.

To explain further, the natural instincts include a fundamental drive toward increasing and affirming life. Self-preservation and reproduction confirm this drive. Strength and power are directed primarily toward self-defense or limited territorial defense. The natural instinct to kill is the instinct to hunt and again to preserve territorial boundaries. This instinct does not include the acquisition of territory for greed. Cooperation is a collective endeavor to give strength and efficiency. Even passivity serves growth and renewal in terms of rest and the restoration of strength. Of course, any of these instincts may become negative when taken too far in the complex, densely populated, modern world. Reproduction, for example, cannot be considered life-enhancing in the face of overpopulation, disease, and famine. That's why we must develop consciousness to mediate our instinctual responses in a 20th century manner, once we have regained them.

To become a man, a boy must develop enough power, usually in the form of aggression, to survive the competitiveness of adolescence and the development of masculinity in general. He needs to be confident that he has and can win something in the face of opposition. This opportunity may take form in sports, academics, or challenging nature programs such as Outward Bound or camp. Without these experiences, he may try negative ways to develop his power by defying teachers, parents, or the law to win his self-respect. Most boys will show some defiance of authority anyway, and this rebellion is important for the formation of their identities.

Competitive activities also involve losing. Whenever we compete, we know someone must lose. This scares us because we know we will surely lose at some point in our life and, indeed, we have no assurance of ever winning. Men must be familiar with the experience of losing in order to learn how to restore their vitality and to show compassion when they win. From these experiences boys develop their masculine power.

Some men either never quite outgrow this period in their life, or they seem to become attached to this early exercise of power. We recognize them in later life when their competitiveness spills into almost everything they do and has a slightly adolescent tint to it. Ken Kesey comments on power:

> And you had to . . . you had to court. Boys no longer court girls. This loss of the ability to court means that men are losing their power, and when you lose power, you begin to use force. I have this theory that power does not corrupt, it purifies. Real power, when you have it, cleans you out. When you don't have power, you have to use force. That's why rape has gone up in the United States.[1]

Two of the most significant emotions connected to our instinctual side are anger and sorrow. In my earlier discussion of the dogs and instincts, I discussed the negative aspects of instinctual anger, and said that we must learn to use anger consciously and appropriately. Consciously directed anger can move mountains. The anger of one mother against drunk drivers started a movement that has done a great deal to stop the slaughter on our highways that we previously accepted in such a blase manner. Christ knew what he was doing when he unleashed his anger on the money-changers in the temple. Anger becomes dangerous if we refuse to recognize it within ourselves and it then comes out in unknown or explosive ways.

Instinctual sorrow reflects true grief and suffering. It is not about self-pity, depression, or the frustration of a belief that we should be happy and life should be easy. This sorrow may be reflected as depression if we try to repress or deny it. This sorrow is the dark side of the spark from the tinder box. Instinctual sorrow falls into these categories—loss of innocence and true adversity. The first is the sorrow from our loss

---

[1] Ken Kesey and Robert Stone, "Blows to the Spirit," in *Esquire*, June, 1986, p. 93.

of innocence as the shocks in life help us progress to new consciousness. Each shock, from early childhood on, involves a painful loss of innocence, sometimes large and sometimes small. These shocks cannot be avoided, and attempting to do so only makes life more difficult, or results in withdrawal from living, which carries its own penalties. Men who are soldiering through life try to repress the awareness of this kind of suffering. The cost for this denial is losing the warmth and support of others as well as losing important participation in the collective human process. Successful men in middle age are often aware of what they have lost in their process of advancement, and some feel they "sold out" their youthful fire and ideals.

The second type of sorrow is caused by true adversities in life. Death, illness, accident, divorce, and bankruptcy may happen to anyone. Our efforts to build a better world do little to alleviate the suffering from these sorrows. However, like the soldier, consciousness can help us learn how to use the tinder box, direct the instincts, and maintain them as friendly companions; we also learn the difference between actual suffering and our emotional response to neurotic suffering.

In reality, a lot of contemporary suffering is neurotic or inauthentic suffering. Neurotic suffering reflects our inability to accept the fact that life is difficult. Furthermore, we suffer inauthentically because we fight our own growth process. For many reasons we are not struggling to become ourselves. We are too busy wishing we were, or trying to become somebody else—someone we think is together and happy. This someone else may be a real person, made up of the characteristics of several real people, or may simply be ideal images planted in our minds along the way of our development. Many neurotic "sufferers" moan and groan about their burdens and problems, as if they thought life should be easy and they should always be happy and secure. They react emotionally, anxious and depressed, carrying on their tune of "poor me, isn't it awful," as if life's difficulties are a special illness inflicted on them. Inauthentic and neurotic suffering erodes our personalities, while the acceptance of true suffering deepens them and leads to wisdom. Genuine self-confidence and esteem comes from confronting, handling, and sometimes just enduring life's challenges—not from looking for an easy way out.

When we become grounded in ourselves, our perspective on suffering begins to change. Through consciousness we learn to suffer and by accepting the "chain of suffering" in life, we increase our ability to maintain an objective perspective, sometimes even a critical distance, on our suffering. Viktor Frankl wrote a lot about this process of dealing with suffering.[2] The more we become aware of our neurotic suffering and accept that life is difficult, the less we feel that life is a personal attack on us. Then we begin to understand that we must live with the cards life has dealt us—fate—and at the same time choose to live out our destiny—our individuation process.

A good way to begin discriminating between actual and inauthentic or neurotic suffering is to keep in mind the Buddhist maxim, "Desirousness is the cause of all suffering." Our Western version of suffering is not entirely comparable with the Buddhist version. But our self-created (and culturally created) need for things (money, achievement, materialism) can often lead to a chain of anxiety and suffering that only ends with death. Frequently, another person, such as a psychotherapist, can help us sort out our suffering. When we accept that life is difficult and we experience the suffering, we start breaking through our personal boundaries and realize we are participating in the pain and darkness of life itself. Suffering should not be repressed or denied, but rather experienced in its depth with a realization that it unites us all in common humanity. Many older people have learned this as part of the wisdom of living.

Knowledge of our own instincts and emotions is the first step that enables us to integrate instinct and emotion into our conscious personality. We must be aware of the existence of

---

[2]See especially Frankl's book *The Doctor and the Soul: From Psychotherapy to Logotherapy* (New York: Random House, 1986).

these parts of ourselves—both the useful and the destructive components. With this knowledge we can discriminate and direct our feelings and our inner strength. The search for this knowledge is hard and unending, and I hope this book is helpful to those who are searching. The positive sides of our instincts and emotions will enable us to act with conviction, passion, and strength and to live with vitality. Men must find this deep power available to them for living and renewal.

Princess

The soldier uses the dog to bring the princess to him. I mentioned in the last chapter that the presence of the princess symbolized that the soldier's feminine side was free of the mother, and his potential for growth into romance, sexuality, and relationship was established. At this stage in the tale, the princess represents the second general stage in the development of a man's feminine side. This is referred to as the "lover." In this stage the young man (and often older ones) find the beloved utterly desirable, irresistible, and magical. We are all familiar with this romantic version of love. Psychologically, the man has projected his feminine side and its ideals onto a real woman. Two distinct features in such a situation are 1) the relationship is an unconscious one, and almost everyone except the two people involved are aware of this; and, 2) once the man gets the woman, he discovers he has not got what he wanted at all.

This is why all great love stories are tragedies; they are stories of mutual projections by men and women, which by their very nature can never attain satisfaction. Sometimes disillusionment is sudden and painful, especially when one is young. The situation is more unfortunate when these projections lead to marriage and children. Then, the disillusionment creeps in with the stress of everyday life. Some people continually seek to maintain the magic through serial divorces or relationships. Some become so wounded they steer clear of committed relationships. Paradoxically, hopelessness and exhaustion in these circumstances can also be viewed as a call to a new level—conscious awareness leading to greater maturity. A fresh new projection is often the middle-aged man's first call to awaken to the feminine part of himself that he has rejected for so long.

Examining the continuing symbolism in the tale gives a sense that these are the soldier's circumstances. First he can only meet the princess via his instincts—the dog. The dog assisting him is the lowest level dog, the one guarding the copper, symbol of common people and Aphrodite, the goddess of instinctual love. Because the transaction is at night and the princess never awakens, we can surmise that this transaction is highly unconscious. Of course he kisses the princess, and we all know that kisses are usually magic and transforming in fairy tales. Kisses break spells and restore bewitched persons to their original conditions, usually one of beauty. We, too, are never the same after our first experience of love.

But do not forget that our soldier has been following a maturational process. A young man's life is enriched by his first experience of love, his first contact with the princess (inner and outer), if he has developed his "I-entity," separated from mother and built some inner strength. If a young man has not followed this process, he will be approaching the rocky road to relationships, interdependence, and self-knowledge with a deformity of masculine spirit. This road can be scary enough at best and most of us in reality approach it in a mixed state. At its best, this new experience can bring a new tenderness, new intuition, and a new connection to the world of nature in a man's inner life. Life is animated, the sky may be blue, the grass greener and the air fresher.

The sons of absent fathers in a world of denigrated masculinity and heroism recurrently sink into their passivity, and computer games (as Dungeons and Dragons). For the man with a defective masculine spirit who gets past his passivity, this first experience may wound him terribly, leading to the compulsive pursuit of romance, disillusionment, fear and contempt of women, or sex, or love.

The wound from a first love can be a wound for life. The image of the woman in this wound can influence and haunt a man's psyche continually. Larry was such a man. He was 53, divorced twice, and still cherished the pictures of his first love at their senior prom. For over thirty years she had appeared in his dreams, often giving him a warm feeling upon awakening. He still felt he was in love with her even though he had not seen her for decades, and consciously realized the irrationality of his feelings. When he daydreamed, it was still her he impressed with his successes.

When they had broken up all those years ago, he had been devastated. He felt he had caused the breakup because he was afraid of the intensity of their romance. Larry knew when he married his first wife that it was not out of love, but to grow up and to help him find a place in the adult world. They had four children and eventually divorced. During his entire marriage, he felt tremendous guilt, because he knew he had married a woman he could never fully love. From the ashes of his divorce he married again. But this time he adopted a new role, that of the maternal man. His new wife liked him in this role and wanted to remain emotionally dependent while espousing the latest persona offered by the feminist movement. Her emotional attitude was one of infantile entitlement insisting that he "be her emotional nurse even on her good days." As Larry's emotional life and vitality was being suffocated, his old girl friend came back into his dreams. This time she did not give him warmth. She appeared crippled, deformed, or obese. This scared Larry, and he began to work intensely in psychotherapy.

The second marriage also ended in divorce. Now, a few years later, Larry is still working in therapy, struggling to find his own instinctual masculine and feminine selves and to live them out with real people. He has not dreamed of *her* for two years.

If the young man's initial encounter with the opposite gender is mixed with sexuality, an even deeper conflict may begin. When pushed onward by personal psychological needs as well as hormones he can attempt to use sexuality to sate his psychological needs in a manner destructive to love and intimacy. Likewise, the fear of being immoral, breaking strict religious taboos, causing pregnancy, "taking advantage of girls," can cause an emotional split in a young man's personality that continues for years. Even if only petting to a climax, twenty years later he may still be carrying this burden of guilt and fear. With this burden he may be unable to allow himself to experience his deep emotional needs and to enter into a full instinctual life with his wife.

Vince went with a high school girl friend for two years with no sex. Finally, one night in a drive-in, she performed oral sex on him. With adolescent enthusiasm and stupidity he told a "few" friends. Of course, the word was soon out. She suffered and he suffered, and she never spoke to him again. He still dreams and fantasizes about her sometimes, always feeling a mixture of excitement followed by guilt. Other men wounded in similar ways may dream of prostitutes and venereal diseases. When I continuously read statements such as this:

> ... recreational sex had always been part of the traditional male repertoire. Whether in 1950 or 1980 casual sex had always been the macho symbol, and very few men were complaining as long as they controlled the action.[3]

I am disgusted at the shallowness of the people who claim to study our culture. I realize how much more we need to study with *depth, compassion,* and *understanding,* and get out of this endless rut of collecting statistics to support political or polemic viewpoints.

We see the soldier's potential relationship beginning, but we also see that instinctual romantic love, forming an uncon-

---

[3]Barbara Ehrenreich, Elizabeth Hess, Gloria Jacobs, "The Politics of Promiscuity," in *New Age Magazine,* November/December, 1986, p. 31.

scious connection, is not enough. Something else is needed to bring about a marriage and to bring renewal to the realm.

Love

The mystery and experience of love is too overpowering to be simply dismissed as a projection or as a romantic illusion, even though some of both are usually involved. Young men and women think they know what love is while older folks, if they have not rejected love by becoming cynical or blase, tend to acknowledge love's mystery and power. Love happens, and it is often a miraculous, transforming, and transcending experience that must not be destroyed by trying to reduce it to a simple set of psychological propositions. Projections are important and may provide the spirit of love, and the seed of understanding the "other," that helps men and women through some difficult periods. Projections must be moved through, recollected, in order to truly love and relate to the unique individuality of the other person. The soldier must consciously meet the princess in the light of day when she is fully awake, not coming to him on the back of a dog.

When we can make the transformation from relating through our fantasies and desires and be true to our own deepest needs, paradoxically, we are then most likely to serve the other's needs also. This is true because if a man and woman become lost in each other, they lose the possibility for each to develop a broader personality. Maintaining one's identity while becoming involved in the emotional life of another is a difficult challenge. Lovers and partners who cannot say "no" to each other begin to find that they have a diminishing capacity to say "yes" to each other and to themselves as well. In fact, when the boundaries are lost, two people can no longer encounter each other for there is no common ground left on which to meet. This is why the soldier and the princess must meet when fully awake, conscious. Once the fusion and projections of romantic love are experienced, a man and woman must begin to reestablish their identities and have love be a bridge between them.

We can only meet each other honestly from the standpoint of our own needs. This kind of honesty is fundamental in any love relationship, including our relationships with ourselves. Without this awareness and honesty we are doomed to pursue an endless cycle of manipulating each other, endless battles, or withdrawing into the icy isolation of a relationship that is either like two armed camps, or has the *proper* form and behavior, but no heart.

A great deal of strength, "Iron John" strength, is required to find our deepest needs and voice them. Men have a lot of trouble voicing their deepest needs, even to themselves.

Men must first get in touch with their deep masculine strength before they can relate to their feminine side or to women. Getting in touch with the feminine before learning about the masculine can thwart the entire process. More is required than simply talking about emotions and "feelings." I have known plenty of women and some men who can emote and talk about feelings seemingly forever, but who have great difficulty discriminating and acknowledging deep inner needs. In my experience of working with couples, the most destructive anger comes from either disguised hurt or from long repressed feelings that some essential bottom line has been violated of which neither person was conscious.

When a man denies essential parts of himself in order to meet the ideal of marriage, of his wife, of the culture, or in many cases of the mother in his own unconscious, he is denying himself, his wife, and their relationship the opportunity for conscious growth in their fullest possibilities. He is also constructing a situation where he may subtly poison the atmosphere of the home, affecting his children and even his grandchildren. Irene de Castillejo maintains: "It is all heartbreakingly difficult. Mutual service without betraying one's deepest trust is the paradox at the very centre of the art of living."[4] No one can know for certain the needs of the other person; however, we can try to know our own. One of the most loving things we can do in a relationship is to deal honestly with the other person from this knowledge of ourselves, dealing honestly within the context of love and not letting honesty become an excuse for brutality. Without this clarity, I doubt that love can grow for very long between two people in our turbulent world.

Frequently, men are terrified of expressing their deepest needs. We fear dependence, and we fear vulnerability. We think, if others know how needy we are, we will either be rejected or they will use this knowledge to hurt us. And sometimes they do. We need the full support of "Iron John" to present these needs strongly. Paradoxically, we find that in this process our strength, rather than our vulnerability, increases. After all, if the other person does use these vulnerabilities to try to hurt us, we know we need to pull out the sword and fight or else cut the relationship off.

Remember that the strongest knights, Lancelot and Tristan, were the most tortured by love. King Arthur, the king who brought law, wisdom and justice to the land, was also constantly being torn between his positive ideals, love of friends, romantic love, and desire. To be alive and to be masculine is to risk pain. To try to placate potential pain by being good is to be forever a mother's son, and to try to avoid it, is to avoid the experience of living.

Caught by the King and Queen

The princess naively told the queen she had a dream of what had happened. The queen instinctively knew the truth of the dream, and used the wiles of the negative feminine to outsmart the dog and trap the soldier. The king then had him arrested, put in jail, and sentenced to hang.

---

[4]Irene Claremont de Castillejo, *Knowing Woman* (New York: Putnam, 1973), p. 124.

The soldier has encountered a number of obstacles that he has had to overcome on his symbolic quest for consciousness and independence. These situations have been crucial in helping him determine and develop the strength of his masculine power and energy. Now he is approaching the final transition in this journey. Paradoxically, masculine instinctual power is not the facilitator for this transition.

The king and queen represent older parental images that have now turned negative and are thwarting conscious development that would foster health in the personality/kingdom. Both are binding the princess to the past and are creating tension by the use of repression (imprisonment) as new attitudes attempt to become conscious. At this period in the tale, the king and queen represent what we might call the cultural parents, not actual parents. In this context, they reflect the negative side of our society—its institutions, norms, values, ideas, and technology and the effects these have on us, especially through interpersonal relationships. In essence, they represent pressure to conform to cultural norms in their negative sense.

The soldier is imprisoned by this final psychological complex, one which affects us all in both the outer and inner worlds. Ask anyone who has made a major life change that varies from the norm how their bosses, neighbors, parents, and spouses responded. Even people getting divorced, or leaving a large company or profession to start their own business, may receive a lot of outside pressure to maintain the status quo. When I left my corporate career to start my own business, my parents, my boss, and many friends thought I was crazy. When I decided to sell out that business and return to graduate school and change careers, I believe that they were then fully convinced that I was nuts. I found maintaining my marriage and most friendships throughout this change impossible. When one makes a major change, the first assumption of most people is that the person is in trouble, not that this change could be a creative and challenging adventure for the entire family. Of course, creative and challenging adventures also have another side which involves hard work, pain, and loneliness.

In our inner world we are often assailed by many inner doubts resulting from cultural pressures. We doubt the validity of our inner needs and dreams. We doubt whether we can achieve them. We doubt that if we do achieve them, they will have been worth the cost and effort. We envision catastrophe if we fail, much as we envision catastrophes when we stand on our own inner truth in relationships. Hanging, in its original sacrificial form, included emasculation and represented an ignominious death. Strangulation, cutting off the breath, in ancient symbolism is cutting off the intake of spirit that fills us all with life.

We must remember the power of the needs and hungers of the instinctive natural self. As I have pointed out, the instinctive self needs to be integrated into our consciousness, without which it can take no real form. But consciousness also needs the instinctive natural self with its depth and power, or one has great difficulty finding meaning and individual authenticity in the world. Jung writes: "The criterion of adulthood does not consist in being a member of certain sects, groups or nations, but in submitting to the spirit of one's own independence."[5]

---

[5]C. G. Jung, Collected Works, Vol. 11, *Psychology and Religion, West and East*, Bollingen Series, Vol. XX, ¶. 276.

10

THE
FINAL TRANSITION

The soldier sat in the dark of his cell, having left his tinder box at his hotel. As the next day dawned, he could see many people coming to witness his execution. Drums were beating and soldiers were lining up. The king and queen, the judge and the royal councilors were all to be there. Then the soldier spied a little apprentice, who was in such a hurry he had lost a shoe. The soldier struck a bargain with him to fetch his tinder box. The boy ran off to the soldier's hotel, now named the Golden Angel, and returned with the tinder box.

In these dire circumstances the soldier needed to retain his hope, his endurance, and his sense of shrewdness. This predicament was a real test of the amount of conscious (ego) strength he had developed. Through this strength, even as he was marching to his execution, he was able to spot a small boy, an apprentice or helper to a skilled man, and enlist his aid by offering him money, symbolic energy.

The appearance of the boy represents a turning point in the individuation of the man. The boy indicates to us that a new personal attitude is required in the man. A new type of human reaction is needed to meet this final situation. As man has continued developing his intellectual differentiation, he has also denigrated and repressed the primitive child within, symbolizing his estrangement from nature and the meaning of life.

Aniela Jaffe tells us: "Every step forward on the way to individuation is at the same time a step backwards into the past and the mysteries of one's own nature."[1] The child represents a renewed and conscious relationship with the inner self. Each step we take forward in consciousness requires that we reground ourselves in the inner world to maintain our balance in life. The child is the taproot of our nature that returns us to the matrix where our life began.

The boy is an apt symbol of the soldier's self. He represents the soldier's future potential and at the same time the undeveloped facets of the soldier's individuality, areas of his personality that were cut off and repressed while he was soldiering through life and developing his ego strength. Paradoxically, we need a strong conscious development in order to relate to and often bargain with our inner child rather than becoming childish ourselves. We must continue to be able to contact the innocence and wonder of the child within us during our most imprisoned periods of life in order to maintain our vision of renewal and the ongoing potential of life. To lose this connection is to become cynical and defensive, cutting off life, growth, and renewal. The recognition of this psychic-boy image at this new level, the threat of psychic and masculine death, and the transaction with the boy allowed the soldier to regain contact with his masculine flint, steel, and fire.

These energies mobilized the soldier's instinctual strength, saved him, and freed the princess. The dogs then tossed the king and queen into the air, and they were dashed to pieces when they hit the ground. The king's soldiers made our soldier the king and had him marry the princess. The land rejoiced for eight days, and the dogs sat by and stared.

This ending of the old king and queen signifies that the soldier/ego has reached full adulthood. He is now independent of his real parents and the parental influence of the culture. He can function independently and authentically, ruling his own realm. We must get to this state in order to be able to relate to the feminine on both the inner and outer levels.

---

[1] Aniela Jaffe, *The Myth of Meaning in the Work of C. G. Jung* (Zurich: Daimon, 1984), p. 149.

Now that the princess is freed and the soldier has become a king, we can look at the meaning of their marriage. The marriage symbolizes the union of the soldier with his feminine side, and at this point he enters into a full relationship with her. In this relationship she will provide life, creativity, and renewal to the realm. We can now view the realm as the total Self in which the soldier is the ego or center of consciousness. If the marriage and reign continue in a positive manner, the princess will provide wisdom and compassion to balance his masculine qualities of strength, initiative and generativity. If the reign turns negative, we will have much the same situation as we did with the former king and queen.

The tale ends with eight days of celebration. Symbolically, the number eight represents the joining of two worlds—mind and matter. This joining suggests that the structure of the personality is whole, completed, and related to the eternal process of life, just as the number eight turned sideways is the symbol of infinity. If we consider the soldier, the princess, and the three dogs together from the standpoint of number symbolism we have the quintessential man. There is the masculine I-entity with his natural instinctive sides joined with the feminine—five aspects together. Please note no mention is made of anyone living happily ever after. The story is complete for illustrating this psychological process of masculine development. The story goes no further in how the couple grows, develops, has children and ages. Those are other stories. Life will continue to be a struggle, and nature continues to follow its rhythms and cycles.

This tale illustrates the journey men must go through to reach full maturity. We see that a man must ruthlessly divest himself of psychic domination first by his mother, then his father, and then the negative pressures of the culture. During this process, he must carefully discriminate what is necessary and not necessary, and be willing to bear the ups and downs of his progression. He must develop his authentic and independent conscious identity, grounded and rooted in his instinctual and shadow sides. Once this development is accomplished, he may then relate to his feminine side as it has evolved. This side can add life, creativity, eros and balance to his masculine qualities of logos, strength and action. The combination of the masculine and the feminine gives him the potential for strength, action, wisdom, compassion, and tenderness.

One can readily see what a long and involved struggle this is for men. As a culture we have lost the thread (much like Theseus in the Labyrinth) that runs through our masculine development. Most men are fixated between the two stages Erikson calls adolescence and young adulthood.[2] Men in this position will grow older, but they will not fully clarify their identities, and the ability for love and intimacy will remain wounded. Many of these men are still attached in some way to the mother, either personal or cultural. Some are trying to relate to the feminine without having developed their masculine identities. Others have become scared or confused, and have either fled the field or continue to suffer and struggle. Adult men are going to have to make a determined, conscious decision to overcome these problems every day until our culture can change enough to bring young men into manhood in a healthy way.

The following chapter will examine what makes up the process of transformation and how this process may begin. After this discussion, I have selected five of the areas my experience has shown to be the most confusing for men today in order to scrutinize these areas more carefully. The first of these will study men's feelings, emotions, and the instinctual/shadow side. In the succeeding chapters I will discuss masculine values, masculine eros, men's feminine sides and the essentials of fathering. In the final chapter I will talk about how these elements can combine to form a life that is vital, personal, and contributes to culture.

---

[2]Erik H. Erikson, *The Life Cycle Completed* (New York: Norton, 1982), p. 55.

PART
III

TRANSFORMATION AND THE REBUILDING OF MASCULINITY

FINDING
THE THREAD

It is only when we have lost our thread that life
seems purposeless, lacking in significance and
unacceptable.

—Irene Claremont de Castillejo[1]

As a culture we no longer have a path that will show us how
to attain manhood. We seem to expect boys (and men, because
this is not a brand new problem) to just grow up and suddenly be men. Moreover, images of what it means to be a man
in our society are scarce. The few images we have are changing and have become terribly confusing. Individually and collectively, we have lost the thread from boyhood to mature
manhood. This loss has presented us with a social crisis that
has resulted in men who are passive in various ways.

If we consider what brings about change and transformation, we see that in our century two methods stand out—
revolution and education. Revolution has become a
catchword since the 60s. Several social revolutions have had
profound effects. Others have failed. The ones that succeed
often set up countervailing trends of conservatism and fundamentalism. In many areas of the world, revolutions are

---

[1]Irene Claremont de Castillejo, *Knowing Woman* (New York: Putnam & Sons, 1973), p.
137.

degenerating into chaos and brutality. Because of our faith in the ability of science and technology to lead us to prosperity, we began to see education as a saving and transforming enlightenment—not, unfortunately, as a source of better or deeper thinkers—but leading us to the promised land of "better living through _____." Education, as a modern notion of enlightenment, has increased our standard of living, but has failed as an agent of deep social change. We have found that educating everyone is a difficult task. Our idealistic belief in mass education has forced its institutionalization and has forced it to become a practical process geared to its economic value (the job market), teaching skills, and providing information needed to live in a complex society. This concept is not bad if we take our idealistic notion of education and accept it for what it is—institutionalized skills training. I do not believe that enlightenment, even when it happens, is sufficient for producing great social change or promoting human growth.

What brings about deep change and evolution is the process of transformation (that I mentioned in the foreword), a process we all participate in whether we like it or not. The majority of us do not realize how personally involved we are in the process of evolution—our culture's and mankind's in general. In other words, we are participating unconsciously. Our American personalities are geared toward speed and therefore toward revolution. We are on a constant search for quick fixes, rapid weight loss, new looks, new personalities, new research, new social programs and so on. Often this approach is useful. In fact, we can even say that revolution is part of the bigger picture of evolution. The problem is that we have lost touch with the deeper process of evolution, the cycles of life, death, and rebirth, that illustrate the real components of transformation. Evolution, or transformation, is not something that we have to participate in unconsciously, and at this point enlightenment can help. To participate consciously in this evolution, however, requires a deeper understanding of our nature than participating in a revolution does. Conscious participation in our own evolution opens the doors to change and growth that may never open as long as we live unconsciously. Conscious participation in life requires a religious devotion to the search for self-knowledge, because we are usually trapped by presuming that we are conscious when in fact we are not.

Transformation

Transformation includes the continuous cycles of death and rebirth. Psychologically, transformation means the death of old ideas, attitudes, perspectives, and often our old identities—our old ego (the king). This process of death involves suffering, because giving up the old way is hard, and forming a new identity is risky and painful. Every major transition period unleashes inner conflict as the mental status quo is challenged. New consciousness is born in the midst of old values breaking down. Time and again the process involves the betrayal of our naive and innocent attitudes about how life should be. The process also requires, as in the legend of the unicorn, that our spirit return to a state of virginal quiet and receptivity often needed for change and growth. This process does not mean we must throw our old lives away; instead, it means we must fully participate in our own evolution, integrating the old and the new, and developing another standpoint based on both.

Several attitudes are helpful if we are going to participate in our own transformation. The first of these is a decision to become involved—*to pay attention*. Involvement means to heed our calls, to listen not only to our thoughts and feelings, but also to the unconscious, and to respect physical and emotional symptoms. Involvement means taking these things seriously and personally, rather than blaming everything on something or someone out there. Being involved is the process of paying attention to ourselves mentally, physically, emotionally, and spiritually. This initial involvement is the real preparation for change and growth.

The second important attitude is that of *questioning* and the best place to begin is usually with our immediate situation. What is really going on in our personal world? Who else is involved? How does our external situation affect us? Where, when, and how are the important things in our lives happening, or have the important things in our lives seemed to have stopped happening? Are we drying up?

Once we start this exploration, we can begin to question the meaning and the emotions in each part of our life and look for underlying reasons behind them. The attitude of involvement and attention needs to be maintained throughout this process. Often we may need to get out of our environment for a short time to follow this process from a fresh perspective. Some people may go away for a period of time. Some find this time during a therapy hour, and others simply take some time alone each day. At this stage the thoughts, emotions and situations need to be amplified rather than the problems solved. Amplification means to enlarge and to intentionally expand and elaborate what is going on. Then we can see more clearly subtle nuances that we hate to acknowledge, are afraid of, and perhaps wish to keep out of consciousness. Looking at messages from the unconscious that come in the form of idle thoughts, fantasies, and dreams, or using the ideas I discussed earlier in men's sexual fantasies and visions can be helpful in this search. We are, in fact, attempting to both question and listen to all parts of ourselves.

Following these attitudes will lead us into an *attitude of reflection*. This is difficult for many American men because of the one-sided focus on extroversion and activity in our culture. I will talk about this difficulty at length in later chapters. Reflection allows all that one has developed so far to percolate within the mind. Then either alternatives may be developed or experience may be sifted down to the essence of what is going on. This sifting down leads us to a better understanding of ourselves, and then we can usually focus on a path or find a thread. Events in the outer world lead into the psychological world and then become transformed back into the external world. If we miss the path—or cannot find the thread—we need to continue the process of involvement, questioning, and reflection.

These attitudes require courage. A great deal of courage is required just to admit something is out of whack somewhere in our lives and to give ourselves the time to attend to it, no matter what other demands are being placed on us. The real test of courage comes when we try to take our new attitudes or new consciousness back into the world to live out our inner experiences. We might learn that we missed the thread again and have to repeat the process. Most of all, we will find a lot of interpersonal and cultural pressure to push us back to our old selves. All of us, as well as society, seem to maintain a special form of inertia toward others who change. Maintaining our direction under this pressure takes courage.

We can see from this discussion that transformation as evolution can continue for a lifetime. By participation, we can not only hasten and expand it, we can also hope to avoid some of the more traumatic calls to change which are very dangerous (heart attacks, for example). Now let us take another look at the fairy tale as a psychological model of masculine evolution.

The Tale as a Model

If we examine the tale as a model of the growth of masculinity, we detect a skeleton that outlines six fundamental phases with several underlying themes. This skeleton provides a developmental roadmap that will help us understand where we are and where we may want to intervene in our development.

In the beginning of the tale we saw that the soldier, an ordinary man, had already reached what we might call functional manhood. He has some identity and has developed the skills to perform the basic business of living. This situation shows us that the first phase in the development has taken place. In the *first phase*, the mother image is nurturing, life-giving, and is an elementary influence in our growing experiences. Because of our schools and sophisticated culture, most of us make it through this stage with some sense of identity and we develop basic social and educational skills. Of course, many traumatic events can wound or disturb us during this period, and psychology in general deals with this part to a great extent. However, our theme begins after that stage.

In the *second phase* of development, the witch appears. The mother image turns sour, and we begin to become conscious of the fact that in spite of her nourishing characteristics, she is also a source of inhibition, constraint and guilt. To gain our emotional autonomy, we must separate from this maternal image and work toward individuality and independence. Unfortunately, we do not entirely give up our needs for dependency; we just reduce these needs. We must become able to live with them individually, no longer requiring a prohibitive maternal environment to ensure our existence. We must leave the pleasant world of having no responsibilities and take up our masculine commitments. If we do not, we can never fully experience ourselves and function adequately without the certainty that someone is taking care of us. Underlying our personality will be a passive masculinity, manipulating, elusive, and filled with rage or envy. Time and again our dependency needs may recycle during our lives as we go through changes, and we may have to slay the witch more than once. This struggle takes a great deal of courage, but it is a vital testing and develops strength and resolve.

In the *third phase*, we begin consciously to identify and discriminate our masculinity. In the discussion of the tale, I outlined how we find this masculine element in the earth, try it out within the family during adolescence, and then in young adulthood bring it out into the world and into relationships. We need to overdevelop this masculine side of ourselves early in life to complete our transition from the maternal environment. Work, peers, models of leadership (hopefully including fathers), and education should help bring us to the sense of identity that leads us into the next phase.

In the *fourth phase*, we begin to develop relationships and intimacy. In this part the soldier hears of the princess and begins to contact her. In life we begin trying to relate to women; we attempt to identify and discriminate the feminine side of ourselves. This phase helps us balance the one-sidedness we developed while growing into manhood.

Frequently, while we are in the midst of the fourth phase, we bump into the *fifth phase*. In this phase we come up against our own egocentric position that is too identified with the culture, its roles and expectations. These cultural expectations are represented by the old patriarchal king and supported by the matriarchal queen. Here, the soldier must muster all his resources in order to overthrow the old regime and develop his own sense of values, authenticity, and psychological autonomy. Here, we stop being the children of our parents, both individually and culturally. We stop living out hand-me-down values, or seeking the approval and disapproval of images that we may have internalized into our minds or projected onto our bosses, girl friends or wives.

In the *sixth phase*, where the soldier marries the princess, he brings everything together and integrates his maturing personality. He then has a fully functioning personality, a new consciousness that promotes prosperity with the whole personality. The meaning is not that we live happily ever after, that we never have to endure these struggles again, or that we cease to grow or transform, but that we have entered adulthood, and have the capacities to be productive, creative, and can give life and caring to others.

Overall, we move from the dependent instinctuality of childhood into the pursuit of consciousness. This consciousness includes discriminating our masculine and feminine sides and integrating emotions and earth strength (adult masculine instinctuality) into our inner and outer worlds to form a coherent personality and an authentic identity. Recognition of the process of evolution, transformation, death, and rebirth is fundamental to participate consciously in growth and change. As happened to the soldier, before each phase of evolution, we will be caught in a metaphorical place of darkness or prison (as in depression or a feeling of stagnation) before the old conscious attitudes die. In recognizing this process in ourselves, we can also recognize the continuous chance we have for new growth (the little boy apprentice) which provides the vital thread to ongoing life in the personality.

Putting the phases in the form of a model may do the injustice of implying this process is the normal form of development. Assuming the process is natural is dangerous, because our culture has wounded and thwarted this natural process. We must protect and enhance this process, just as we are finding we must protect and enhance many other natural processes. Another danger is that we have a tendency to equate developmental phases with age. Actually they often correlate with chronological age, but many elements based on individual and cultural circumstances can influence the process. The awareness needed for transformations commonly made in adolescence and early adulthood can come at any age. Often when we are older, the risks seem greater; at this time psychotherapy can truly help because it supports and teaches courage and transformation.

The Thread—Individuation and Wholeness

Most of us would readily agree that we are still in the dark ages when it comes to understanding ourselves and the universe we live in. Even the most rational people will now admit a large part of our mind is contained in the unconscious— whatever that is. The realities we must face about our lives, including our dreams, fantasies, slips of the tongue, compulsions, fears, intuitions, and addictions, force us to accept that we do not know, control, or understand many things about ourselves. Those of us who spend a great deal of time working with the unconscious find evidence that in the midst or beneath all of this mystery is an ordering factor that becomes the matrix of consciousness.

The history of working with the unconscious is long; however, Freud unquestionably brought it into the forefront of modern culture. Freud and his initial followers tended to view the unconscious as the home of instincts and as a repository of the primitive, the antisocial and the evil within a person. This view implies that at best the unconscious is unsavory and, at worst, it is the home of deep mental disturbances. Furthermore, Freud implied that we all have an unconscious death wish as well as a wish to live. This death wish resided in the unconscious depths and became the source of outer aggression. Of course, these ideas are an oversimplification of Freudian concepts. Both he and his followers evolved a set of theories far beyond these simple ideas, but the point is that the initial process of promoting the study of the unconscious to a wide scope in the world also tended to give the unconscious an image of darkness and fearfulness. Some even considered it a dark abyss into which the mentally ill had fallen. Many people still share this fear and prejudice, and often the most rational people we know are the most afraid of their own inner mystery.

The outstanding contribution made by Freud was that he undertook the first major scientific attempt to study the whole personality. He tried to envision a total person living partly in reality / consciousness and partly through the unconscious. Therefore, the Freudian man is capable of rational thoughts and actions, but he is also beset by conflicts and inner contradictions, buffeted by unknown forces, moved by aspirations beyond his grasp, and alternately confused and clear-thinking, frustrated and satisfied, hopeful and despairing, self-centered and humanitarian. This view has an essential validity that fits the complexity of our living experience.

Both Freud and Jung were concerned with more than just treatment of the disturbed personality. Ultimately both were concerned with the nature of reality and man's place in the scheme of the universe. To Jung fell the responsibility for reorienting our perception of the unconscious. Jung pointed out that mystery, darkness, or the unknown is not necessarily evil, unsavory, and undesirable, although each of us has some of these negative traits. Moreover, he also discovered an ordering principle in the personality that operated on an objective level beneath our personal repressions and complexes, both good and bad. Jung's view of the personality is generally positive, but not naively optimistic. He did not foresee an inevitable triumph of "good" or an inevitable triumph of the death instinct.

Jung considers the objective ordering system of the personality (which he terms the Self) the source of what we have been talking about as the individuation process. This ordering system is therefore dynamic, and will aid us in unfolding the potentialities we have as unique human beings. Therefore, the path to self-knowledge lies in making the unconscious conscious. The idea of looking for meaning in symptoms and looking for missing parts of ourselves in sexual fantasies, for instance, illustrates some useful ways to make the unconscious conscious. Freud and Jung studied many additional ways of bringing unconscious material to consciousness, dream analysis being a well known one.

As we make more of the unconscious conscious, we are, of course, enlarging our realm of consciousness in relation to the unconscious. Remember the important points in this process: first, the relationship of consciousness to the unconscious is important. Consciousness, in our discussion represented by the ego also meaning I or we, must have a receptive attitude toward the unconscious and its messages. However, the ego retains the responsibility for running our lives and concrete decision making. I consider the relationship of the ego and the unconscious somewhat like a corporate business structure. The ego functions like the president and the unconscious like the board of directors. The president/ego runs the company and makes decisions with the input and support of the directors/unconscious. While the president/ego has responsibility for operating the company, he must do so within the overall philosophy and direction of the directors/unconscious, or they will begin to give him problems.

Often the more objective wisdom of the board / unconscious will be needed either to steer the president / ego in new directions or to take a more complete long-term perspective on events. In clinical experience we most often find that mental disturbances are based on a disturbed relationship between consciousness and the unconscious and not on some dark bogey from the abyss.

The second important point to remember is the role of consciousness in the individuation process. Consciousness itself is not a goal. The goal or thread we follow through life is individuation. Self-knowledge through consciousness is the tool that helps us continue to find this thread, but it only has meaning in a life being actively lived.

Wholeness and balance through self-knowledge is becoming popular terminology to many on the fringes of depth psychology. These terms are generally explained as the conscious knowledge of our many parts and sides so that we may consciously use them when appropriate and also regulate them. Now I must admit, this model sounds pretty good to me. As a matter of fact, it sounds a little too good, like well meaning self-help books telling us how to do everything better. So I am beginning to find the concepts of wholeness and balance a little frightening. These two words are in danger of sliding over into the pop-psych idealism of new age consciousness and becoming meaningless and wholeness may no longer indicate the search for our own authenticity.

Conscious one-sidedness can give us the greatest personalities. I cannot imagine Winston Churchill as a slender, quiet person—not smoking a cigar, not sipping brandy, or being crusty and garrulous. Nothing would convince me that a more balanced approach to living (physical or mental) could have made him a more individuated man. In this discussion of wholeness and individuation I do not mean that men should become vapid and sterilized! The appearance of balance and "getting it right" does not mean a depth of soul. It generally means we have missed the point of individuation.

If someone comes to me who wants to pursue wholeness and develop and integrate their many sides, I think they are off the track. My interpretation of individuation is to live out—as authentically as possible—who I am with as much consciousness and humor as I can muster, particularly about my participation in my own process of transformation. The individual process is the process of constantly transforming into our most authentic selves.

Conscious One-Sidedness—King Arthur

The unicorn myth, one of the earliest myths of the masculine spirit and the hunt for regeneration, renewal, and survival, still has symbolic force in our culture. A more recent myth that I have referred to several times is that of *King Arthur and the Search for the Holy Grail*. This myth, with its specific characters and spiritual values, is not as primitive as the unicorn myth, but note that it touches the same themes.

King Arthur brought law, order, and justice to his realm. He changed men's attitudes into using strength for justice and nobility, ceasing petty selfish wars and squabbles, uniting in fellowship, working for values greater than and outside of themselves and seeking higher spiritual meaning. He urged the development of masculine strength and values to protect the weak and to honor the feminine (symbolized by women in the story) rather than raping, ravishing, or trading them for power and political purposes. Arthur was a *king* par excellence, but in other aspects of his life, he had great difficulty. If we look at some of the other aspects of masculinity in his life, we see the following:

As a father: His son was born through passion and enchantment. He never fathered him well and lived to see his son turn his own values against him and cause his downfall.

As a husband/lover: We all know the problems he had with his queen and his best friend that sadly hastened his downfall.

He had no true love or romantic ideal of marriage as we think of it and no so-called "intimate" relationship with women that lasted.

As a wise man: He was no seer, magician, or healer. He constantly planted the seeds of his own destruction. He was haunted by the loss of Merlin and unable to heal the splits in his own home and in his kingdom.

As a warrior: He was not the greatest. Many were greater, including Lancelot. He occasionally made a fool of himself, as in his first arrogant encounter with Lancelot, in which he was defeated.

As a spiritual man: Again, many were ahead of him. He was not included in the search for the Holy Grail even though it was his kingship that empowered and enabled the search.

But throughout all his triumphs, and his misery, and even during his downfall, he sure as hell was *King Arthur*, and he stood for his vision and values even though they helped lead to his greatest losses. Moreover, he stood for eros, bearing the tension and agony of trying to reclaim his son (who lost his life in their final battle, still under the influence of the witch, incidentally)—honoring his wife and best friend, and holding them within his circle of principles and affection, while suffering the knowledge that after his reign, the kingdom would be in chaos because it had no potential new king.

So we see that Arthur was not the greatest warrior and had trouble as a lover, as a husband, as a father, and he was neither a priest nor a seer. He was not a "balanced" personality. But he was conscious of his weakness and his failings, and more important, he was conscious of his vision, strength, and values (conscious authenticity). Because of this consciousness and his stance, even though he failed at establishing his kingdom and had it crumble around him, his legacy of justice, law, order, and peace has lived on, and his legend has haunted and fascinated Western man ever since. He taught us to integrate our animal strength and reconcile it with the values of society. He achieved immortality!

Men who live passionately, have visions, take stances and risks are also going to have this energy spill over into some negative areas. Life is a struggle: perhaps perfect balance— stasis—is death.

We have become so shallow in our culture that we dishonor men because of their struggles. Our society would rather see the media pick them to bits over their weaknesses and be titillated by their affairs than honor the importance of their visions and the sum of the life they have lived.

Proceeding to Specifics

Now we have a story, a model, and a process. We have examined attitudes toward transformation and the eternal cycle of death and rebirth within ourselves. We have seen how the conscious and unconscious must work together as our individuation process unfolds. We can see the two threads of masculine development and individuation. Both are intertwined, or perhaps it is easier to say that the thread of masculine development makes the texture in the weaving of the fabric of a man's individuation.

Rebuilding masculinity becomes the process of finding where we lost our transformation process (where we dropped the thread) and how this process can be reestablished within the context of our culture. In the next few chapters, I will attempt to flesh out the skeleton of our model by specifically discussing several areas that my experience has shown are troubling and confusing to men today.

12

MASCULINE FEELINGS

We must educate your feeling and persuade you
to experience it like a man and not like a maimed,
dull child.

—Dr. von Haller[1]

During the discussion of the fairy tale, we have seen that
growing (developing) conscious masculinity must go through
phases. To develop enough strength and independence to separate from the control of the mother image, men must first discover the inner depth of their personality. During this
separation process they must contact the deep masculine
through self-knowledge which has instinctual power, which is
fed from the shadow side, but which is based on the fire of
passion, enthusiasm, and emotion rooted in masculine feelings and values (which I will discuss next). Once the young
man has separated from the mother image, he must also separate from his father image, and the negative—or imprisoning—properties of our cultural norms. Once he has made
these transitions, he has integrated within his personality his
deep masculine instincts, passions, and feelings, and is
grounded enough in his masculine power and identity to
begin coming into a full relationship with his feminine side.

---

[1]Robertson Davies, *The Deptford Trilogy* (London & New York: Penguin, 1983), p. 326.

In the beginning of this book and throughout at various points, I have based my discussion on the suggestion that our culture has become too one-sided in certain masculine values. To many of us this point is self-evident, but to others perhaps it is not so clear. As I pursue a more detailed discussion of masculine feelings and values, I would also like to examine this one-sidedness carefully in order to explain it clearly. I am going to develop this discussion within the context of different styles of consciousness as illustrated by Jung's theory of psychological types.

Styles of Consciousness

Attempts to categorize men based on personality and temperament go back to some of our earlier efforts to understand behavior. In early history, Aristotle attempted to describe human behavior in accordance with Hippocrates' fundamental categories, first published four hundred years before the birth of Christ. Based on the conception that there were four basic essences—earth, fire, air, and water—the argument was that four basic "humors" or liquids made up the body— blood, phlegm, black bile or melancholy, and yellow bile or choler. These attempts progressed in various fields up through Freud into modern psychology. Freud, with more sophistication, categorized people into neurotic characters fixated at various stages of psychosexual development—oral, anal, phallic, and genital. Currently we have an amazing array of classifications in psychology and the social sciences. Moreover, many other fields, ranging from astrology to business have joined this attempt. Although many of these efforts are useful, some are misleading, some are merely fun, and others are purely fanciful.

Jung developed his theory to illustrate how consciousness works in practice. He was also interested in helping us understand individual differences better by explaining how consciousness works in different ways in different people. Jung attempted to define the components of consciousness present in all of us. For example, everyone makes decisions, such as buying a new car. One person may approach this decision by conducting a financial analysis. This person is interested in the economics of the decision, cost, resale value, maintenance cost, and other things affecting the "bottom line." Such a person may carefully research consumer bulletins and reports. A second person may be interested in how the car drives. Such a person is interested in acceleration, cornering, braking, and will study motor magazines. A third person may buy a car because he likes the name, the style, the color, or the feel of the upholstery. All three decisions are equally valid for a particular person but have very different contents and different styles of consciousness interacting in the decision-making process. You might also imagine that combining all three of these processes could result in a more balanced and satisfying decision.

This theory is not intended to be a theory of personality. Pigeon-holing people into conceptual categories would undermine the whole idea of individuation. Nevertheless, practical knowledge of these styles helps us understand ourselves and helps us appreciate and understand the differences between ourselves and others. Figure 1 on page 172 will give a quick, though very restricted version of the components of this theory. The letters in the parentheses are simply the abbreviations of the words in the boxes as they are used in the Myers-Briggs Type Indicator[2] (a psychological inventory to help determine styles). This theory gives us a good tool for examining individual differences on a group basis and for helping us understand a wide variety of attitudes and experiences. All of the styles and preferences are equally valid psychologically and, in fact, need one another. We all have each of them in some degree, but one of each pair is usually preferred

---

[2]Isabel Briggs Myers, *The Myers Briggs Type Indicator* (manual). A lot of information is available on Jung's theory and its application from the Center for Applications of Psychological Type, Inc., 414 Southwest 7th Terrace, Gainesville, Florida 32601. I have relied heavily on their publications.

and better developed. Our personal style is determined by taking the preference we develop for each one of the four pairs of opposites and combining them. Our styles are not considered fixed and may change as we live and grow.

We begin with two different but complementary attitudes toward the world—*extroversion* and *introversion*. The extrovert's essential stimulation comes from the outer world of

I PREFER:

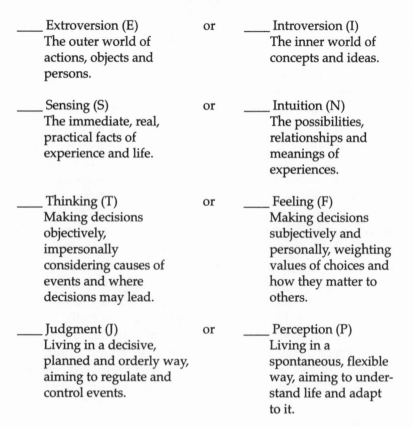

____ Extroversion (E)   or   ____ Introversion (I)
The outer world of   The inner world of
actions, objects and   concepts and ideas.
persons.

____ Sensing (S)   or   ____ Intuition (N)
The immediate, real,   The possibilities,
practical facts of   relationships and
experience and life.   meanings of
                                experiences.

____ Thinking (T)   or   ____ Feeling (F)
Making decisions   Making decisions
objectively,   subjectively and
impersonally   personally, weighting
considering causes of   values of choices and
events and where   how they matter to
decisions may lead.   others.

____ Judgment (J)   or   ____ Perception (P)
Living in a decisive,   Living in a
planned and orderly way,   spontaneous, flexible
aiming to regulate and   way, aiming to under-
control events.   stand life and adapt
                                to it.

Figure 1. The four preferences scored to generated types on the Myers-Briggs Type Indicator (adapted from the Type Table in The Type Reporter, *1986, 3/2).*

people and things, his environment. Inherent in this attitude is a desire to act on the environment to affirm and increase its importance. Characteristically, extroverts feel pulled outward by external claims and conditions, energized by other people, and may act and then (perhaps) reflect. On the other hand, introverts find their essential stimulation in the inner world of thought and reflection. Introverts feel pushed inward by external demands and intrusions. They are energized by inner resources, internal experiences, and may reflect, then (perhaps) act. One can readily see that these definitions are a little different from our normal social definitions of extroverted and introverted. Likewise, one can easily imagine the various potentials introverts and extroverts have for misunderstanding each other.

Next are the two perceiving functions that explain the ways we gather information. People who prefer *sensing* take in information by way of the five senses—sight, sound, feel, taste, and smell. Sensing people tend to look at specific parts and pieces, live in the present, and prefer to handle practical matters. They are often described as grounded in reality. They notice the concrete facts and want to deal with things that are definite and measurable. People who prefer *intuition*, by contrast, may seem somewhat bothered by reality, preferring to live in the realm of possibilities and in anticipation of the future. Intuitive people prefer to gather information through their intuition, a sort of instinctual knowing through imagination, that depends more on the mind as part of the complex sensitivity of the total organism than as just a receptor of data from one of the five senses. Characteristically, intuitives look at patterns and relationships, follow hunches, and enjoy change. To sensing people, intuitives often seem flighty, and intuitives may think sensing people are boring and literal.

Once we gather information, we then have to decide what to do with it or make decisions based on it. To do this we use either *thinking* or *feeling*. Those who prefer thinking decide with the "head" on the basis of logic and objective considerations. Good development of the thinking function leads to powers of analysis and an ability to weigh facts objectively, including consequences, unintended as well as intended. Thinking people may appear cold, distant, and seem spontaneously to find flaws and criticize. People who prefer feeling make decisions on the basis of personal subjective values. These people apply personal priorities and weigh human values and motives, both their own and others. They tend to see things as participants, from within a situation rather than as observers. Feeling people often seem totally irrational to thinking people, because the thinking person is not aware of, or does not understand, the personal value system of the feeling person. Typically, people preferring feeling try to understand other people, wish to affiliate with them, and desire harmony in relationships. Good development of the feeling function leads to warmth, empathy, compassion, and decisions from the "heart." As you can see, this definition of feeling is very different from our common use of the word "feelings" as emotions.

Finally, we come to *judgment* and *perception* as complementary lifestyles. A *judging lifestyle* is decisive, planned, and orderly. Judging people like to have life under control and are goal-oriented. They enjoy deciding and planning, organizing, and scheduling, having clear limits and deadlines, and like to wrap things up, even though they may not have enough information for making clear decisions. At their best they are characterized as responsible, dependable, and decisive.

A *perceptive lifestyle* is flexible, adaptable, and spontaneous. These people tend to experience life as it happens, enjoying the surprises as they occur, and enjoying the freedom to explore in an open way. They meet deadlines in a last-minute panic and often wait so long and gather so much information when trying to make a decision, they miss the opportunity. At their best, perceptive people are considered spontaneous, receptive, understanding, and flexible. Judging people may appear rigid and demanding to perceiving folks, who in turn often appear disorganized and irresponsible to the judging people.

Tom's style is introverted, intuitive, feeling and perceiving (INFP). His wife, Mary, is extroverted, sensing, feeling and judging (ESFJ). Right away you can note many areas of potential conflict. For example, since Mary is sensing (concrete) and judging (wanting a decision), she has probably planned next year's vacation. Since Tom is intuitive (not wanting to be bothered by reality) and perceiving (wanting to be open-ended), he is still not quite sure of his schedule this afternoon. Even worse, as an introvert (mostly concerned with his inner process), Tom has probably already agreed to a vacation without paying attention to what he said. When the time comes for the vacation, Tom will find it a shock, and Mary's feelings may be hurt because he had not taken this event seriously. One can easily see common ground for disagreements, not only with our wives and children, but also in any group process. Understanding different styles is important for harmonious interpersonal functioning and balanced decision making. For us to manage well in all kinds of situations, all of the preferences should be available to make their needed contribution:

> Thinking should facilitate cognition and judgment, feeling should tell us how and to what extent a thing is important or unimportant for us, sensation should convey concrete reality to us through seeing, hearing, tasting, etc., and intuition should enable us to divine the hidden possibilities in the background, since these too belong to the complete picture of a given situation.[3]

Out of Balance

Where have we as men become out of balance in our culture, and what does that imbalance mean? Our one-sidedness developed first from our desire to create a country out of the wilderness, thus forcing an extroverted emphasis that still

---

[3]C. G. Jung, *Collected Works*, Vol. 6, *Psychological Types*, Bollingen Series, Vol. XX, ¶. 518.

continues. The success of this venture, "progress," became intoxicating to us, and we became almost frantic in the pursuit of it and our hopes for a better world through "progress." This pursuit was greatly facilitated through the fantastic breakthroughs of science and technology. Technology was based primarily on sensation (facts) and thinking (logic) with specialized intuition.

First, we have the emphasis on extroversion. We are a nation of "salesmen" and a "can-do" culture building a better world. Introverted men were accepted in roles supportive of this view in such fields as science and teaching. Other types of introverted men and boys seemed outside the cultural norm and often felt like social misfits, experiencing the pain of never being able to become a successful extrovert. Grammar school and high school are often extremely painful for introverts since the school system tends to reward extroverts, and introverts are often slow in developing social skills. The social norm for men in our culture has been extroversion with introversion taking a back seat.

We have an interesting situation with perception. Our educational system, reinforced by technology, is oriented toward facts, reality, and the concrete. Scientific management attempted to follow in this orientation. True scientists, however, make good use of intuition. I think we have split intuition into two areas. The first follows the path of inferential statistics. If we can divide it, analyze it, reduce it to specific variables extracted from a proper sample, then we can generalize it. This is a reductive, linear form of intuition, often very good. However, with a hunch or "gut feeling," something we know but cannot explain the basis for, we think twice before taking a stand for it in a management meeting. We then end up with a cultural norm of linear intuition and with the other forms of intuition taking a back seat.

When it comes to the thinking and feeling processes, it is obvious that men and the institutions in our culture value analyzing the situation, weighing the facts objectively, and reaching an impersonal decision. Feelings, the subjective valuing process, take a back seat in the world of men.

In the judgment and perceiving preferences, judgment is the masculine cultura! ideal. Judgment as a preference falls right into line with sensing and thinking. We want men who can make decisions, who can "make things happen"—control events. Men in management and administration think their success depends on organizing and controlling. A whole new industry has developed to teach people in all areas, especially management and administration, how to more effectively plan and organize time. One can take seminars and buy elaborate books to facilitate this skill. I doubt if a perceiving type could ever be a one-minute manager, so perceiving has taken a back seat to judging as a preference.

We developed a masculine cultural profile reinforced by parents, schools and institutions that looks like this:

Extroverted: Geared to action and the outer world.

Sensation: Emphasis on the concrete, facts, the immediate, the real, and the practical with linear intuition being accepted.

Thinking: Analysis, objectively considering the facts, impersonal, logical, reductive decision making.

Judgment: Decisive, planned, organized, regulating life and controlling events.

So what has our culture done with the rest of masculine introversion, intuition, feeling, and perceiving as preferences? They have become labeled as inferior, repressed out of men's conscious identities into their unconscious shadow sides, and by and large projected onto women. All of these preferences that have what could be considered "irrational" attributes when considered from the perspective of the sensing/thinking profile have been projected onto the feminine in our culture.

This phenomenon was much easier to see up until the 1960s because, before then, the task of women included the feeling values, such as maintaining relationships, the ambiance of the home, nagging the family into going to church, and performing social niceties—such as remembering birthdays, anniversaries, and sending thank-you notes. Symbolically, men wanted to keep women at home (introverted), behind the closed door, so to speak, to mediate the family process. The wife was the custodian of her husband's personal taste as well, often picked out his clothes, made sure his tie matched his suit and made him participate in a social life reconfirming men's inability to deal with "feeling" functions without the guiding hand of women. A major part of this process also included her guiding him (or nagging him) to give sufficient time and patience to feeling activities such as the marital relationship, children, and social causes. Women could get away with introversion because they were supposed to be moody and "have that time of the month" anyway. They could also get away with being perceiving types because we depended on them for spontaneity: decisive, controlling women were considered unfeminine. I do not blame women a bit for rebelling against the ever-increasing burden of carrying all of these qualities for the culture.

The business world is beginning to swing away from this one-sided perspective. Roy Rowan, in *The Intuitive Manager*,[4] takes a new look at intuition. He proposes that American managers are too rational, contained, and control-oriented. Planning and analyzing more precisely, the theology of MBAs, has resulted in what he terms "analysis paralysis."

> "Constantly accumulating new information . . . without giving the mind a chance to percolate and come to a conclusion intuitively, can delay any important

---

[4]Roy Rowan, "The Eureka Factor," in *The Intuitive Manager* (New York: Berkley Publishers, 1991), p. 65.

decision until the time for action expires," he says. "That is substituting study for courage."[5]

Within the context of our discussion, Rowan is discussing not only intuition, but also the lack of sufficient introverted time to give the "mind a chance to percolate." He proceeds to tell us that intuition is often the driving instinctual link that can make a big difference. As he sees it, an important part of intuition is the sifting of personal experience. This concept is close to the Peters and Waterman notion of "Management by Walking Around," and "hands-on" experience which gives managers not necessarily facts, but the intuition resulting from the wisdom of lived experience. They continue, stating that the analytic approach taken too far leads to a "heartless" philosophy. They also tackle the notion of other rejected preferences, reminding managers that "soft is hard." The stuff that has been rejected for a long time as intractable (irrational, intuitive, informal, receptive, value-oriented) is important and has been successfully utilized in the way the best companies get things done.[6] Some new institutional awareness is dawning, as well as personal awareness reflected in current literature.

The initial task is not to get in touch with the feminine. Our initial task, like the soldier's, is to return via self-knowledge to a fuller state of masculine values. Until we have made this journey and withdrawn our projections from women, I doubt if we can figure out what our masculine identity is, and we certainly cannot understand how our own feminine sides differ from real women.

From the perspective of feelings in the context of Jung's theory, I am going to discuss emotions and then how emotions, feelings, and the notion of shadow come together to help form the repressed, powerful instinctual man in our psyches.

---

[5] *The Intuitive Manager*, p. 65.
[6] T. J. Peters and R. H. Waterman, Jr., *In Search of Excellence* (New York: Warner, 1983), p. 11.

Emotions

Feeling in the psychological sense is an act of personal valuing. It is the rational faculty that assigns value to human experience. Feeling as a process can lead to harmony, warmth, and empathy. It may also be negative, selfish, and cold, depending on one's subjective valuing system. If we are asked how we feel about something, we may reply that it feels good or bad, terrible or wonderful. These responses indicate that we have assigned a value based on feeling. Because feeling is a rational act of valuing, it is not necessarily volatile, hot or cold, like emotions.

A typical psychology book defines emotions as a state of arousal that has psychological, situational, and cognitive components. Therefore, to a greater or lesser degree, when we experience emotions, the possibility always exists that we might be so totally seized that our rationality may be overwhelmed. This danger is one reason that many men are afraid of emotions. The stronger the emotion, the less likely we can handle it with our preferred adaptive processes of the concrete, practical, and logical. An emotion can at once be a response to a situation (as fear is to a threat) and can also have motivating characteristics (as anger can motivate aggression). We may behave in certain ways in order to experience an emotion such as love or joy, thereby making it a goal in itself.

Robert Johnson defines emotion as, "a sum of energy that occurs or is set off in a person by meaningful experience."[7] He uses the term energy to characterize emotion and concludes it is morally neutral. Emotion may be good or destructive depending on the situation. This definition makes emotions easier to understand. While emotions may be morally neutral, they follow a natural law. If they are denied or repressed too much, they will turn on a person by developing an illness or seeking escape in an unconscious, irrational manner, that is either embarrassing or destructive. An example is the quiet,

---

[7]Robert Johnson, *He* (New York: Perennial, 1984), p. 32.

mild-mannered man who one day murders someone. On the other hand, if we become too emotional, we have difficulty functioning in life.

In the fairy tale, the soldier learned how to use the tinder box. Symbolically, this knowledge represents the development of his ability to relate to his instincts and emotions, and to strike an emotional spark when it is needed to create change and transformation. Psychologically, the intensity of the emotional flame or energy is a barometer of the inner life of the individual. Emotion is always the energy that mediates further psychological development. Emotions often indicate the presence of psychological conflicts as well. They also represent the degree to which we participate in the process of living. People with no emotions appear "dead." On the other hand, emotional control is often important. In many crisis situations, a "cool" head is necessary and practical, but men have overdone their control of emotions in the pursuit of rationality. Thus we have developed the tyranny of objectivity, logic, and reason. As a result, we often find we have made ourselves virtually helpless in relationships.

When confronted by an irrational woman or child, masculine rationality usually does little good, so we are then helpless. We have no power because our preferred process is useless, and we have nothing in between rationality and brute force, which is socially unacceptable. Even if we finally explode, we may simply terrify the other person by our reaction and do little to solve the issue or understand and further the interaction. On the other hand, if we deny our emotions to those closest to us, we are both denying them the possibility of fully relating to us, and denying the relationship one of the major catalysts for growth and transformation. Just as the soldier learned to direct this power and only call on it when appropriate and needed, we must do the same. One of the primary methods for directing emotional power is to become conscious of our feeling values and to protect them (often with emotion) before they are violated.

Shadow and Feeling

Early in my discussion of the fairy tale, I pointed out that in the process of developing our ego strength and identity, we go through a process of selecting certain portions of our personality that become our favored way of dealing with the world. These propensities are usually based on social norms and reinforced by parents and social institutions. During this process, other qualities that could have been part of one's conscious personality (the ego), but did not fit the perceived norms, are rejected and repressed into the shadow or dark side of the personality. Theoretically, the shadow also includes the unlived potentialities of the personality, and processes one is not aware of that go on in the mind. It contains the inferior and undeveloped attitudes and components of conscious styles, as well as characteristics unacceptable to the ego, particularly as the ego is expressed by the values of one's public face.

Introversion is often considered passive and feminine in the masculine world, because introversion does represent a certain type of receptivity. Introversion, by nature, is receptive to the life, ideas, and processes of the inner world. However, it is not passive; it only appears so to those with an extroverted bias. It may also be very oriented toward the masculine, depending on the other preferences. We have previously discussed both intuition and perceiving as preferences, and I think it is enough to say they are also generally repressed into the shadow of men on a cultural level.

The feeling side as repressed in men will come out in inferior and irrational ways. When not being expressed as anger, this side may be overly sentimental, childish, and hidden. It may remain entirely tied to the mother and never reach adulthood. We have ended up living a cultural stereotype that looks like this:

He is rational. She is emotional.

However, the flip side of the fact that he is rational is that in his feeling process, he is most likely irrational because that side is undeveloped and unconscious. As a corollary, he will be less able to deal with his emotions in a conscious manner. Men need to develop a conscious feeling process as a valuing function.

The chthonic masculine includes all that is underground, all that is unconscious. In our fairly tale, this area included the masculine instincts, their energy, and the treasure of self-knowledge. This model fits very well with the picture of men today. The masculine instincts of brutal, blunt, hairy, primitive, power, aggression, as well as emotion, have been pushed into the shadow. Also included in the shadow is the primitive potential of each of these attributes. Knowledge of the value and wisdom contained in the positive or bright side of these attributes has also been submerged.

Often the primitive masculine makes its first appearance in our dreams. Many of the men I have worked with have dreams in which they are being chased or threatened by thugs, robbers, or other dark masculine figures. Frequently they have ethnic characteristics of people with whom the dreamer may have negative associations. One middle-aged southern professional man with a cultural mother-complex, unable to recognize his masculine power and get out from under the smothering influence of his wife, dreamed:

> I was in bed with my wife and she was lying on top of me. A huge man, a redneck type in jeans and a t-shirt started breaking down the door. He looked gross and strong, but had a large beer belly. I was scared and knew I must get up to defend us, but I couldn't push her off of me and she was totally unaware of the danger.

Laurens van der Post[8] credits earthy instinctuality as the source of individuality. He states that a most formidable com-

---

[8]Laurens van der Post, "Appointment with a Rhinoceros," in *Testament to the Wilderness: Ten Essays on an Address,* by C. A. Meier (Zurich: Lapis Press, 1985), p. 120.

bination of instincts in serving life determines the personality and demands that we live individually.

Marie-Louise von Franz suggests that instinctual wisdom is of the highest value and is creative, spontaneous, and essentially unforeseeable, therefore almost impossible to corrupt.[9]

If the valuing system of feelings can be brought into consciousness, and consciously supported by the power of the chthonic masculine, then we may live the following statement of Robert Bly:

> The deep nourishing and spiritually radiant energy of the male lies not in the feminine side, but in the deep masculine. . . . The kind of energy I'm talking about is not the same as macho brute strength. . . . It's forceful action undertaken, not with compassion, but with resolve.[10]

---

[9]Marie-Louise von Franz, *Shadow and Evil in Fairy Tales* (Dallas: Spring, 1980), p. 247.
[10]Keith Thompson, "What Men Really Want: A New Age Interview with Robert Bly," in *New Age Magazine*, May, 1982, p. 34.

13

MASCULINE VALUES —ANOTHER LOOK AT JOHN WAYNE

Don't apologize, Mister—it's a sign of weakness.

—John Wayne as
Captain Nathan Biddles[1]

We have examined the male cultural profile that has evolved emphasizing extroversion, facts, concrete perception, analysis, rationality, logical decision making, action, planning, and control of events. Other values, such as introversion, receptivity, nonlinear intuition, feeling as a valuing function, spontaneity, and a flexible approach to life have been repressed into our shadow sides and often projected onto women. We also took a look at emotions as the barometer of our feeling values and our participation in the process of living. We noted that emotions are often threatening to men because they tend to prohibit men's preferred way of dealing with problems (rationality and control), and they violate the cultural norms for masculine behavior, leaving men helpless as long as they are caught in the cultural-mother complex. In addition, we discussed the shadow side of men and the chthonic masculine as the source of renewal for masculine power, giving men the primordial energy for courage, resolve, creativity and life.

---

[1] From the 1949 movie, *She Wore a Yellow Ribbon* (The Nostalgic Merchant, Suite 1019, 6255 Sunset Boulevard, Hollywood, CA 90028).

The shadow is much more involved than the consideration I have given it as a concept in this discussion. The dark aspects of the shadow certainly contain the potential for evil and destruction. Many books discussing the shadow are available if you would like more information.[2] My intention is to stick with the shadow concept only as I have discussed it, as consisting of contents a person chooses not to admit to or not to show because they seem weak or socially undesirable. Many people ask me how to figure out what their shadow qualities are. We have repressed these contents so far from our consciousness (ego awareness) that finding them is extremely difficult. We may feel quite virtuous that we have pushed down these offensive qualities, or we may think we are subscribing to a cultural norm that does the same thing.

One good way to identify our shadow is to notice what qualities in others make us angry or irritated. I do not mean we should not get angry or irritated, or that these emotions are due only to shadow. But the qualities that arouse these emotions inside us are often indications that we have hidden in our own nature some of the same qualities. Any quality that is totally rejected will find a niche in the shadow. Then our tendency is to see it outside of ourselves, as a projection, in other persons, images, nations, and objects. Good or bad, what we have not admitted to in ourselves, we have difficulty tolerating in others. Our culture does the same thing on a collective scale. I have already discussed the masculine attributes that have been repressed in this way. Now I would like to take a look in depth at a figure that has become a major shadow image in our culture during the last decade. We can then examine the "bright" shadow values we have ignored and lost as we rejected this image of John Wayne.

---

[2]Three that come to mind are Mary Ann Mattoon, *Jungian Psychology in Perspective* (New York: The Free Press, 1981); John G. Sanford, *The Invisible Partners* (New York: Paulist Press, 1980); and John G. Sanford, *Evil: The Shadow Side of Reality* (New York: Crossroads, 1981).

Another Look at John Wayne

Mark Gerzon, in his book *A Choice of Heroes: The Changing Face of American Manhood*, summarizes what has become the negative image of the John Wayne version of manhood.

> The John Wayne syndrome meant keeping emotions buried:

> The John Wayne syndrome is an explicit, if unwritten, code of conduct, a set of masculine traits we have been taught to revere since childhood. It means to be hard, tough, unemotional, ruthless and competitive; to be in Lifton's words, "a no-nonsense, sexual conqueror for whom women were either inferior, inscrutable or at best weaker creatures."

> The soldier is an ancient figure. His image as epitomized by John Wayne—whether against Indians (in innumerable films), Mexicans (in *The Alamo*), Viet Cong (in *The Green Berets*) or other more contemporary villains—is but the last in a long line of military heroes that have excited men's imagination.[3]

D. L. Stewart contemporizes this negative image of John Wayne in the lead-in to an article saying: "It's not always easy for the head of the house to stop thinking like John Wayne—and start talking like Alan Alda."[4]

I must admit that I think Mark Gerzon's book is one of the best I have read for it challenges us to rethink our definitions of manhood. I believe he is correct when stating *The Sands of Iwo Jima* is a warrior's tale, but I do not think it is in any way the tale of a war-lover. *The Green Berets* was a propaganda film of sorts, but to me it only indicates that John Wayne fell into the mess of Vietnam along with the whole nation. *The Alamo* was

---

[3]Mark Gerzon, *A Choice of Heroes* (Boston: Houghton Mifflin, 1982), pp. 33, 34, 35.
[4]D. L. Stewart, "Hey Son, I Love You Too," in *Reader's Digest*, 128 (Feb. 1986), pp. 131, 132.

not about soldiers, but about frontiersmen and adventurers. No American soldiers were at the Alamo. The frontiersmen and cowboy images are also two images that have great shadow power in our culture. This power is evident in our movies and cigarette ads and illustrated by people who wear jeans, cowboy boots and hats and drive pick-up trucks around in our great monuments to progress and technology, cities and shopping center parking lots.

If we look at the great trilogy of John Ford cavalry westerns (*Rio Grande, Fort Apache, She Wore a Yellow Ribbon*), we can get some idea of the values in the mainstream of John Wayne movies. All three of these stories were primarily about men, about men's honor, duty, development and love for each other, and young men being trained into adulthood by older men. John Wayne stood for commitment and honor. He related to Indians in a straightforward, respectful manner. He stood for peace. Little violence was in these movies and certainly no slaughter of Native Americans. The only slaughter happened to the cavalry in *Fort Apache* when the commanding officer (Henry Fonda) held too rigidly and dramatically to his desire for glory and advancement. John Wayne survived the slaughter, having been relieved of his command and sent to the rear because he refused to behave in a manner he thought dishonorable. God only knows how our recent history could have been affected if more officers had responded this way in Vietnam, placing personal ethics and honor ahead of advancement or just getting by. We can see TV shows almost every evening that show more raw violence and gore than was in all three of these movies combined.

The art of soldiering has many positive characteristics, such as focusing on an objective, discipline, and the pursuit of collective values larger than oneself. But we need to know who we are soldiering for and why. We need to choose how we soldier and be careful we do not use soldiering attributes for defensive adaptation or dominance.

The women in these films were never inferior, dumb or weak. They were traditional, as suited that era of history. Family life was treated with care and respect. In a very touching scene, Captain Biddles (John Wayne) was shown watering the flowers on his wife's grave and talking to her as he had done in the evening before her death.

His characters were clearly feeling men, tough, but compassionate. He even shed a few tears in *She Wore a Yellow Ribbon*. All of these films honored our past, including several ethnic groups and former Confederate soldiers now melded and working together. Another poignant scene in *She Wore a Yellow Ribbon* showed the funeral of a former Confederate general serving as U. S. Trooper John Smith.

The Horse Soldiers had only one real battle scene. In it, John Wayne, the commander, did not fire a shot or carry a weapon, and he got drunk with sorrow, anger, and disgust after the battle. In his great movies, not his wartime propaganda films, he pursued soldiering competently and with dedication, but hated killing, reflecting General MacArthur's observation that the soldier hates war because he is the one in it. John Wayne was never a war-lover.

In *The Quiet Man*, he played a man running away from the accidental slaying of another man in a boxing match. This beautiful movie does the best job of showing the relationship between archetypal masculine and feminine feelings of any movie I have seen. Maureen O'Hara co-starred as she did in several of his movies. Patricia Neal co-starred in several similar roles. John Wayne never played the ideal lover or the "sexual conqueror" in his movies. Nor were his women co-stars the sexy sirens of men's imagination. They played strong, intelligent, independent, feisty women—never clinging vines. They would run over today's "soft men" like a freight train.

In *The Searchers* (another John Ford western), John Wayne played a relentless pursuer, dedicated for years to a vengeful search but ending it with love and compassion. In *Three Godfathers*, John Wayne and his two companions delivered a baby in the desert and gave their lives and freedom to preserve its life.

In *True Grit* and *The Shootist*, we see a tour-de-force of an older man, living his final years in the integrity and authenticity of his personality. When I look at many of our old men today, I am scared. So many look fragile, so helpless—they putter absent-mindedly like children, and they are treated just like children. I like the pattern of seeing old age and death reflect a life lived.

Earth Strength

I love two things about the classic John Wayne movies. The first is that they contain the earthy strength of the masculine, not the airy or sky strength of the lofty spiritual or intellectual type man. In these movies, the image is of basic feeling values supported by commitment and perseverance. To me, this picture is the "resolve" that Robert Bly speaks of so eloquently. I do not see any of these values in conflict with the newer values of sensitivity and nurturance among men.

I think the new values, roles, opportunities, and options for men are important and hope they really reflect new growth in our consciousness. I support them. But if we choose these values, we must do so because they express our deepest needs— not to satisfy someone else, or because they are the latest fad in the culture. Masculine values are needed more than ever in the world, for they give a man the inner strength and endurance to stand for his beliefs—even those such as sensitivity—in a harsh world that runs roughshod over our feeling values. I am not saying that we need to master our inner strength to be better "new men." I am saying that having the strength to stand for sensitivity and eros is one of the results of fully developed masculinity—and it has been that way for centuries.

Fathers and Sons

The second thing I love about the classic John Wayne movies is the conflict they illustrate between fathers and sons, quite clear in *Rio Bravo* and *In Harm's Way*. John Wayne has in each case failed at fathering during his son's early years. He has been distant, aloof, and threatening as a father figure. He succeeds as a father by taking a stance, like a tower, at a crucial time in the father/son interaction that forces the son into manhood and ends in their reconciliation. In these movies, John Wayne will not compromise his beliefs and will not help (mother) his son to a safer, more successful position.

These movies illustrate that in many ways a man can fail at fathering and then still make the critical difference if he can help his son make the one transition out from under the control of the mother-image. The second step in this process is standing for letting the son be who he really is—letting him risk young adulthood in his own way, even if the result is being a private rather than an officer (as in *Rio Bravo*) or gentleman. Fathers must give their children the respect needed for them to develop their own authentic identities and independence, no matter whether or not they ever reach their potential to be great brain surgeons, score high on the SAT, or go to fine universities. This earth wisdom of fathers, once expressed during the initiation rites of puberty, must take a stance for life, realizing that separation, independence, and authenticity are vital in the lives of their sons. If their sons are designed for greatness, this stance for the son's authenticity will hasten that process, and if they are not designed for greatness, living authentically is better than waking up at midlife or retirement and discovering one has lived the ghostly life of others' expectations and values.

Negative mothering includes anxious nursing and guarding of the child when the latter does not need it or no longer needs it, lack of confidence in the child's strength and independence, and interference with its development. Mothers seem almost naturally to turn negative in this sense during a son's adolescence, especially when the father is distant or absent. Kids today in their mid-twenties are still often dependent on their home and parents. They are having trouble making the break we discussed at length in interpreting the fairy tale. Men have to take a stand and intercede in this situation in spite of the mother's anxiety, even if she appears right and is upheld by the culture, and even if the father's intervention is misjudged as being brutal and non-caring.

Actually, fathers often need to step in earlier than adolescence. Our cultural mother-complex, with either the acquiescence or absence of most fathers, already starts hounding grammar school kids (with teachers and the schools' assistance) to realize and fully develop their so-called "potential."[5] This attitude increases as the child grows—in school, in extra activities (all wonderful of course), in the way he dresses, and in the way he is appealed to and influenced by TV advertising and shows. Fathers need to step in with their earth strength and wisdom and stand for the value of life—let kids be kids, and let them play and develop.

As I said earlier in this book, our culture has made mothering an impossible role. I do not see how anyone can be a mother without being filled with self-doubt and self-criticism.

However, becoming the kind of father just discussed may not always make one's wife happy. She may prefer that you behave more in the sensitive role women have projected on Alan Alda. But be of good cheer. Most men will recognize that Alan Alda is successful in his craft, which means he most likely had some lean years, and had to maintain his commitment, work hard, balance career and family, and gain some knowledge and wisdom with age. His life evidences plenty of masculine strength joined with eros, which I will discuss in the next chapter.

Feelings and Logos

I have discussed John Wayne and his movies to illustrate two specific points in this chapter: 1) showing how attributes become rejected and repressed into shadow sides, and how

---

[5]For a full amplification of this problem, read David Elkind's *The Hurried Child: Growing Up Too Fast Too Soon* (Reading, MA: Addison-Wesley, 1981).

this process may also rob us of needed, positive virtues; and 2), illustrating the earth strength of the masculine and the necessity of this masculine, not feminine, earth strength to take a certain stand for growth and life. The earth strength of masculine supporting feeling values is the best answer we have to the one-sidedness of our culture's technological thinking and pursuit of progress—and the reclamation of our masculine souls.

MASCULINE EROS

> We have to reach back and get hold of our deaths and our births and our marriages and our children, and bring them back to us instead of turning them over to "Sesame Street" and the mortician on the corner and a school board that you don't want any part of.
>
> —Ken Kesey[1]

In Chapter 12 we saw that *feeling* as a psychological function is a process of making judgments based on subjective personal values and convictions. Feeling type people are often described as making decisions with the "heart" in contrast to making decisions with the "head." Personal attitudes resulting from a well-developed feeling function include an understanding of people, a wish to affiliate with them, a desire for harmony, and a capacity for warmth, empathy, and compassion. People who prefer feeling usually take an immediate and personal view of situations, seeing things as a participant from within that situation rather than as an outside observer. Remember that in psychological language, this definition of feelings contains an impor-

---

[1] Ken Kesey and Robert Stone, "Blows to the Spirit," in *Esquire Magazine* (June, 1986), p. 274.

tant difference from our normal use of the word to describe emotions.

We also noted that in our culture, extroverted dynamism and "hard" factual thinking processes have become preferred over the "soft" subjective processes of introversion, intuition, and feeling. Tom Peters and Nancy Austin, in *A Passion for Excellence*, surprise us by spending a lot of space informing us that our best companies did not buy this cultural norm, and that others need to develop their disowned "soft" processes in order to improve their companies. They discuss people, values, and trust in several sections of their book. They include a section labeled "Emotion and Feel: Being Human." They devote their entire chapter 16 to "Attention, Symbols, Drama—and Love." Who could believe that we would end up with a book on business leadership talking about love? All of the above terms, of course, fall into the category we consider the feeling function. They proceed, discussing at length "Integrity" and "Bone Deep Beliefs"—commitment on the John Wayne level of standing for beliefs and values. Part Four of their book is called "People, People, People," and in it they state:

> Make no mistake about it, "Techniques" don't produce quality products, educate children, or pick up the garbage on time; people do, people who care, people who are treated as creatively contributing adults.[2]

Bob Waterman is quoted as saying, "Attention is all there is."[3] James Hillman relates these notions to the realm of personal psychology (our relation to ourselves) and to our personal relationships.

[2]Thomas J. Peters and Nancy Austin, *A Passion for Excellence* (London: HarperCollins, 1985), p. 201.
[3]Thomas J. Peters and Robert H. Waterman, Jr., *A Search for Excellence* (New York: Warner, 1983), p. 401.

Personal relationships require personal feelings. Here the emphasis is on the small. The mystics can instruct us. We like to believe that the great mystics occupy themselves with the vaster cosmic things, but they usually talk about small things, very small things. With the feeling function they reduce intellectual speculation to matters close at hand, personal issues of food and nature. Their laughter is born of trivia. Our spoiled feelings are usually resentments over small things, those little mistakes that have been neglected as one goes along. Then life turns sour; one has soured one's life by missing the small feeling opportunities and one is left with festering minor irritations. To miss the small is to miss with one's feeling function. Therefore, personal feeling needs to be expressed in small ways: personal favours, personal sharing, personal remarks about exactly what one likes in the other. The feeling function, by recognizing the other person's virtues connects him to these parts giving him belief in himself.[4]

Culturally, men are taught to desire and respect things that are inflated, hypertense, high pressured, big, fast, and technologically complicated. Even for hobbies and relaxation, we look to Porsches, complex stereos, power boats, power lawn mowers that are more expensive and complicated than tractors were twenty years ago. Patience is boring, and simple means dull or stupid. We have lost the art of finding pleasure and meaning in small, natural things or activities. We can see from Hillman's remarks that expression of feeling, personal values, is often a matter of taking time, choosing patience to give attention to small things.

When we consistently do not have time for someone, whether wife, child, or employee, the person begins to get the

---

[4]Marie-Louise von Franz and James Hillman, *Jung's Typology* (Dallas: Spring, 1979), p. 140.

idea we do not value him or her much. Frequently this feeling reflects the truth, but just as often this idea is a misunderstanding. I have continually met couples in therapy where the wife felt undervalued because the husband spent too much time at work, and the husband felt his work and the resulting income was an expression of his love for her and the family. However, even when the above case is true, we could get some sense that the husband's feeling function is not fully developed, or he would have already taken the time to dialogue with her about this. The time we spend indicates the value of the person or process to us. In business or personal relationships, if we have no time for someone, the implicit feeling messages are as follows.

Things are more important than people;

Money is more important than people;

My work is more important than our relationship;

I love you—when I have nothing better to do.

The development of the feeling function does much to heal or bridge the separation between the ego and the shadow. It does this because feeling determines the value given to each side in every conflict, so as men we have to go further than working out a "rational" solution and ask questions like the following:

What does all this have to do with me?

How do I feel about this?

What does it mean to me? To them?

What does it say about me?

This process of differentiating and evaluating (using feeling to further thinking) goes hand in hand with a harmonious cooperation between the principles of the masculine and the feminine, which are also opposites, yet complementary.

A man's quest to develop his feeling function is a confusing and difficult task. New feeling values may consistently conflict with the old thinking process. Often we have difficulty figuring out whether feeling is developing or thinking is just deteriorating when we are feeling discouraged over the whole process. Back in the 70s when I thought I was well on the way to becoming a "liberated man," I went into a store I owned and went over a list of things to do with the store manager. I looked up and saw that she and all the employees were staring at me. I said, "What's wrong? I said that in a friendly way."

She answered, "Sure, in your friendly voice of command." Attempting this change from thinking to feeling requires courage, because we may be hurt or appear stupid in some situations. Sacrificing the old viewpoint is painful in itself, and doubly painful if we then fail at the new. I was stunned to realize that my executive persona had become so ingrained that I had difficulty changing it even when I tried to, and in fact thought I had succeeded. My children increased my chagrin by confirming this reality and telling me how pressured and distant from me they felt as a result.

We must realize that preferring thinking over feeling as a style of consciousness causes our feeling function to remain primitive and underdeveloped. The experience of beginning to use it later in life is like trying to write with your left hand after being right-handed all your life. The underdeveloped function may be like a child and is often shown as a child in dreams. We have to nurture, guide, direct, and educate this function in its development. Frequently I have seen fathers who have been distant from their children (particularly in cases of divorce) try out their new "feeling" approaches, only to be met with anger and hostility. Actually, kids need to finally be able to express their anger at their dads, and this expression shows a new level of intimacy developing. However, such an outburst is not exactly reinforcing to a dad who is attempting to change. Consequently, the ego (the conscious personality) must consistently do the hard work of discriminating which path to take and trying to understand the results. We need to explore and experiment again and again: trying, testing, succeeding, and failing is the only way we can learn to use what is inside us. We must have experience to develop any new potential.

Eros and Feeling

The false equating of eros with the feeling function has plagued Jungian psychology for many years. Early in this book I presented a description of eros as the feminine principle and logos as the masculine principle. Eros, as I described it, means relatedness, interest in relationships, and an attitude that works for conciliation and reconciliation. Eros values self-integration, subjectivity, and the concerns of individuals. Eros is rooted in the material universe and the earthy qualities such as passivity and receptivity. The word logos was used to signify power, meaning, and deed. Logos stands for objectivity, structure, meaning, discrimination, generativity, and intrusiveness. Logos is often equated with the spiritual in the sense of the nonmaterial. I also stressed that both eros and logos are equally necessary in human life and complement each other.

We may recognize that eros is the personification of love based on the ancient Greek god Eros. Adolf Guggenbuhl-Craig suggests that eros is an attribute that makes both gods and humans loving, creative, and involved. He observes:

> Here love is understood to include the entire spectrum of emotional attachment, from sexuality and friendship to involvement with profession, hobbies, and art. Eros is at work in the love men have for women and women for men. Eros is also present in politicians whose "love" is politics, or in mathematicians whose passion is mathematics, or in flower fanciers who live for their roses.[5]

---

[5]Adolf Guggenbuhl-Craig, *Eros on Crutches* (Dallas: Spring, 1980), pp. 26–27.

Eros, however, is not intended as a panacea for the world's problems. Eros can lead to suffering, conflicts, frustrations, tragedy, and comedy, as well as satisfaction and joy. Eros can be primitive and instinctual (primitive sexuality), or lofty and idealistic, and all of these expressions can be worthwhile at times.

Eros as the feminine principle does not define or determine what is feminine in individual women or men. It is a principle and a process that informs and guides both women and men in the area of relatedness to self, to others, to nature and to the world. Jung may have used this particular term as a result of his own enculturation. Eros is a misleading term for the feminine function, because while it appears to men via projection and motherhood that women have a special "relatedness" to life, we will see in the following discussion and in the next chapter that the feminine side of men *does not* contribute much to men's ability to relate once they have passed the instinctual and symbiotic (sexual and romantic love) stage of development.

We saw in chapter 12 that women have no monopoly on feeling. The fact that we men have made feeling alien to ourselves and have projected it onto women does not make it feminine. We have certainly learned that men do not possess a monopoly on thinking either—plenty of women are doing well in thinking-type jobs and professions.

Eros represents relatedness and value reached primarily, but not exclusively, through feeling. That is, through the psychological function of feeling. I will soon explain that eros does have a very special relationship to both logos and the feminine. When a man thinks or feels, he does so as a man because his primary personality identification is masculine, and he develops upon this foundation. Likewise, when a woman thinks and feels, she does so as a woman. The more we develop individually, the more the process of eros will reflect our individuality and personal identity rather than psychological principles.

Of course, we must always keep the exceptions in mind, as Jung points out:

As we can hardly ever make a psychological proposition without immediately having to reverse it; instances to the contrary leap to the eye at once: men who care nothing for discrimination, judgment, and insight and women who display an almost excessively masculine proficiency in this respect. . . .[6]

Eros and the Woman Within

I would like to make a few comments on the effects the anima has on eros in their special relationship inside of a man. For the most part, however, I am saving my discussion of the anima (man's feminine side) for the next chapter. In the discussion of the fairy tale, once the soldier separated from the mother, he was ready for the next stage of development, which led him to his feminine side. The next step is the growth into romance and sexuality, leading to the potential for relationship with the opposite sex.

Men and boys are not without eros up until this time. They are simply involved in another kind of love that may also develop and continue throughout their lives. This other kind of love includes the love of doing, such as sports, studies, jobs, hobbies, professions, and so on, and the eros that men have for men. Often this eros is centered around some joint activity, for example, men who are on teams, who soldier together. As a result, they may develop a special type of eros or love for each other. Some men and boys develop close friendships that last for years. Unfortunately, our society has become so competitive, so isolated in work and living styles, and so child-oriented that we have lost or devalued many of the opportunities men used to have for eros with other men.

With our sexual instinct, the inner woman leads a man into the first and perhaps many involvements with girls or

---

[6]C. G. Jung, *Collected Works*, Vol. 14, *Mysterium Coniunctionis*, Bollingen Series, Vol. XX, ¶. 225.

women. The inner woman's part in this process is to get the whole thing started and to get the man emotionally involved as well as sexually involved. As I mentioned earlier, the inner woman works by projection. Generally, in this process, she totally unhinges our feeling function. We have more feeling awareness and emotional fluctuations than we ever dreamed possible. Then she pulls out and leaves us sitting all alone, or even turns bitchy on us—the romance has worn off in the relationship. The man must then reestablish his own identity and work on loving the other person for who she really is (eros) and work to develop a real relationship with that person (again, eros). If we do not begin to develop eros and relationship, then the situation will turn bitter and destructive in either the inner or outer world and eventually in both. The anima therefore leads us into situations that have potential for eros and, in a manner of speaking, expects us to then make the best of it. She is primarily involved in individual relationships, since group projections are rare, and she can turn very negative on a man if he does not continue toward the development of eros.

Whenever the anima is involved in projections, a need for fusion and symbiosis is present. Projection of the inner woman always seems to include a portion of our inner need for completeness and our inner longing for both paradise and growth.

ANIMA ⟶ FUSION

The anima has to recede and the projections withdrawn before eros can really begin.

EROS ⟶ RELATIONSHIP

Otherwise, we simply end up trying to manipulate the other person to fill our needs. However, the other person must also have a "hook" inside for us to hang our projection on. A shade of truth exists in what we perceived.

PROJECTION ————————➤ HOOK

This hook means that we have seen a vision of the best in the other person. We have seen a vision of the positive potential in the other person's personality that even they may not be aware of consciously. Unfortunately, we can do nothing to bring this vision to reality. In fact, the more we try, the worse we make the relationship, because it then becomes one of power and manipulation. The other person's individuation is his or her responsibility. Developing eros and relationship must be with the real here-and-now person.

As we withdraw the projections, we can see how much of ourselves and our needs and wants were reflected in the image we had of them. This time can be painful and disillusioning, but it can also be a great source of new understanding about ourselves.

As many emotions and conflicts are stirred up, we also have the opportunity to deepen our feeling function. If we become more aware of our emotions and follow them back through our feeling function in order to become more conscious of our values, we will also find that we are making our inner woman more conscious.

So in summary, we see that our inner woman in primitive form attempts to lead (or force) us into eros and higher consciousness. The anima's vital principle, the principle of life, involves the feeling function in life. That process of involvement may lead to growth, or to bitterness. Then comes the potential for eros to lead us back to increased consciousness about the inner feminine. Of course, this process is often long and turbulent, a process we must courageously live through and then seek to understand. Attempting this process through focused consciousness and rationality is a sure way to miss the meaning of it and end up wondering how everything started so nicely and ended up so terribly.

Too often, men in our culture—the soft man, the Peter Pan, the maternal man, and the pseudo-liberated man—take a passive role in eros. Such a man's eros is like a child's. He wants to be loved, enveloped, and enclosed. He seeks the nourishment and magic circle of the mother figure. He almost expects the world, personified by his lover, to force happiness on him. As we remember the fairy tale, we know that he has not yet slain the witch. To learn more about this situation, a man can develop and talk to some women friends; they are all familiar with this problem in men and often do not know how to deal with it.

Because we have projected so much of the process of eros onto women, we have difficulty distinguishing eros from the feminine in our own psyches. As I further explain eros in this chapter and the anima in the next, you will see many similarities, especially in their developmental stages. Several differences may be kept in mind to help differentiate between them. Eros is an energetic process with the goal of relating to an object. This object may be inner (as part of our personality), but is most often an outer object (as another person). The anima is an inner function of the personality and affects processes and behavior, often dramatically, but this function entails no specific series of actions. Eros can be consciously developed, whereas development of the anima is primarily a result of the development of the full personality. When projected, the anima desires fusion, overcoming the distance between the subject and object, and making them become one. Eros desires closeness and relationship, but not fusion. Eros desires to maintain and respect separateness and identity between subject and object and to build a bridge of relationship between them.

Eros and Logos

Eros and logos follow a parallel course of development throughout our lives. The stages in this developmental process represent potential patterns of orientation which influence our lives in varying degrees, either consciously or unconsciously. These stages are never as differentiated as I am presenting them because we move back and forth in them, depending on the circumstances of our lives. Ideally, eros and logos will develop together, complementing each other. If they do not (and for most of us, they do not), we will become one-sided and will be left vulnerable in the side that is underdeveloped. The following figures give a brief summary of the developmental stages of eros and logos. Figure 2 includes some words that reflect the broader meaning of each stage, even though this presentation is still oversimplified. Figure 3 shows the interaction of the feminine qualities with the stages of development of logos and eros.

Two things are apparent when we study these two figures. First, the stages in both eros and logos build on and depend on prior stages. As we grow, we need them all. For example, Meaning without Power (vitality) is just a ghost hav-

LOGOS	EROS
POWER—muscle, potency, superiority, authority, control, endurance, potential, vigor, energy	MATERNAL—sheltered, source, protection, fostering, instinctual, love, risk-free, primary, containment, elemental
ACTION—doing, moving, initiate, achieve, acting, intrusive, deed, implement, campaign, war	LOVER—attraction, appeal, desire, energize, ardor, passion, lust, pleasure, symmetry, elegance
KNOWLEDGE—data, language, factual truth, judgment, analysis, science, discrimination, information	RELIGION—spiritual, natural, mysteries, virtue, inner life, realization of a great power, concern with more than ourselves
MEANING—intellect, spirit, understanding, consciousness, self-consciousness, psyche, mind, metapsychology	WISDOM—authenticity, soul, trust, receptivity, sageness, tolerance, compassion, living experience, foresight

Figure 2. Developmental stages of logos and eros.

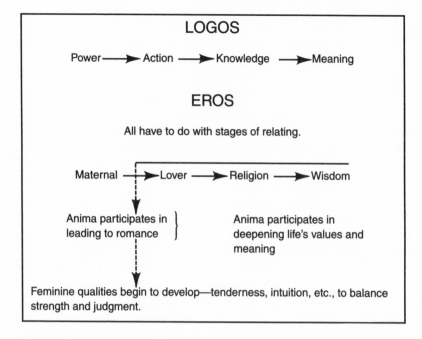

Figure 3. Interaction of the feminine in the development of eros and logos.

ing no form or body. Also, both eros and logos need to develop in a parallel manner, or we become one-sided. Power without Widsom (compassion) is simply brutal.

Second, from previous discussions, we have seen that men in our culture developed an extreme one-sidedness in logos qualities with the exception of Power, the foundation of the whole process (because many of the attributes of strength are culturally unpopular). My discussion has also pointed out that many American men have not developed their eros past the Maternal/Lover stage. We can also note that American men tend to project everything in the area of eros onto women.

Our culture is in critical need of men who have the strength to stand not only for their values and ideals, but also for *eros*! The future of relationships, families, and perhaps our world, may depend on this strength. Throughout history, we have had a few men who could totally combine all I have outlined here and take a stand for eros: Buddha, Christ, St. Francis, Gandhi, and Martin Luther King, Jr., to name a few.

Unfortunately, I am not on the path to becoming a Christ or Buddha, and actually, I do not want to become one, either. So what kind of practical meaning do eros and logos have for me as an ordinary American male, perhaps having previously been a soft-man or a manipulating man? To answer this question, I will look at Dagwood in a certain situation and see how the ingredients of our discussion could add up to create some new responses to his situation.

Dagwood

Once we take a look at Dagwood's experience and discuss some of the implications and pitfalls involved in it, I plan to give several short scenarios showing different ways he can respond. In these scenarios (see pages 211, 212), I will suggest response patterns that illustrate different levels of the development of logos and eros. I will not provide any formulas to follow because understanding needs to be developed from within. As we develop understanding, we can see better who we are and who we may become. So the intention of these illustrations is to help develop an understanding of the situation at hand that will enable us to better decide how to choose to behave, and how to learn from the process of our own living experience.

One can easily see from this comic strip that both Blondie and Dagwood are living emotionally immature roles. Dagwood, of course, is behaving like a little boy, another one of the kids. Blondie is behaving in the style of the "managerial wife." She is also assuming a maternal role with Dagwood, perhaps thinking of men as little boys in her heart. As a result of this stance, she not only tolerates this behavior on his part, but also manages it and probably uses it to her own advantage at times.

If Dagwood decides to become an adult man, a father, and a true husband, he is going to have to begin with a basic

decision. This first decision is to follow the path of the soldier in the fairy tale and separate from the mother complex that allows him to be a son/child in his own marriage.

Then he has a judgment call to make. If Blondie is this intent on the value of spring cleaning, she probably has a critical mother complex of her own. He must be aware that if he crosses this complex, she will respond to him emotionally with anger and perhaps hurt. He will have to be willing to stand up to her wrath for what he feels are higher values.

Currently, many women who are caught in a mother complex feel totally responsible for household responsibilities, and unhelped, and unappreciated. When questioned or confronted by a man, they become angry, frustrated, overwhelmed, and seem quite irrational to the man. They seem to know what should be done and exactly how it should be done and are only interested in seeing it done in an often over-perfectionistic way. They want the man to do "his share" and share the responsibility as they (or their critical mother complex) define it. They are not open to masculine logos, clarity, and simplification in this area. The woman may also be experiencing deeper conflicts, such as:

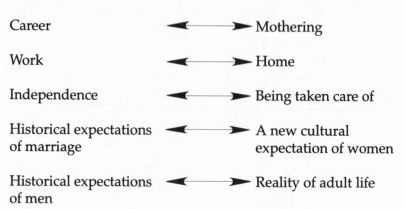

Career	←——→	Mothering
Work	←——→	Home
Independence	←——→	Being taken care of
Historical expectations of marriage	←——→	A new cultural expectation of women
Historical expectations of men	←——→	Reality of adult life

Dagwood will have to use his own masculine judgment to determine if all or part of this mother complex is involved, or if he and his wife are functioning according to habit or out-dated models they would both like to get out of.

This discrimination is important, because it will help him judge on a feeling level how much anger he is willing to deal with in the process of evolving out of this situation. Continually giving in can be destructive to her as well as to him. It belittles and destroys him, and since she is caught in a complex, the situation probably leaves her very unhappy at a deep level and confused about how to get out of the situation. His growth, her growth, and the growth of the relationship need this strong intercession. But he must assess each step, because people easily become enraged and irrational when dealing with complexes, and irretrievable bottom lines may be crossed unintentionally.

The first response that he might make could come straight from the caveman masculine: he could tell her to "bug off." This response is obviously blunt and brutal, and will do little to further their relationship or enhance his standing as a husband.

He could also respond from what I like to call the "eros masculine." The two primary characteristics in this response are 1) to maintain his position as an adult and father by not fleeing the home and facilitating the kids' flight; and, 2) to talk about it—even if simply and clumsily. Talk about it. Talk about what everyone has planned for the day. Look at the values of play, friendship, recreation, and physical activities as well as the value of housecleaning and Blondie's feeling about it. Often, just the discussion of these values on a true eros/feeling level can alleviate much of the stress and lead to cooperation and solution. His ability to stand firm and initiate a feeling dialogue in the family can make a great deal of difference. If he just gives her an intellectual discourse on values, he can probably expect a war. This type of talking is tough to do, because it requires conscious, careful relating in a context of eros, without giving in. Husbands and fathers need to learn how to both STAND FOR THEIR VALUES AND STAND FOR EROS AND RELATIONSHIP! This stance provides a crucible for working out differences, evolving more consciousness, and at the same time developing a more caring and enhancing relationship among family members.

This process can be moved up the eros/logos ladder even further. Intuitions can be used by Dagwood. If he knows spring cleaning is a value to Blondie, he can initiate both planning and discussions of it. If she is struggling with a complex, he can use compassion as well as strength and objectivity. He can use both eros and logos to help plan and decide who does what when. He can also discuss with her whether she would like to share some eros with him in a joint activity or whether they would both rather do something individually. Even though Blondie acts like a stern mother grabbing them by the ear, I think from the perspective of eros, she felt hurt and lonely when everyone ran out on her the way they did.

The important point for me is that men, husbands, and fathers need to learn to both stand for their values and also stand for eros. This stance can force the transcendence of a situation rather than the disintegration of it. It may also force the others to clarify their values, which you may not like to hear, but even this process results in more honest relating and less manipulative and passive-aggressive behavior. Each relationship then has the potential for both people in it to be continuously transformed, and it becomes a relationship of growth and authenticity as well as struggle.

15

THE WOMAN WITHIN

Barbara Walters:	"... and what about women?"
John Wayne:	"I'm scared to death of them."
Barbara Walters:	"You, John Wayne—why?"
John Wayne:	"Because they can hurt you so much."[1]

At the end of the fairy tale the soldier married the princess and thus came into full relationship with his feminine side. Symbolically, this is the sacred, mystical marriage of antiquity signifying the completion of one's personality and the unity of the masculine and feminine within one's self. Since then we have taken a careful look at men's feelings, values, and eros. As we proceed, an understanding of these characteristics of men's personalities will help us discover what the illusive girl deep inside every man really is, as well as what she is not. In general, men have been taught to see feminine attributes negatively and often to repress them. We are learning, however, that they are not all negative—many are positive. We know from recent experience that some of these attributes are cultural, and as men we disguise some so-called feminine characteristics in a process of self-deception. For example, dependence is often seen as a negative quality. But any man who functions in a large corporation or institution can only do so much personally

---

[1]This is from a Barbara Walters television interview with John Wayne as I recall it.

and is then dependent on others, both above and below him. Many businessmen and administrators function well and instinctively in this environment, but would feel very threatened if they were labeled "dependent." But deeper than this, and in spite of macho dispositions, what man at some point in his life does not long to let that far away little boy in himself cuddle comfortably up in the arms of a lover?

In general, I am not speaking of our enculturation, even though it greatly affects our concept of the feminine. Of course, we cannot escape enculturation because it affects all of our perspectives, even up to the words we choose to use. The feminine side of man (the anima) is considered an ingrained psychological figure that in her positive form can inspire us (as the muse of ideas and wisdom) and in her negative form (as the unvalued hag or witch) can destroy us. She includes the feminine psychological characteristics in our personality, such as vague feelings, moods, some intuition or hunches, receptivity, an orientation toward personal, erotic and romantic love, feelings for nature, and the bridge connecting us to our deep inner life as our outer face (our persona) connects us to the external world. We have seen that this inner damsel is often mistaken for the feeling function, and that the psychological functions of feelings, intuition, and perceiving have been projected onto the feminine in our culture. In the same manner, the principle of eros, the binding force in life, has been confused and often thought of as the feminine in a man. I have noted that even if the eros principle is considered the feminine principle, it does not define the woman within, although it has a special relationship to her.

In psychological discussions, parts of the personality are often personified as in the above paragraph, where I begin speaking of the feminine side of a man, name her anima, and then refer to the anima as "she," girl, damsel, and woman. This type of personification is simply a short way of using words as a metaphor to enable us more easily to explain and discuss human experience. In the next section, notice the names men have given the different stages and aspects of this illusive part of themselves. These names portray our experience of this mystical dimension of ourselves that attracts us so strongly and we try to avoid so stubbornly, because we fear whatever is in our nature that we do not understand. Jung called this dimension *anima* as I have pointed out. Robertson Davies gives a beautiful literary illustration of this dimension:

> She is not a soul as Christianity conceives it. She is the feminine part of your nature: she is all that you are able to see, and experience, in woman: she is not your mother, or any single one of the women you have loved, but you have seen all of them—at least in part—in terms of her. If you love a woman you project this image upon her, at least at the beginning, and if you hate a woman it is again the Anima at work, because she has a very disagreeable side which is not at all like the smiling sibyl in the blue mantle. She has given rise to some of the world's greatest art and poetry. She is Cleopatra, the enchantress, and she is Faithful Griselda, the patient enduring woman; she is Beatrice, who glorifies the life of Dante, and she is Nimue, who imprisons Merlin in a thornbush. She is the Maiden who is wooed, the Wife who bears the sons, and she is the Hag who lays out her man for his last rest. She is an angel, and she may also be a witch. She is Woman as she appears to every man, and to every man she appears somewhat differently though essentially the same.[2]

When we personify this way psychologically, we talk of these parts of our personality as if they are not part of us. We must

---

[2]Robertson Davies, *The Deptford Trilogy* (London: Penguin, 1983), pp. 433–434.

remember that they are, and we should not allow the discussion of our experience to simply become an intellectual exercise. On the other hand, our psychological processes seem to have a certain amount of autonomy. Moods, emotions, romance, and so forth, are often hard to control consciously. We are only too familiar with slips of the tongue, forgetfulness, spontaneous replies, and irritabilities that transpire without thinking or against our wishes. Please keep these incidents in mind as I discuss the anima "as if" she were autonomous.

Stages of the Feminine in Men

In addition to the above comments on the anima, I mentioned earlier that she is the function that "animates" a man's life. As a rough guide to study and to help us gain more self-understanding, stages of development of the inner woman have been outlined, illustrating the various experiences and manifestations of these experiences as the personality grows and matures. As in our discussion of other concepts and stages (styles of consciousness, eros, and logos), this formulation is stylized and incomplete. We do not develop through these stages in a linear manner. We often move back and forth in them; they always seem to overlap. We may experience several at once, and we often seem to recycle through them. The four developmental stages of the inner woman are frequently spoken of as Eve, Helen of Troy, Mary, and Sophia.

We discussed the first two stages at length in our consideration of the fairy tale. The first stage, Eve, depicts a degree of unself-consciousness in which the anima is not really differentiated from the mother-image. This inner woman on this lowest level of differentiation represents purely instinctual and biological relations. Figuratively, this is our connection to the great goddess of ancient times. Psychologically, this stage portrays what Goethe called the "world of the Mothers," the deep unconscious world we all begin to evolve from in infancy. In more academic terms, we simply call this the unconscious, the home of the archetypes, the matrix that forms human experience and consciousness. Primitives considered this the underworld, the dream world, but the "world of the Mothers" is an appropriate metaphor. This metaphor suggests the unconscious as the mother and matrix of human experience and the world of the mother as paradise to the individual from which one is eventually expelled. From this, we can understand why worship of the Mother does not come from the heart of man but from the depths of his innards, often from his very core. Dependency on this primitive level can keep the "heart" of a man forever imprisoned.

The second level, Helen of Troy, represents a higher level of beauty and aesthetic values. This level moves us toward eros by the process of personal romantic and erotic thoughts, fantasies, and love. The inner woman in this stage also facilitates the development of some feminine qualities in the personality, such as tenderness and intuition, to balance masculine strength and judgment.

Helen enriches our fantasy life as the source of our erotic fantasies. For over three thousand years she has been the incarnation of Aphrodite, the Goddess of Love, and often represents man's sexual urges in conflict with social inhibitions. In history she caused the launching of a thousand ships and the great Trojan War that involved gods, goddesses, and men in mortal combat affecting the course of world history. Psychologically, she may also represent the conflict between the conscious (civilization) and the unconscious (instinctual) minds.

When a man is too rational, too one-sided, too caught up in himself and his career, Helen is likely to appear with beauty and irresistible sluttish charm. Usually, she is projected onto a real woman, and an otherwise sensible man seems compelled to love her, no matter what her past is or what he knows about her. Politicians have self-destructive affairs, evangelists see prostitutes, priests fall in love, and professors divorce their wives to marry young students. When Helen appears early in our life in positive form we fall in love and learn the joys of romance. If we deny her and shut her out causing her to come

218 / C. T. B. Harris

after us in a negative way, we can find the most practical of
men making astonishing reversals of what seemed to be their
basic natures.

The third stage is represented by Mary (the spiritual
mother), who personifies the ability to raise love (eros) to the
level of spiritual devotion or the possibility of a relationship
with God. Other psychological thinkers consider this stage that
of Mary Creatrix, the Muse. They mean by this concept that if a
man has a relationship with his inner woman based on true values, she will be the mother of and the inspiration for his creativity. Writing, poetry, composing music, sculpting, and painting
are often identified with this Muse. Of course, men can express
this side of themselves in many more ways. Tying flies, making
furniture, or even conceptualizing and starting a new business
can be creative, masculine experiences urged on by their Muse.
The attitude of patience and receptivity, instead of aggressive
achievement, differentiates the presence of the Muse (which
does not mean that committed activity may not follow her
inspiration). When a man projects this stage of his inner feminine development onto a woman, he will think that she is the
source of his inspiration. Some women do function in this role,
but they serve to connect the man to himself, and make it difficult for him to relate to her as a person with her own identity. In
Greek mythology, the Muses were originally the goddesses of
songs. Song is a combination of intellect (words) and emotion
(music). The marriage of these two give birth to inspiration. If
men become lost in or dominated by their creativity, they may
ignore the practical and material sides of their lives and the
existence of other people. The great inquisitors of the Middle
Ages—who tortured and murdered so many thousands in the
name of the Mother Church—show how destructive a vision-
ary or idealist may become when in an "other-worldly state."
Rigid or off in the air, they are separated from eros and the practical reality of flesh-and-blood people.

The fourth stage is that of Sophia, who represents the
principles of relationship to the highest wisdom, the feminine
personification of God's wisdom. Some scholars consider the

Mona Lisa and the Holy Spirit to symbolize this stage. The Gnostics considered her the personification of both wisdom and the world soul. Other learned religious men visualized the Black Madonna as Sophia, combining the wholeness, the glory, and the wisdom of God with the rich, maternal black earth—a combination foreign to the conventional Christian mind. Personally, I experience this level more along the lines of the wisdom of nature, the wise old woman, knowledgeable, patient, immortal, and close to God. Psychologically, she is the connection of the conscious personality to the greater Self and the universal family of man. Sophia provides man with the mystical perception that allows him to know with his heart what his mind knows is true but cannot prove. In any event, when we consider the problems of the feminine in man in our culture, the soft-male, the Peter Pan, the maternal man, and the pseudo-liberated man, we see the problems we are most vitally concerned with are in the Eve and the Helen stages.

I find it interesting that Jung and Jungians have given such high sounding names to the stages of anima development. This naming is in particular contrast to the naming of the stages of the masculine side of women. In fact, women's masculine side has less esoteric names and they are not so commonly used. The inner image of man in a woman, the animus, has stages usually called the Lover, the Warrior, the Wizard, and the Child. Many men, even psychologists, seem uncomfortable with these terms, even if they are describing "her" inner man. The very word anima is the Latin word for "soul." In addition to Eve, Helen, Delilah, Mary, Muse, and Sophia, terms such as spiritual guide, Holy Grail, Beatrice (from Dante, ". . . she who makes my mind a paradise"), vamp, and siren or seductress are commonly used. This projected idealization and spiritualization shows how violently we have repressed our eros, sensitivity, and creativity—illustrating our loss of soul—and our need to reconnect with our feminine selves and nature. With the onset of rationality and the resulting Cartesian mind/body (spirit/matter) dichotomy, we have consistently attempted to intellectually spiritualize these values and needs, without remembering that the wisdom of the earth and the ordinary (humanness) is just as important. In fact, the wisdom of the earth and the ordinary may be the way to the Grail as Christ was the word (logos) made flesh (matter created from earth).

The lack of the feminine has become an important issue in our culture and in our psychology—and rightfully so. However, we must be careful that our need and our one-sidedness do not force us to look for too simple an answer. We can clearly see that soft-men are not the answer, and in reality "the feminine" is not the answer. The feminine is not the Buddha. The feminine is a part of the answer and a stage in the ongoing process of development. If a psychological answer exists, it lies more in the full development of the psyche. This development of man's understanding, character, and personality allows him to appreciate the higher manifestations of his anima. As I pointed out in the last chapter, her stages of development are tied directly to his full personality development and rarely change independently. We must try to understand and relate to all our parts—to become men of "substance" and if necessary use intelligence, will power, and discrimination to make a conscious sacrifice of some parts. Growth at any cost can sometimes be terrible, as "progress" is teaching us.

The inner feminine also has a negative side. The more a man attempts to reject and repress her, the more she will come out in unconscious negative feelings and moods. A man in the midst of this negative constellation acts like an inferior woman who is upset about something. Underneath, he can be moody, resentful, spiteful, and jealous. Or he may become increasingly rigid, expressing less and less until he is emotionally dry and brittle. A mood may fall on a man instantly without his being aware of it. Often a small disappointment or remark will cause it. A man needs to have two responses to this possession by his inner woman. First, he needs to be able to determine his real feelings and values and express them and, if need be, take a stand for them—to give them value and look for the meaning in them. Often, he may need an avenue to express his authenticity in a creative manner. Remember the engineer in chapter 8 who needed to paint. A man also needs to learn where to stop with this process. To give it value does not mean to give in to or to be controlled by our moods. A man who is controlled by his moods loses initiative, ambition, and toughness that he needs to keep.

Men's Feminine Side and Women

Separating the feminine side from real women is an almost lifelong task. Our mother-image is the mother of all of our feminine images. Our first image of the feminine comes from our early perception of the mother and dwells on some level of the unconscious from that point on. Throughout our lives, the women in our world affect the development of our inner woman and our inner woman in turn has an effect on the outer woman. The development of our inner feminine is intertwined not only with the development of our masculinity and our total personality, but also with all of the women and images of women that we interact with.

In the past, men have had a tendency to want to relate to women in the abstract. They sentimentalize and idealize women whenever they project their anima on them, trying to make them into "Dream Girls." When men go about making Dream Girls out of flesh-and-blood girls, it has the most awful effect on the girl. Some fall for it, and try to embody the dream, and that is horribly phony and invites trouble; others become perfect bitches because they can't stand it.[3] Often, the "affair" is a search to be able to continue this process of projection. As soon as the woman involved becomes "real," the affair usually ends. Men who do the same with fantasies and with sexuality are often more comfortable with movies, books, and magazines than with real women. The anima, though, is a psychological function—a real woman is flesh and blood and includes everything in her personality plus life. Learning to

---

[3]Robertson Davies, *What's Bred in the Bone* (New York: Viking, 1985), p. 307.

know and relate to real women is one of the best ways to learn to differentiate the anima and her projections from the real woman. We find that once we begin to know, relate to, and live with women in a real way, they no longer have to live out all that idealistic, spiritual, and sentimental claptrap that we keep trying to project onto them. Romance does not have to end, but we must relate to a real person, not a vision. We still need to be able to bring romance out of the closet on special evenings, weekends, and vacations. The anima can add joy, creativity, tenderness, and spontaneity to these times if she is not bogged down trying to live as a daily projection.

Relating to a real woman is helpful in another way. She can tell a man a lot about his moods. She usually recognizes them right away, because she senses his withdrawal, and she has difficulty getting through to him. She can help him recognize his moods if she does so with kindness. If both can realize it is not her problem and neither expects her to "fix it," then women can be a great source of help to men as they try to understand the cause and meaning of their moods. This time is difficult for a woman, because when in a mood, a man does not want knowledge, he wants mothering, and he may be very critical of the nearest woman. A man who has become too unaware of his inner woman can also become too personally involved in what he is doing, too compulsively subjective, and lacking in objectivity and humor. Such a man may justify this involvement by claiming he works in a jungle, by giving the impression his career is constantly beset by life-or-death crises, or by making his work impossibly idealistic. A good relationship with a human woman can do much to help him regain his sense of equilibrium and perspective.

Often, this process can be indirect and unconscious. The real woman may be expressing discontent that also is voicing a deep level of discontent in the man's anima. The real woman may be complaining about her husband, when he is, in fact, pretty good. She may have a list of complaints, or just a vague restlessness and dissatisfaction that he cannot understand.

The man may be hard-working, successful, and committed to the relationship and the family. First, he needs to be able to stand up and say he does all these good things and wants to be appreciated for them. Then he needs to be able to listen very carefully to what is going on. Though he is expressing love through what he does, he may have fallen into the pattern of doing so by "soldiering." His contribution should be valued and appreciated, but if his eros and spontaneity are drying up, both his inner woman and the outer one will become restless and discontent.

Tom, a middle-aged attorney, was puzzled by the way his wife seemed to become more flighty and emotional as he attempted to become more logical (as you can guess—in his crisp courtroom manner) in their interactions, in almost inverse proportions. Her behavior tended to get him more entrenched in his position, in order to bring some "sanity" to the situation. This predicament really indicated that it was time for him to get to know his own inner woman better and to let her develop. When he was able to let his own feminine side contribute a little emotion and irrational behavior to his marriage, the situation with his wife eased.

Several times I mentioned that the woman within develops in tandem with the full personality, meaning that we cannot consciously develop her. However, our conscious attitude toward her can affect her development, as I have implied. If we respect and embrace her, she supports, comforts, and inspires us; if we repress and deny her, she turns sour and bitchy. Another attitude that has grown insidiously in our culture to the point that it is a major concern is *fear*. We see the fear of women evidenced in the men described in chapter 1. Often we see the fear of displeasing the mother, but also we see the fear of our vulnerability. In the previous interview with John Wayne, Barbara Walters asked him about women. He replied that he was scared to death of them. When asked why, his response was, "Because they can hurt you so much." Again, this fear and vulnerability is intertwined among our inner and outer women. We are sensitive and vulnerable and we are angry that we are this way. Our fear of women's anger seems to be deeper than the still-living sensitivities we gathered from the disapproval of our mothers and teachers. However, these experiences are intense and should not be underrated. Perhaps our fear may even trail back to primordial times when men were completely at the mercy of nature, and feared the devouring aspect of the great goddess. No matter how deeply buried this fear is, or where it comes from, we are often angry about having it. We hate to bring up unpleasant things in relationships because we are afraid of her anger, of our anger, of rejection, of appearing stupid and petty, or of the deep inner pain we may feel. We have seen that developing our masculine strength, feeling, values, and eros is necessary for adult manhood. Our ability to express ourselves (anger and other emotions), and to stand for our values and still stand for relationship, is an important part of maturing manhood. Yet, I am afraid we are losing another dimension, namely "courage of the heart." This courage, I believe, comes from the inner woman. Without this ability to risk our deepest vulnerability, relationships with both our inner and outer women become dry and lifeless. The courage of the heart commits us to life. We need this courage to open ourselves to relationships within and without. Instead of relationships that close us off, we need those that open us to ourselves and help us be more than we have been. Merle Shain comments:

> And most of us have had to protect ourselves so much at times that we've given up the high road and taken the low. But independence carried to the furthest extreme is just loneliness and death, nothing more than another defense, and there is no growth in it, only a safe harbor for a while. The answer doesn't lie in learning how to protect ourselves from life—it lies in learning how to become strong enough to let a bit more of it in.[4]

---

[4]Merle Shain, *When Lovers Are Friends* (New York: Lippincott, 1978), p. 14.

We start on the road to developing this courage early in our lives, when we first get up the nerve to finally ask a girl for a date. Before courtship or dating was all over, we had to risk rejection and having our dreams shattered over and over. I have heard middle-aged men after divorce talk about how the terror of being 13 came back repeatedly every time they called someone for a date. But this risking develops courage and strength. Ken Kesey and Robert Stone dialogue about this:

> Kesey: We kept losing our heroes, losing all of the stuff we believed in. One after the other, until finally, we had to strike out on a new philosophical path. We became Krishnas. We went to India, took acid, began to develop the yin side of maleness, instead of just relying on the yang side. And during that period, the Sixties and Seventies, the yin part of us grew bigger than the yang. The whole business of allowing women to browbeat us—

> Stone: Is that new?

> Kesey: Well, they didn't used to be so obvious about it.

> Stone: It used to just come with the territory?

> Kesey: Yes. Today they think they have a right. Not only a right, they have an OBLIGATION to do it. Things have flop-rolled over to such an extent that I never saw my sons ever phone girls during high school or college. Girls called them. The boys I know—for them to make a phone call to get a date with a girl, they just don't do it. They'd be crushed if they were turned down. They just can't even consider doing it. So there is a whole new kind of narcissistic consciousness developed in young men. I never thought of myself, ever, as being pretty, or even handsome, or desirable. All you wanted to be was . . . PASSABLE. Stomachable.

Stone: So you could persuade women to do this awful thing, which you knew that they didn't want to do.

Kesey: And you had to . . . you had to court. Boys no longer COURT girls. This loss of the ability to court means that men are losing their power, and when you lose power, you begin to use force. I have this theory that power does not corrupt, it purifies. Real power, when you have it, cleans you out. When you don't have power, you have to use force. That's why rape has gone up and up in the United States.[5]

This kind of narcissism is another kind of yearning for mother and obviously is a failure to slay the witch and proceed.

In a final word on the woman within and real women, remember that we do not relate to women through our inner woman. The inner woman leads us to relationship through projections (the "Dream Girl") which must be withdrawn in order for eros and relationship to build. When the inner woman gets hold of our emotions, she intensifies, falsifies, and exaggerates the whole matter—in short, she is too supersensitive for real relationships. James Hillman suggests that if we want relationship, the inner woman should not be part of it:

She makes moods, distortions, illusions, which serve human relatedness only where the persons concerned share the same mood or fantasy. If we want to "relate," then anima be gone! Nothing disturbs more the accurate feeling between persons than anima.[6]

Ambiance and Renewal

The anima plays an important part in two other processes. The first of these concerns the ambiance of our lives. The

---

[5]Ken Kesey and Robert Stone, "Blows to the Spirit," in *Esquire Magazine* (June, 1986), p. 268.
[6]James Hillman, *Anima* (Dallas: Spring, 1981), p. 39.

anima contributes more than beauty and inspiration. In a sense, she balances the functioning of the masculine identity by adding art, what von Franz calls subtlety.[7] The inner woman provides men with a subtle rather than a coarse attitude, enabling them to have both a more sophisticated understanding of problems and at the same time a receptivity for life as it is, bringing a subtle feeling touch into their judgments. This subtlety gives a certain realistic flexibility to men, helping them avoid psychological rigidity. Men who have this quality can adapt to a situation, see it intimately and have a feeling about it beyond the general cultural reaction.

As a man's receptivity develops, he will find himself being led further into the functions of introversion and intuition. He will become more receptive to the "unknown possibility." This ambiance and receptivity will lead the man further into his feeling function as well. The inner woman is in a sense the guardian of compassion and nurturance, the male feeling values that he expresses through eros. These values keep us connected to life as life and help us maintain an atmosphere around us that is nourishing and renewing.

The inner woman as the "archetype of life" in a man impels him to connect with life in all of its forms and possibilities—the life of the intellect, the instincts, the flesh, and the concrete and earthy emotionality directed through eros toward people, involvement, and the community. When he becomes too entangled in logos, she attempts to restore his feeling connections and his connections with his own inner depths. As the "archetype of life," the inner woman includes the psychological cycles of death and rebirth. The nourishing, life-sustaining form can come from the earth-mother side of Eve or from Mary (the Muse), the mother of creativity. Rebirth means new life in the personality. Often this rebirth occurs as we differentiate our moods and emotions in order to understand what we really want. But growth and rebirth require energy, and if our energy is tied up in our mother-complex

---

[7]Marie-Louise von Franz, *The Feminine in Fairy Tales* (Dallas: Spring, 1976), p. 192.

and soldiering, our life can get deader and deader, even up to the point where we are threatened with a real physical illness or death. Often, a man may become so compulsive in his behavior that even a vacation is over-active and pressured or done for "others." In that case, the anima can cause him to have an illness or a heart attack to lead him to enough introversion to consider his inner life. Of course, some of us are hardy enough to get through all of this input from the inner woman and become increasingly rigid and defensive. Others are not so "fortunate."

I remember the story of one man I knew. He married late in life to a woman thought of as "good" for him by all his family and friends. He was a capable fellow, always having good jobs no matter what other problems were going on. After ten or twelve years, he developed a slight drinking problem. Then to everyone's surprise, he up and divorced his wife and ran off with another woman. For a long time he knew something was wrong but could not figure out what to do about it. His new relationship did not work out, and he became an alcoholic. His ex-wife had remained friends with his family and relatives. Finally he came back to her, and as a "good" woman, she took him back, helped him stop drinking, and his family and friends breathed a sigh of relief that he had come to his senses. By age 47, he had died of cancer. He was not able to figure out how to answer his call and ended up returning to the situation (filled comfortably with the hand-me-down values of society and family) that he had been called away from. We do not get too many calls for renewal, and "courage of the heart" is required to risk answering and pursuing them.

Deeper Authenticity

As the inner woman evolves and becomes a more conscious part of our lives, we need to give her an attitude of respect and receptivity. In addition, we need the strength to suffer through our emotions and the courage to maintain our conscious awareness of them, and to allow them to lead us to risk our vulnerability in relationships with other people. As we go through this process, we become more aware of our own inner values and feelings, how to express them and, if necessary, how to stand for them. In this way the inner woman leads us deeper into our lives and helps us live more authentically. Each step on this path requires that we more clearly define or understand some part of ourselves. One does not have to be a guru contemplating oneself and new age consciousness, or a new male, to experience this process of deepening authenticity. In discussing the book *The Man in the Gray Flannel Suit*, the book that became a cliché about conformity in business in the 1950s, James F. Bene, Chief Executive Officer of Borg-Warner, speaking of Tom Rath, the book's main character, said:

> What he learned was that at no point in your life should you stop asking questions: What is the purpose of my life? Why am I here? What am I doing?
>
> These seem like pretty simple questions. But they are the questions that ultimately made *The Man in the Gray Flannel Suit* a success story.[8]

The continuing cultural spiral of over-emphasis on logos and progress set the stage for the women's liberation movement. Women's liberation is helping to force men to withdraw many of their projections on women as women seek their own identities. As these projections are taken back by men (or thrown back by women), we must look for a place to put them within ourselves. We must also find the strength, courage, and eros to come out from hiding behind our defensive posture in order to develop our masculine spirit and balance the growth of women so the process can continue. Otherwise, as currently seems to be the case, women will overdevelop their masculine

---

[8]B. Greene, "The Man in the Gray Flannel Suit," in *Esquire Magazine* (June, 1966), p. 213.

sides to fill the gap left by men, and the feminine in the culture will continue to be wounded.

Men confident in their masculinity, and in touch with eros and their own feminine sides, will not be nearly as threatened by the evolution of roles in society. They will not have to prove their manhood by mastering weaker men, women, and children. They can be like a tower—secure in what they stand for—confident in their masculine identities, but living with a creative eye on the feminine.

16

Foundations
of Fatherhood

> Our Father who art in heaven, hallowed be thy
> name, thy kingdom come, thy will be done on
> earth as it is in heaven.
>
> —The Lord's Prayer

Is fatherhood dead or alive in America? Not so long ago, a
father was regarded as the most important and powerful (at
least on the surface) member of the family. In a few short
decades, the "king in his own castle" has become a weak figure. Earlier, I noted his caricature in comic strips and television
shows. He seems to be either absent or emotionally absent (or
both) in the majority of our families. Clinically, we know that
this absence results in de-individualized sons and wounded
daughters. De-individualized is the expression for a particular
state of alienation a boy develops when he does not have a
father to identify with—and to rebel against—in the formation
of his own identity. What else happens to our sons when they
have a vacancy in their spirits and personalities in the place
"reserved so significantly for the fathers of the world?"[1] They
have trouble relating to others as adults, particularly their own
wives and children. They may strive to become the man their

---

[1]Laurens Van Der Post, *Jung and the Story of Our Time* (New York: Viking Penguin, 1976), p. 141.

father was not, and with no intimate model, they run the risk of creating grandiose ideals to compensate for the lack of masculinity in their development (such as Rambo). They will have difficulty shouldering their adult responsibility. They may also succumb to mother and end up spending their lives seeking direction from women and living to please them.

As the status of the father has declined, one can understandably wonder if women, buoyed by the feminine movement, have moved in to assume the father's former power and authority. This situation may appear to be the case in many modern families, but my clinical experience consistently indicates that the position of the mother has become almost as impossible, and practically as uncertain as that of the father. Nevertheless, we must acknowledge that the rhetoric against our patriarchal heritage has contributed to the decline in the role of paternal authority.

One result of this rhetoric is the emergence of a new kind of father, the nurturing father. Often, this kind of father turns out to be the safe, nurturant, seemingly expressive man that some feminists suggest all men should become. But we need to question whether this man is just the "soft-male" turned father, and if so, will he have the other qualities needed to be a father? Our societal rhetoric has labeled the old father as being an absolute monarch who cared little about intimacy and emotions. Patriarchal in this sense means insensitive power; it means Edith bringing Archie his slippers while he relaxes in his favorite chair, and it also means being right and self-justified in order to maintain control and authority. And this picture contains some truth. Technology and a competitive culture infect many men with goals of power and achievement, and many women know that thrusting himself into his career is easier for a man than pursuing the perilous path toward developing intimacy.

Psychologically, our cultural picture is more complicated. Like personal transformation, cultural transformation involves history, death, and rebirth, as reflected in the evolution of our images. Cultural change culminates as the collective expres-

sion of individual experience, and consequently, in their interplay, the individual and the collective shape and form each
other.

On a personal level, fatherhood always means beginning
a new level of experience. Fatherhood means new feelings of
responsibility and adulthood, whether one is ready or not—
often frightening! The implied responsibilities may appear
staggering or overwhelming. The responsibility of supporting
a family can be frightening, but now many men doubt
whether they can fully support a family, and even if they
could, how would their wives feel about their shouldering all
of the financial responsibility? Working out a satisfying marriage has also become a very complicated issue. Moreover,
most men have not been trained or brought up to play the
nurturing role or to negotiate personal relationships. Furthermore, men in general do not want the old patriarchal asper-
sions cast on them. The models have vanished, and the images
of fatherhood have become dim and confused. One thing does
seem to be apparent, though: If a man can wade through this
muddle, he has the opportunity for a deeper emotional experience and a gain in self-knowledge that has never before been
so available to men.

As the representative of the patriarchy and the father
principle that had become stale, dry, inattentive, and
exploitive, the old king in fairy tales was ready to be overthrown. The new king—representing renewal and a new
potent principle of living (or set of principles)—always was
coupled with a new queen, a new connection with the feminine necessary for the renewal of life. Overthrowing the old
king does not mean doing away with fathers or the principles
of fathering. It suggests symbolically the transformation of
what we perceive as the dominant masculine principles in
our culture. As a society, our concept of masculine and patriarchal principles has been divided since the founding of our
country.

When the American colonies split from England, we
could say that metaphorically the old king, the King of Eng-

land, had become rigid, uncommunicative, inattentive, and exploitive. As we severed from England, we developed two dominant political perspectives. The colonial gentry wanted a new benevolent father-government that protected the rights of responsible citizens (generally considered property owners), one that guided, listened, and responded to the citizens, but did not control them except under voluntary restraints. The second perspective reflected the concepts of Tom Paine to a large degree, and desired the creation of a nation of brotherhood, brothers with no government that functioned in a fatherly way. This division in our political perspective lives on and is reflected in some of the ways we try to maintain individualistic illusions in a mass society. We have faced a continuous question as to whether we can generate energy by holding the tension between these polar views, or whether we will be torn apart between them. Our cultural split with patriarchal authority began long before the modern women's movement, and the role of fatherhood on the collective level is just as much of a problem as it is on the personal level.

As we begin to discuss politics, we begin to broaden our concepts of masculinity and fatherhood. Within this broader context, the problem of one-sidedness is more dramatic than in the previous problems discussed in styles of consciousness. In this previous discussion, I noted how men developed a cultural model of conscious styles consisting of extroversion, sensing, thinking, and judging, and they repressed other functions considered inferior and projected them onto women. This process left men not just needing the feminine for balance in their own personalities, but of more importance, needing to reclaim their own personality potentials and a unitive perspective. Now we need to examine the political issue of how patriarchal power works to hinder this reclamation and how it has robbed us of masculine as well as feminine authority.

The remainder of this chapter will deal with images of patriarchal power and the purpose of fatherhood from a psychological and a cultural perspective. This chapter is not a "how to father" manual, but a discussion meant to help provide the foundation on which to build personal styles of fathering.

Images and Reality

When we overthrow an old king, we discharge an old mental image in order to bring in a new one that promises life and rejuvenation. As we make this change, we participate in the process of changing our perception of reality, which thereby changes our reality. We accomplish this change just as artists and poets do, by changing our mental images. Our perception is based on images. Creation of new images or new ways of perceiving old images creates a new functional reality for us. Paradoxically, reality rests in the imagination rather than out in the world of things and events. Our imagery, our imagination, can convey and contain the complexities of life, its mysteries and its abundance of meanings. This thinking is not far out or esoteric. Ask those who have started their own business, and they can quickly tell you how they had to create and recreate their own reality. They know that the reality of the world (90 percent or more of small businesses fail in the first year) as seen by parents, "mature" friends, and bankers is usually death to their vision. These entrepreneurs treasure the few close people who can share their vision, their images, and by doing so, empower their personal reality.

Dreams, fantasies, reality, and indeed culture, itself, all include our images and are based on them. Images represent the inner and the outer world—the concrete, the factual, and the subjective. The degree of our intellectual and personality development is often determined and measured by our facility and command of images and symbols (words are an obvious example), and our ability to relate them (again, language is an obvious example). One could even say that growth in consciousness can be reflected in our ability to both create new imagery and to transform old images, giving them new and more complex meanings. Consequently, we know imagination is vital to the developing child, the poet, the artist, the scientist, the businessman, and, in fact, to all of us all of the time. To lose it is to become regressive in the art of living. The essence of protecting our imagination is to accept it as a vibrant and indispensable process in our personality. The personal, authentic imagination is important. We do not have to imagine like a child, although getting in touch with the intellectual and emotional openness of our "inner child" may help if we have become too rigid or "mature" in our attitudes. Imagining in the ways of our parents, teachers, new age gurus, or authors of books on creative thinking is not so important. Many people downplay or give up the excitement of their imagination because they think only creative artists or so-called intellectuals have the criteria for creative imagining and others are just flakes or childish. Each life, and each area of life is based on imagination and the construction and use of images. We all have the ability to imagine in our own unique form.

Depatriarching Masculinity

A few thousand years before Christ, as civilization as we know it began to emerge, the male image was pushed into cultural ascendancy. The great goddess and her queens and priestesses faded into the mists of history and the unconscious. As animals were domesticated and the Iron Age, cities, and primitive technology commenced, the ancients shifted their images of deities to reflect their changing experience. King gods evolved, replacing the great goddess. Zeus, for example, came to Greece with his personal animal, the bull. The fertility of the bull, of course, provided stability for people who depended on herds. Communities grew and clan chiefs evolved into kings and then into dynasties of sacred kings. These kings, considered empowered by the gods, were often the head of the priesthood and the military as well as the government. The genesis of western masculine thought began with this transition of images. An almost totally masculine heroic sense of values emerged, giving the sense that everything could be overcome, nothing was impossible, and stability could be attained if one had the will and courage to persevere and fight through to the end or goal. These values were necessary to thrust mankind out of the province of nature and into the march toward civilization. The stories and myths of these ancient people gloried in the tales of heroic journeys, battles, and conquests, reflecting—and at the same time supporting—this new evolution of values.

The sacred kings personified two kinds of potency: the fostering of life and the promotion of order. These kingly figures from antiquity have left us a heritage, imprinted deep in our psyches, of two significant images that are fundamental to our concept of masculinity: fertility and commanding authority. The depth and strength of these masculine images are still vividly illustrated in our society. A figure such as Lee Iacocca in a television commercial illustrates commanding authority. The use of experts and scientific appearing illustrations in commercials also illustrates the effort to identify with the authority of medicine or science. Considering the issue of fertility, note how uneasy many men become over the thought of having a vasectomy, even when they are middle-aged and have all the children they want or ever hope to have. Many men still have a strong prejudice against even using a condom. Far below a man's rational mind, fertility is still linked to power. Many men have difficulty giving up their fertility and would prefer that women take the responsibility for birth control.

The ancient traditions went even further by imaging the sacred king as the father of his tribe, the shepherd of his people, and the center of the realm. Social order was a reflection of the order of the gods. As monotheism developed, the king of the gods developed into God, the king/father as Jehovah in Israel, and Allah in the Islamic world. Kings ruled by the grace of God and/or were inspired by God. This concept helped compel the civilizations forward toward modernity, reinforcing the masculine value system, hero-warrior and enforcer of order on man and nature with mandates for obedience from the Divine. As this God/King-commander/father image evolved, we developed the imprint, the style and the definition of masculine authority, power, and aggression that led us into civilization. However, about the time of the Renaissance and the beginning of the industrial revolution, this God/king-commander/father image began to rigidify and become stagnant. Since then, we are finding that in our more modern culture, the emphasis on will, aggression, and separateness (individualism) is leaving us alienated and trapped in a narrowing focus of awareness.

So we have this heritage of centuries that combines the images of God, king, and father into one interrelated image on the collective level. Moreover, this God/king-commander/father image was also the central unifying figure of the culture as the representative of divine power and authority.

From the psychological perspective, an interesting event took place as the patriarchal king-image of Jehovah lost some of its cultural numinosity. As the Old Testament patriarchal God, Jehovah was the creator, the stern admonisher, the giver of laws and the appointer of kings and prophets. As this image became moribund for the culture, it evolved and split into three new images: the Father, the Son, and the Holy Ghost. These new images brought new strength, rejuvenation, and increased consciousness to religious life.

The birth of Christ resulted in the revision of religious customs, revaluing human relationships, man's relationship to God, and providing a charge of energy that spread throughout the Western world. This prime example shows how images split and evolve from a psychological standpoint. This example shows how the severing and evolution of old images that have lost their mystery and strength can give birth to new images that can empower the life of a culture. The transformation of old images, like the overthrow of the old king, indicates a growth in consciousness, increased awareness and a finer discrimination of human potential. Unfortunately, it took only a few short centuries to incorporate this new energy into an older form of patriarchal institution. Religion again became a matter of obedience, and Christ failed to continue as a numinous mode of manhood.

Images are vital to our perception and experience of reality. The evolution of images and our imagination both form our reality and compel us toward greater awareness and consciousness. In the province of masculine psychology, we see that through the centuries we have inherited a powerful traditional image of God/king-commander/father that is so deeply imprinted in our psyches, we are often unaware of how the operation of this image affects our behavior and attitudes. Throughout history, this image has maintained both positive and negative qualities. For example:

The thrust of power to gain control of the outer world by individualism ar.d will power also results in separation and alienation.

The giving of laws makes civilization possible by regulating ethics, morality, and human relationships, but we can also become petrified in legalism.

The emphasis on controlling the outer world can result in losing touch with the inner world and can also lead to the lust for dominance over others.

The accent on superior rational intellect can result in losing touch with feeling values, the feminine values, the cycles of life, and our own bodies.

Since this image began to rigidify, we have found ourselves and the world suffering more and more from the effects of the negative qualities. People who identify with dominant images that are becoming rigid have two characteristics. They never doubt themselves, and they will go to almost any length to preserve their power. Simone de Beauvoir comments on how this rigidifying image affects women: "For the Jews, Mohammedans and Christians among others, man is the master by divine right, the fear of God will therefore repress any impulse towards revolt in the downtrodden female."[2] Women, of course, are not alone in this problem. As long as men have this image of God/king-commander-father as a model, they are trapped in an increasingly narrow mold for living. Having to live up to this image with its heroic undertones (either at home or at work) is a hell of a job for a man to deal with in today's world. The rigidifying of the image means we do not allow for human weakness. A scandal, an affair made public, and other signs of human frailty can ruin a career or a marriage, even though our ideals are so high, rigid, and unrealistic almost no one can live up to them. What does a king-commander/father/hero do if:

He is scared?

He hates being a commander?

He is gentle, or if the world has penetrated to a gentle spot in his soul and he cannot stand it any more?

He needs a hug?

He is in the middle of a family fight, his wife and kids are screaming at him, and he just wants to burst into tears?

In King Arthur's day, this masculine image was not as rigid. Lancelot, for instance, was able to have a bad romance and run off naked into the woods and be crazy for a few days. Everyone was sad, but this event did not ruin his reputation as the king's champion. They hoped he would recover and return. He was not crucified by the *National Enquirer, People* magazine and the eleven o'clock news. Since this old model has rigidified, we do not have that kind of flexibility anymore. Of course, I am not suggesting that we go back to King Arthur's days. The answer is, if mythic truths are eternal, to bring this flexibility back into our present world.

---

[2]Barbara Walker, *The Women's Encyclopedia of Myths and Secrets* (San Francisco: Harper-Collins, 1983), p. 921.

To accomplish this return, men need to look at these mythic images in order to separate and deliteralize them as a primary step in renewing cultural masculinity as well as man's spiritual attitudes. Separating these images and their entangled concepts of authority is exactly what I mean as "depatriarching the masculine," removing the notion of divinity or divine right from masculine authority both personally and collectively. True masculine strength has nothing to do with ruling and domination. This separation allows us to bring new consciousness and new awareness to each of these images. My concern is primarily with the image of father. Taking away the image of God and king leaves a lot more flexibility in developing the images of the father. We can begin developing a clear image of what a father can be in our culture, based on each man's personal authenticity and values without the contamination of the divine and heroic. We can more clearly define the psychological functions of a father—his strengths, his dark side, and his place in our psychological development. For today's men, we need a whole new array of fathering images that are both flexible enough to fit individual styles and are also grounded in the psychological principles necessary for healthy child development. This transformation cannot be accomplished overnight, because the old image, though horribly abstract, is deeply embedded, and new images are fuzzy. But this transformation must be pursued with masculine resolve. The next section in this chapter will examine the above issues more closely.

The current lack of images leaves us with a dangerous problem. Images are needed as models for personal development; images as models assist the search for personal identity. Fathers have not been doing much to pass models and images down. By their default, sons (and men) are left vulnerable to the changing, consuming images of advertising, the media, and social movements. The world of these images does not exist, and identifying with these images simultaneously increases alienation and destroys one's sense of self-worth.

Thinking about and defining our masculinity enables us to take responsibility for ourselves.

Perspective

Fathering has no simple formula. The great child psychiatrist D. W. Winnicott[3] talks about the role of the father based upon the assumption that the father is necessary in his own identity, not as a nurturing duplication of the mother. Of course, sometimes maternal men can be very helpful and may make better mothers than their wives; nevertheless, Winnicott thinks that a father's taking on the role of mothering must interfere to some extent with his function as a father.

The expectant father is traditionally thought of as a nervous, bumbling sort who can do little but get in the way during late pregnancy, birth, and the early weeks in the baby's life. Men in the last couple of decades have become more active in participating in and supporting their wives during the birth process. However, Winnicott considers another role of the father crucial during this period. This role of the father is to provide a "protective covering" for the mother so that she can turn her full attention to the birth process and the bearing and nursing of the baby. Psychotherapists currently know that many deep psychological wounds can be inflicted on a child during this period. When the baby emerges from the period of complete dependence on the mother, the father continues to be important as a familiar figure, but one who is also different from the mother. The presence of this additional parent reduces stress for both the mother and the child and adds balance and stability to the family situation.

As the children continue to grow, getting to know their fathers as individuals helps them learn more about relationships that include love and respect without idealization. The

---

[3]Madeleine Davis and David Wallbridge, *Boundary and Space* (New York: Brunner-Mazel, 1981), pp. 136–138.

father should let enough of himself be known to his children so that they will not idealize him in a god-like way.

By virtue of his difference from the mother, including different interests and views, he can open up a whole new perspective of life for his children. When he joins them in play and activities or takes them out, he adds valuable new elements to their experience and helps them see the world through a new pair of eyes.

In depth psychology we see the father as having additional functions, most of which I have mentioned already.

The father is a model for his son of how to live and operate in the world and a partial model to his daughter. This modeling does not denigrate the mother; she also can model competency in the world, but due to her biological function, she cannot model separateness from herself.

The father operates first as a persona model for the son and then as an image from which he must differentiate his own masculine identity.

The father is the first image that begins the development of his daughter's image of her own inner male or masculine side.

The father must be able to facilitate his son's separation from the mother image and, if possible, support the mother emotionally as well during this period of separation.

Our culture is in great danger when fathers do not perform these functions. I have already talked at length about absent fathers and said that an absent father dumps the problem of differentiation onto the child. But what is the danger when the "soft-male" gets into fathering? If the father gets so far into the nurturing role that he is another mother, or even may usurp the mothering role, then his sons will have difficulty establishing their masculine identity and functioning in society. A father does not have to present a macho image or disdain nurturing, but he needs to have some conscious awareness and clarity about himself and his values as a man.

The father's clarity and values are just as important for a daughter's development. As she grows up, her emotional and psychological development is deeply affected by her relationship to her father. As the first masculine figure in her life, he affects not only how she relates to her own masculine side, but also how she relates to men, and to her own uniqueness and individuality. The way he relates to her femininity affects the way she grows into her womanhood, just as his modeling affects the way his sons grow into manhood. His attitude toward the world, work relationships, and competency will affect the attitudes of his daughters as well as those of his sons. If he is insecure and afraid, she may take on his fearful attitudes as well. He provides a model of authority, responsibility, decision-making, objectivity, order, and discipline for all his children. When we throw out the old "patriarchal authority" (which is in reality dominance and therefore a false authority), we need to replace it with a model of authority based on values and inner authenticity. Developing confidence in their own inner sense or "voice" of personal authority is vital psychologically for both sons and daughters.

As both sons and daughters become old enough, the father must be willing to step back, and, if necessary, take a stand that insists that his children individualize their values and ideals. They may internalize some of his values and they may also need to clarify some values of their own through conflict with his stance. The father's stance is necessary for his children's development, but, he must participate in this conflict while not insisting upon the maintenance of his "patriarchal" dominance. He needs to recognize and admit when they are right, and also be willing to lose to them, allowing them to be different from him, and using his stance to help them develop their own perspectives. If he remains too rigid and impersonal in maintaining his position as they try to differentiate from the family, he may force them into more and more serious forms of rebellion against his values. Often, this conflict is painful, but it can also be exciting if he can enjoy seeing his children become individuals. The father needs to realize that the children's lives are their individuation process, and the more he tries to smooth the path past a certain point with "mature" thinking, the more he is actually denying his children's right to struggle and develop consciousness, personality and deep meaning in life.

Time after time, as I have worked with adolescents, I have come to the startling realization that these young people have no idea what their parents' values are. They know they should score high on their SATs and try for a good college (and often feel tremendous parental pressure—do well or you're sunk), but that is about the extent of their awareness. They know a few general values, such as not to murder, steal, or smoke dope; however, these values often appear questionable to them when compared to the behavior of adults and the messages from advertising, TV, and the movies. As money, materialism, and the "pursuit of happiness" have become our cultural focus, communicating the concepts of good and evil, or right and wrong to our children has faded into a forgotten notion. Children know if their parents are obsessed with materialism and have developed an economic mentality in their hearts, and they do not trust these attitudes. Many have the uneasy feeling by adolescence that their parents' hearts and souls are for sale, if not already sold, and they are frightened of where they may fit into these debit and credit transactions. As a result, they seem to become cynical and lethargic toward life. Often we find these two extremes: one child searching for intimacy and values through the drug culture, and another selling his or her personal soul for the perfectionism that leads to anorexia. Many are in between, simply blotting everything out with TV, being depressed (quite a few are suicidal—suicide is the third largest cause of death for teenagers) or growing listlessly into adulthood in a state of passivity.

Fathers still have values, even though I am thoroughly frightened for our future by the number of men I know who are afraid to ask the questions Tom Rath asked (see page 229).

Fathers still have experience in the world but do not know how to convey it to their children. The father's separation from the family has created a void that destroys the communication substructure in father-child relationships, and this separation eventually creates an antagonistic relationship, or a passive, withdrawn father (even if he is authoritarian). In effect, too many fathers have given up. Fathers have got to reclaim their roles and their relationships with their children.

Fathers must struggle and fight to gain a new connection with their children—to explain their values and how these values relate to the way they live. Men's lives have faded so far from home that kids can no longer learn of their fathers' world through osmosis. Fathers have to consciously forge the connecting links between themselves, their worlds, and their children. Fathers need to communicate their values of work, family, professions, and politics to their children. Fathers also need to present a model of living that makes its meaning explicit—a model that cannot be seen is worthless to the family.

One suggestion with which to begin is to be willing to argue with family members within an atmosphere of personal trust, warmth, and feelings. If one is divorced, stand toe-to-toe with the children and listen to their hurt and anger and how they wished they had a normal family, without attempting to be defensive or self-justified. Be able to argue, discuss politics, ethics, and morality, and be able to *listen carefully* to their views and present your own in a thoughtful manner (not in the "I am the parent, I know best," divine right tradition). Be as open to changing your mind as you want them to be, and be open to learn from them.

Adolescence is a time when everything changes, and one is first faced with the great questions of "Who am I?" "Where am I going?" and "What is the meaning of this world?" If we listen to our own adolescent children, we can run across some exciting and provocative insights. But fathers cannot be a blank screen. They must also stand for their deep values as well as letting their children win, changing their minds when appropriate, and not requiring their children to accept all of their beliefs. The final most important thing is to let them go, helping them develop their values as they leave.

Finally, I will mention once again that the father must also intercede for his son's life and his right to be who he is, good or bad, and stand with the strength necessary against the boy's mom and the current cultural values on his son's behalf. What are we all so afraid of? Why are we afraid if our children do not take the SATs over and over, or go to a small state college rather than a large prestigious university, or do not even go to college? Why can we not have some faith that if we live our values openly and clearly and love our children, they will get the picture of life they need?

Courage and Aggression

As a psychotherapist, I am struck by the dwindling of courage, the polarization of aggression in our society, and how rarely we hear discussions of the daily choice of good over evil. As the lofty expanse of our Constitution has narrowed its focus to the "pursuit of happiness," our rationale for how we act has become pragmatic, reasonable, and realistic. In politics, business, and our personal lives, we are therefore justified in becoming "players" in the game of life rather than genuine participants. As our analytical ability and methodology have increased, our sense of right and wrong has seemed to fade away.

Aleksander Solzhenitsyn[4] reflects on this trend as a decline in courage that can be considered a lack of manhood. We are increasingly unable to act with courage and resolve toward the major problems and major threats in our own backyard. More and more, courage and aggression are manifested culturally in the compensatory fantasy performances in movies, TV shows, and athletics. The performers become rich

---

[4]Aleksander I. Solzhenitsyn, "A World Split Apart," in *Solzhenitsyn at Harvard* (Washington: Smithsonian Institute, 1980), edited by Ronald Berman, p. 5.

and famous, fulfilling our fantasies and at the same time underwriting the notion that money is the important product of virtues. One dark effect of this progression is that it leaves a group of people who either are not making it into the "pursuit of happiness" group or are not making it into it fast enough. Many of these folks feel an amplified sense of justification in acting pragmatically to get into the group or to express their alienation violently. Examples are in every sphere of our cultural life—for instance, middle-class drug dealers, crime and violence in general, or the new phenomenon our culture has created, the mass murderer.

As we evolve away from the patriarchal father image, we must keep in mind that the king was also the symbolic custodian of the realm, the family, and the personal values of courage and spirituality. As we create new images of fathering, both individually and collectively, we must carefully take responsibility for helping these new symbols of value become living experience for our society. How each of us does this is again a matter of personal style, but in order to develop our own personal style, we need a sense of our function and some understanding of the nature of aggression as it is currently evolving.

Eric Fromm,[5] writing on human destructiveness, classifies aggression into two categories. The first he calls benign aggression and the second malignant aggression. Malignant aggression is destructive. It is aggression that attempts to control life by destroying life and the spirit of life. Malignant aggression is power-oriented and is often the result of a sense of helplessness and impotence that causes a person to attempt to transcend his negative states of frustration, neglect, and alienation through violence. This kind of violence compensates for impotence and the lack of creativity. Malignant aggression is often paranoid, hoarding possessions, building up power and destructiveness. In an extreme case, a man tries to get out of the role in which he feels stuck by doing violence

---

[5]Eric Fromm, *The Heart of Man* (New York: HarperCollins, 1964).

to others (the rapist, assassin, terrorist, and mass murderer) and to himself. The parallels on a national level are obvious.

Science, weapons, city life and culture, the lack of personal safety, crowding, collectivization and technology accentuate our feelings of alienation and impotence. We are further dehumanized in the myriad of statistical abstracts we become as our names transform into Social Security Numbers and we take our place on polls, tax lists, computer lists, mass mailing lists, and heaven help us feel human if we have to communicate with computers in the confusing array of payments we make each month. Everywhere we turn in our daily transactions it seems increasingly difficult to contact a person who "cares."

As malignant aggression penetrates modern life, anxiety generates a greed that subtly replaces eros. We develop an economic, a legalistic, or a trader's mentality, dividing everything equally or thinking constantly in terms of debits and credits. Good intentions are no protection against this insidious attack. Greed in any form negates what it wants to have. Take, for example, the man and wife who want "the best" for their families. This couple may buy so much, so many "things" and have their children enrolled in so many of the "right schools," sports, and activities that they are hopelessly overburdened financially. As a result, they are constantly overworked and overstressed. In desperation they try to get more and spend more to ease their anguish (even including expensive psychiatric treatment, therapeutic camps, and drug treatment centers for their children).

Unless these parents luck into some insightful psychotherapist who is not caught in the same trap, or find some eye-opening life experience, they never realize they have slipped into a self-destructive cycle greed masked by proper sounding goals. Greed negates life by always demanding more. Their family is dying because there is *no eros*—no love, no true relationship. These hard-working, seemingly "good parents" have become malignant. They think they work hard and suffer unjustly, but they repress the fact that it was their anxious and increasingly narrow perspective that incited them to assume these burdens.

More insidious still is our fascination with the power side of technology. A machine, a gun, or a hand grenade can convert a boy into a man, the impotent into the potent. The man or boy becomes more powerful and potent than others, but in a malignant way. Even more subtle is the way the characteristics of modern technology, when applied to people rather than things, are not the principles of life, but those of lifeless mechanics. With this kind of system, we live under the illusion that we are very much alive when we have many things to own and use. Men begin to admire speed and power. Fast and powerful machinery becomes sexual, giving a "rush," and beauty is attached to competition, cheerleading, or awarding the prize. True relaxation becomes a lost art because all of life runs mechanically and compulsively at too fast a pace. Even our attempts at relaxation, hunting, fishing, and boating become malignant violence to nature and to ourselves as we lose the values of the mystery of life and the experiencing of nature.

We become more interested in machines and technical systems than participating in and experiencing life. We go to sex therapists or the latest book or manual to learn the mechanics of sex. We go to therapists and counselors, or read manuals and take adult education courses to learn the mechanics of relating to others. We have almost become so mechanical that we think if we find the right buttons to push or the right programs to follow, we will find happiness, pleasure, and love and avoid the risks of learning, experimenting, and living. Risks imply the possibility of suffering, and how many of us teach our children how to suffer? We have it all: fast cars, complicated stereos and televisions, personal computers, and God only knows how many gadgets, coffee makers that will do everything but give you a massage when you wake up—yet every psychotherapist will tell you how bone-deep the loneliness is in this country.

What about benign aggression? What does this strange term mean? Benign aggression means both defensiveness in the sense of preserving life, and also having a spirit of adventure and strength in the support of life. This concept involves both preserving life and giving life, fostering life with strength and energy (remember the legacy of King Arthur). The spirit of adventure may have dangers at times, but this spirit furthers the culture as people dare to break cultural traditions or loosen their passions to do things like starting new businesses and pursuing more Spartan, but meaningful careers or spiritual paths, often risking or losing possessions in the process. The most elementary form of benign aggression is to love life and fight death. For the love of life to develop as a principle, it requires security, justice, and the freedom to create, to venture, and to wander. Not the suffocating kind of security, mind you, but enough security in early life to give one a sense of optimism and hope about life.

Where do fathers come into this picture? Fathers must first set an example in discrimination between these forms of aggression, acting with conscious awareness and then modeling this discrimination in how they live. Children, and women, too, need models of benign aggression. The heroic men in the quest for life (Christ, Martin Luther King, Jr., Gandhi, Anwar Sadat, and others) have given us a model of how to create life in a broader form. They transformed the meaning of courage from aggression and conquering to preserving life and pursuing the inner journey. Fathers must also reflect this transformation of courage in adult life—the courage to stand for life, not for conquering or ruling, and the courage to explore oneself and the culture deeply and then to act with self-awareness. Dominance is not a part of benign aggression, but ambition in the service of life is part of it. Without ambition, probably no one would have the drive to achieve any great work. The above heroes also gave us a "sword" in the name of life. The sword, in the fairy tale, is a symbol of masculine consciousness and discrimination. We must pick up this sword and use it in discriminating styles of aggression, in transforming heroic courage from conquering to preserving life, and finally in fully understanding the reality of our culture. Fathers must pick up this sword and wield it against the dragons and beasts in our society.

What about courage and aggression in relationships on a personal level? In my experience as a therapist, women seem to be hungering for positive male aggression. (But I do not mean they want someone to knock their teeth out!) The most common complaint I have heard from women is, "He won't fight with me."

Some men just quietly leave or withdraw. This action may be aggressive, but a lot of men are genuinely confused in this area. Many have no repertoire between giving in and turning brutal. After all, what can a concrete, rational, thinking man do best but give rational, concrete, impersonal answers? This response negates eros. Of course, if he is smart at all, he has probably learned that his best efforts can start a real war. The worst kind of man, however, says, "Yes, dear, whatever you say, dear," while doing exactly as he pleases. In relationships this behavior is malignant aggression.

A man with love and spirit can also openly get angry and argue with his girlfriend or wife, his children, or even his boss. Once out from under the patriarchal image, he can even reclaim his feeling values and develop a container of eros for fighting—continuing to stand both for his values and for eros. He must listen to and share emotions, even while shouting, but respect bottom lines and demand that his be respected in turn—and overall, struggle for clarity, meaning and definition in relationships. At the same time, he must allow himself to be moved and touched by others, responding to their needs and to them personally while maintaining his own integrity and realizing that he does not need to rationally solve their problems for them.

Most therapists know that men who have difficulty relating to women will also have difficulty relating to their children. A number of books currently being published are about the yearning of men to have intimacy with their fathers. I think deep down inside, we all yearn for intimacy, but finding intimacy requires courage, spirit, and action in the service of living—benign aggression.

Reality and the Witch's Curse

In the final war scene of the movie *Excalibur* (a story of King Arthur), Morgana, the mother of Arthur's son Mordred (who was still tightly bound to her as the witch-mother) hoped to defeat Arthur and win the kingdom. By her magic she had maintained her youthful beauty and allure throughout her life. On the night before the battle, which destroyed both sides, the spirit of Merlin appeared to her and caused the release of a great fog, a killing fog, that enshrouded the entire battlefield. The fog emanated from her mouth and, as the fog grew, her true ugliness became apparent. In many fairy tales a witch represents something neglected—she was not asked to the party to participate in the feast, the birth, or the marriage. But eventually she comes anyway, casting a spell of evil and retribution, a state of negative enchantment. This is the Goddess of Strife, and she must be admitted to the feast of life and given due attention. In fact, to deny her is to begin the creation of one's own state of illusion—enchantment—through our own denial of reality.

As we have turned our eyes toward technology and machinery, we have developed an accompanying illusion, a killing fog of negative enchantment, and we are living in a growing cloud of unconsciousness. We compulsively try to hear and know everything. The news media makes crisis chatter out of events, holocausts, and potential catastrophes throughout the world, filling our minds with anxious shadows that we defend against with our illusions. We hear, read, and see more and more without understanding what is going on at all. We have lost touch with the fact that our model for information gathering and rationalism does not give us the ground for understanding reality. We insist on our right to "pursue happiness" but are no longer sure of our right to live, and our children blot it all out by watching endless violence on TV.

We continue our state of enchantment (often called lifestyle), thinking we can avoid suffering and commitment, and struggle to remain unaware of the enormity of unneces-sary suffering going on in the world. Why do we stand for so much crime and misery? Why are so many people turning to fundamentalism? Can turning to a new or old extreme posi-tion (that is in some way the method of the old king) heal, join, mediate or balance these opposing forces, or will these positions simply foster our illusion of control? Why are we not able to bring our ideals of liberty, democracy, and equal-ity back to the level of our daily lives? The masculine spirit needs to awaken. We need men to husband and father our culture.

In an anxious world, the fear of death cannot be allevi-ated by materialism for very long without the help of a state of enchantment. Life has meaning from the way we live it and the value we give it until the time we die, and then beyond in the manner that our life affected the collective consciousness, especially through our children and relationships. Moreover, we need to reclaim the value of death for men in our culture. Michelangelo observed that "Whereas death killed all men, the thought of it had made many." We have lost much of the spirit of living by losing the value of death for we have learned to dissociate from our bodies, we don't deal with the meaning of illness, and we don't allow for the sacredness of death. Ancient cultures—from before the time of the three hundred Spartans up through the time of our Native Ameri-cans—had a masculine meaning for death—more than just dying in battle in the military sense! They had a cultural com-mitment to the value of a man's life as it was lived and the right for life in general.

Even when we try to do good, we force our efforts into the framework of a battlefield or war mentality. We become so focused on winning or losing, and minimizing our costs and casualties that we lose our ethical perspective. As a result we live in a constant state of polarization between winning one thing and banishing everything else from our consciousness. Our focus seems riveted to, and controlled by, media direc-tions and other dramatic efforts. The conscious awareness needed for our time demands that we get out of this polarized mentality and expand our focus to the wider range of problems confronting us. We need to learn to look for longer term and more conscious solutions. No matter what sphere—science, health, politics, or social—we have globally evolved to the point where issues must be dealt with comprehensively and with greater consciousness than that provided by a battlefield or media mentality.

The father's task is to promote social functioning, leading the family into life with a sense of reality, perspective, and culture. No father, if he is living ethically and helping to bring life into this world, can avoid the responsibility of seeking the conscious awareness (the sword) needed to confront the issues of our time. Yes! The authority of the father is needed, authority based on knowledge, creativity, and wisdom—authority based on eros, and not contaminated with power and violence.

The Spirit of Fatherhood

Many men fail at the art of living because they never realized when they were at a fork in the road that required them to make a decision that would affect the foundation of their lives. They are not aware that everyday life asks us questions beginning long before our consciousness is fully developed. Each decision narrows our path. Paradoxically, the little daily decisions set the bricks in the highway men follow and cause them to become collaborators in the demise of their spirit. Boys begin deciding when small how they will be good, what they will rebel against, what they will be or will not be when they grow up. Little decisions such as the desirability of certain playmates, bribes for grades, and attending the right schools cause us gradually to sell out our integrity and undermine our self-worth. We play with the right kids, play the right sports, take the right lessons, and later date the right girls or wrong ones for a short rebellion. We try to pick the sensible college and the right career and try to impress others with our maturity. The inner voices of integrity and conscience weaken against the so-called "more mature" opinions around us, cultural pressure, and the fearful appearance of the world. Obsession with practicality, sensibleness, the promise of happiness with success, and the avoidance of pain and suffering keeps us off the byways that could add depth, meaning, and vitality to our existence. Soon, in adulthood we are so embedded in our "cultural" direction that admitting we were wrong and beginning again becomes terribly difficult and totally disrupts our lives.

My dad died when I was in my early 40s. Our relationship had been full of joys, sorrows, and conflicts. Many of these conflicts were never resolved while my dad was alive so they worked themselves out in a series of dreams I had after his death. The series ended with this final dream:

> I am in the kitchen with my sister. I hear a noise in the carport. I have to kick the garbage away from the door to open it. My stepmother comes in. She says, "Buddy, he's back." I go out to meet him with tears streaming down my cheeks. I put my arm around his shoulder, saying, "I'm glad you're back; there is so much I want to say to you." He says, "There's more than one way to die."

That final sentence, "There's more than one way to die," has haunted me every day in every decision I have made since then. This dream told me about the spirit of fatherhood in a way my dad never could state in real life because of his desire for me to be secure and to suffer less than he did. We must bring back and maintain the eternal questions that Tom Rath asked:

What is the purpose of my life?

Why am I here?

What am I doing?

Each time we avoid these questions, we are unconsciously discovering another way to die—an insidious death of the spirit even though the body still functions.

Asking these questions forces creative living, forces us to listen to our inner voices, and forces us to listen to our inner integrity, asking, "Is this right or is this wrong?" Then when we sacrifice part of ourselves, we do it knowingly, with conscious awareness, because we have asked the right questions. We also know we often have to make choices because we cannot have or do it all. When we make a choice, personal or moral, we do not have to take a poll like a modern politician to find out what to do or who to be if we are already consciously living our values.

This spirit of fatherhood empowers a man in his experience of living with strength and purpose grounded in personal authenticity and cognizance of values greater than himself. He in turn empowers those around him to passionate and creative living.

THE KING,
THE LION,
AND THE UNICORN

As we look back into the childhood of humanity, we find that as our mythology evolved the king, the lion, and the unicorn became connected in the field of human imagery. The lion and the unicorn emerge as symbols of kingship. The lion symbolized the strength and power of the outer masculine world, and the unicorn the depth and energy of the masculine inner world. The king was the intermediary between these two realms, mediating for balance and equilibrium—not by repression, but by holding the tension between these two struggling realities. These three images illustrate a more comprehensive differentiation of our deep masculine energy and its connection to the Self through the royal image of the king.

In one of our simple nursery rhymes we find the lion chasing the unicorn around the city until the whole conflict is drummed out of town. This story reflects a psychological situation where our strong extroverted focus, lacking a mediating king, has forced this entire masculine conflict between inner and outer back into our cultural unconscious where it has been causing no end of social problems ever since. As a result, many people have come to the conclusion that no good can occur whenever masculine energy is in authority. Unfortunately, this perspective is as out of balance as our current situation. It simply swings the pendulum in the opposite direction. Male energy can encompass intelligence, health, compassion, and creativity, and can exercise them in service to the community. Robert Bly notes that all great cultures since the time of the Greeks, except for ours, have lived with images of this energy.[1]

Most of our discussion so far has concerned men's inner lives and their lives in intimate relationships. The focus of this book has been on the individual, but we need to understand how this inner work and work on relationships will benefit our culture. In the long run, our inner and outer work should harmonize, which does not mean the end of struggle or that we should conform to any particular set of norms. It means that these two areas should contribute to each other as we strive to develop, and the results of this struggle should contribute to culture. We need to examine the questions of how strength, values, love, and eros can combine to benefit our society, and, in turn, how bringing this new energy into the society will affect men.

The imaginal field of the lion, the king, and the unicorn presents a model that can help us perceive more clearly these questions and their answers. This model may help guide us out of the avoidant or defensive-manipulative position that many men are sliding into. Along with the above position, a large number of men today are finding it easy to become fascinated with the feminine. We have idealized it for so long and have heard such "bad press" against masculinity that when we step out of the masculine world for a while we easily become engulfed. Nurturing feels good, eros feels good, and often we have missed a lot in caring for our children, cooking, decorating and so forth. But most of us—not all of us—need a broader sense of balance. We need to translate the feminine into a richer way of life with new alternatives. We must not slip back into the tempting influence of the mother image. We do not need to get lost in the feminine realm. As I mentioned in an earlier chapter, in the days of lions, king, and unicorns, if

---

[1]Keith Thompson, "What Men Really Want: A New Age Interview with Robert Bly," in *New Age Magazine* (May, 1982), p. 50.

a knight gave up his deeds and masculine adventures and stayed too long in the castle with his beloved, people feared he would lose his ideals, enterprise, and desire for further spiritual development.

Unfortunately, as women have pursued their need for cultural identity and meaning, they believed that since they did not have it, we (men) did. Many men also believed that we must have it since women felt so strongly that we did, even though deep down we had an uneasy feeling that we did not. The fact is, we do not. The evolution of a mass, information-based, technological society has left the old king dead and petrified on his throne. We all, individually and collectively, need to be revitalized.

The women's movement has shown us that "Sleeping Beauty" is no longer an appropriate fairy tale for our children. Now it is the prince who is asleep—asleep to life—dormant within men's personalities. We need to reawaken and begin again with the deep vigor of masculine nature and the hope and idealism of the prince. We need to forsake our secularized, rational cultural models to seek the transformation of masculine ideals that move us to aspire to become more than we are, that inspire a fuller expression of the life that has evolved throughout the centuries.

The King

When we examined the old king in the fairy tale, I observed that psychologically he symbolized the dominant masculine principle, the father, and the patriarchy on the cultural level. He represented the status quo and conventional cultural values. When he became one-sided and resisted renewal, he brought about his own overthrow. I believe that we have rushed so quickly to overthrow him that we neglected to realize we did not have a prince to become the new king and to beget new male energy into the culture. As a result, we have relied too much on women to define what the cultural masculine should or could be.

As we overthrow the patriarchy, the sick old king of today, we need to look back for the positive values the patriarchy offered. Men have stood for more than nationalism, war, and forcing women into being wives, mothers, and daughters. Men have also stood for the evolution of consciousness, art, culture, and the manifestations of the spiritual in life. They have stood for law, for healing, and adventure in the realm of the mind and spirit. If we do away with the masculine spirit and man's pursuit of cultural spirituality, we may lose our respect for the spirituality of life. Men's commitment to spirituality and values greater than themselves is one of the great protectors of the feminine principle, the principle of life and of nature.

The king[2] as a symbol stands for the rule of the best in humankind and is the carrier of the essence of responsibility, experience, and the nobility of our ancestors. A new king must carry these noble attributes into his own age. The riches of our heritage must be carried into the consciousness of our time, our moment, in order to give birth to the consciousness of the future. The evolution of the king as a ruling psychic principle must be taken up individually with self-discipline and the willingness to undergo the seasoning necessary for this responsibility—the seasoning I have outlined in this book. Such a king symbolizes our truth during a particular moment in our lives and calls for obedience. It is through the king that we can awaken to the realization of *our* authenticity. As I noted in my explanation of the fairy tale, a true king requires a queen for balance, creativity, a connection to the heart, and a human life of relationships. While I am discussing masculine energy, we must not lose sight of the fact that the masculine and feminine principles require each other for wholeness and balance to be present.

It is our responsibility to see where our allegiance lies. Do we have a feeling of uncertainty about the leading principles of our lives? Are we serving our truth, or are we serving an inner politician in the negative sense—manipulating and responding

---

[2]Helen M. Luke, *The Voice Within: Love and Virtue in the Age of Spirit* (New York: Crossroads, 1988), p. 40–51.

to outer trends? Are we too simplistic, thinking it is sufficient to serve as steward or statesman to current conventional values, doing good as we see it and not acknowledging the need for a king? Such a perspective has a nice appearance, but doing good in a shallow manner for outer reasons creates a backlash of evil, as pride, power, or violence creep into the picture, and we may discover that we can even feed on the greed of helping others. It is our psychological task to summon forth, without confusing this psychic truth with the emptiness of our old social institutions, the royal principle within ourselves, a principle that has been buried as deeply as Iron John was.

In mythic terms the king has two companions, the sage and the fool. The sage represents wisdom and the truth of the spirit, but only through the king can this wisdom be put into action. The fool balances the king with the wisdom of absurdity. He reminds us that what is of greatest consequence within ourselves is of no consequence. We must be able to laugh at ourselves and dance with life even when our greatest projects crumble. Robert Moore[3] has written extensively about the king and his companions and our need to summon his return through our imagination. The voice of the king, filled with passion and expressing his vision, can arouse our response, restoring our desire to live and grow.

The king, as mediator between the lion and the unicorn, is a symbol of the Self that brings balance, structure, and unity to our personalities. A king of this nature brings forth love and devotion, and can lead our personalities in an approach to our spiritual dimensions and our inner lives toward inspiration and unity. Of course another option is also available. We may always regress into deeper fragmentation and psychological and spiritual rigidity. As I finish our discussion of the lion and the unicorn, I will provide several examples that give a living picture of the personal meaning of these concepts and the person's choices to grow or regress.

---

[3]Robert Moore, and Douglas Gilette, *The King Within* (New York: William Morrow & Co., 1992).

A Country Without a Royal Principle

Robert Stone, in his dialogue with Ken Kesey, noted that when the Dodgers moved to Los Angeles it gave notice that greed had taken the field. He commented, "It represented the total commercialization of sports. It was finally saying to American men, 'There is nothing you do that is more important than money.' "[4] David Ignatius asked in an editorial, "Where is the Selfless Public Service of Yesteryear?"[5] He quoted General George C. Marshall as saying that indispensable qualities of a public servant should be "Courage. Wisdom. Tolerance. An understanding of the democratic procedures." He quoted an old Marshall aide who said he never once heard Marshall ask, "What's in it for me? How am I going to look?"

In Marshall's era, civil service was regarded as a virtuous endeavor worth personal and financial sacrifices. Ignatius also observed that the Washington of Marshall's era has now become the Washington of Stockman and Deavers. He then lists a sampling of statistical and anecdotal evidence supporting his assertions:

- Rising salaries. The decline in public service ethic has been accompanied by significant increases in pay.

- Growing affluence. The D. C. area is now the richest and best-educated metropolitan area in America.

- The lobbying boom. The number of political action committees has increased more than sixfold in a decade. The number of registered lobbyists has more than doubled since 1976.

- The dearth of negotiations. It used to be typical for officials who disagreed with policy or who felt that their useful service had come to an end to do the proper thing and resign.

---

[4] Ken Kesey and Robert Stone, "Blows to the Spirit," in *Esquire Magazine* (June, 1986), p. 268. The material that follows also comes from this editorial.
[5] David Ignatius, "Where Is the Selfless Public Servant of Yesteryear?" in *International Herald Tribune* (May 8, 1982), p. 6.

Contrast that with the approach of Mr. Stockman who remained in the Reagan administration for more than four years after he concluded that its fiscal politics would have disastrous effects on the economy.

One of the greatest contributions of Western man since the age of the ancient Greeks has been the expression of the culture's values in an organized manner. People who serve the culture as a profession are tremendously important. We need them as well as active citizens. We have learned through many bitter struggles that political systems only work well when they serve a higher, apolitical vision. Our country was founded by men with this tremendous royal energy.

Modern men have moved into a materialistic phase. Sports and politics as well as business have gradually become a pursuit of money. The great energy that once poured into science and research has also become dominated by the bottom line and is frequently reflected in a search for increased materialism. Money is too easy a yardstick to measure things with—especially men. Our religious institutions that once channeled the spiritual aspirations of mystics and saints are staggering bureaucracies that are unable to renew themselves. The highest values from the history of our culture are virtually without a home. We are badly in need of the revitalization offered by a royal vision and deepened by the value of life that comes from the feminine.

Careers—Values

Lillian Rubin asks:

> "Why can't a man be 'self-respecting' unless he can 'take care of his wife and kids'? And why can't a woman respect him unless he's acting in that traditional role? It's easy to point to the social definition of man and woman, wife and husband, and say, 'There, that's why'—as we have done now for the

last decade or more. But the answer no longer satis-
fies. Instead we have questions that beg for understanding.

Why, after so much struggle, does it still happen that
way most of the time?"[6]

The answers to these questions are complicated and troubling.
I believe men need several basic things. Men need a vision
and/or a work culture that gives them identity and meaning.
We also need to be able to stand for something of value. This
value does not have to be financial success, but it must have
value reflecting our stance and commitment, or we are in danger of losing our masculine soul. The value also does not have
to be macho: we can be an artist or a house-husband if we are
firmly committed to that pursuit as a fundamental value.

Statements as strong and varied as the ones I have been
making remind me of another piece of ancient wisdom that
can be retrieved from the story books in nursery rooms. In an
ancient fable a lion was caught in the net of the hunters. A tiny
mouse, befriending him, chewed through his bonds and set
him free. This bit of ancestral wisdom reminds us of the value
of the small, the quiet and the hidden, and how vitality rests
on wholeness and the importance of all things in relationship
to each other.

More and more, in our defensiveness, confusion, and
need to please women (or need to rely on them), men opt for
mediocrity in what they do. Men need to regain their visions.
We need to know what we want to do and then do it. If we
have a royal vision, we give value and purpose to the others
around us and thus to the culture.

A royal perspective is needed for visions both big and
small. It is needed in politics, large corporations, small businesses, and it probably would not hurt anything in science

---

[6]Lillian B. Rubin, *Intimate Strangers: Men and Women Together* (New York: Harper-
Collins, 1983), p. 27.

and education. However, men also need to be doers that are trusted and believed in by the feminine. The days are gone when we can have a nice little woman at home to applaud our daily quest into the asphalt jungle. Now and in the future, we are going to have to do it differently. We are going to have to learn to know the feminine part in ourselves, and be sure that our "doing" reflects deep inner values that incorporate the values of life and nature. This new way will prevent one-sidedness and provide the "feminine" assurance and confirmation we need. The nature- and depth-oriented men will be true to inner values, will be able to contribute to life, and will not just be trying to "please mother."

The Lion

The robustness of the lion is symbolic of the natural strength a man needs to emerge from the protection of his dependency and enter into the risky business of life. This metaphor represents the deep inner masculine vitality necessary to enter the outer world of achievement and accomplishment. Our long journey into consciousness requires that we develop a sense of identity in the outer collective world. We must learn to fight and compete, to measure and be measured. Symbolically we must learn to kill and be killed many times. Whether we like it or not, this process represents the truth of our existence.

Mystics throughout the centuries have recognized this truth. They felt that the "Green Lion," instinct and vitality, full of ardor and courage, exhibiting heroic qualities in the world, was necessary as a precondition for undertaking the journey of spiritual transformation.[7] The Green Lion was the alchemical symbol for the natural man and his strength, fierceness, and virility. Spiritual development in this classical sense came through the taming of the lion and not through the education of the lamb. Our current notion of spirituality as a pious

---

[7]Evelyn Underhill, *Mysticism: A Study in the Nature and Development of Man's Spiritual Consciousness* (New York: Doubleday, 1990), p. 147.

effeminacy, amiable and peaceful, is emphatically contradicted in the great spiritual tradition.

However, we are not animals and we cannot live totally out of our animal values without violating our deeper selves. If we are to be true to ourselves, to our human nature, we must live by an ethic which everyone who is seeking individuation must discover for themselves. This search is an inner search and a spiritual one. Without its direction and balance, represented by the king and the unicorn, our instinctual vitality loses its royal nature. Whether our lion represents brute physical strength or the brute strength of intellect (the lion is also a symbol of the sun), they will become power-oriented and create endless battlefields in our outer world.

The Unicorn

The unicorn represents the creative power of the inner life. It is the white ethereal light that unifies the spectrum of colors. It unifies our inner life and our emotions, bringing them to a spiritual focus. The single horn represents the unified, penetrating power of the spirit in contrast to the diversity of the flesh. Through this dramatic spiritual power, masculine spiritual power, the nature of life can be transformed and the individual can be connected with the transcendent Self.

The legend of the unicorn states that he can only be tamed by a virgin and that he must lay his head down in her lap while she sits in her garden next to the Tree of Life. In this state he will allow his throat to be cut, his red blood to flow, and, in this manner, his transformation is achieved. Often this story is used as a metaphor for a man's developing relationship to his anima. However, I am going to use it in a more general sense. As we must first develop and then sacrifice or tame our lion as our personality matures, we must also develop a strong inner life, our unicorn, and be willing to sacrifice it in order to deepen it and broaden it in the service of our Self and life.

As I mentioned in the introduction to this book, these metaphors represent eternal truths and they go on daily in our

269 / EMASCULATION OF THE UNICORN

lives. We do not do them once and then "get on with our lives." As the king is always evolving through the kingship cycle, the lion and the unicorn are also growing to new levels of strength which will require new levels of sacrifice.

Blood, throughout the ages, has symbolized sacrifice. A blood sacrifice was thought to be healing, causing life's energy to flow back into us at a deeper level. Blood sacrifices were offered to God in an effort toward reconciliation and wholeness. Blood represents passion and the sacrifice is to transform passion to a deeper level. It is the home of the soul and carries our ancestral heritage forward to us and then toward the future in our bloodlines. Sacrifice leads to depth, not just to pleasant feelings and escape. It may lead to joy, but the road to joy is difficult and requires a continual willingness to sacrifice, and along this road life becomes increasingly personal, as we shall see.

◊ ◊ ◊

Dean was a physician in his late forties. He had reached a point in his life where his practice was large and his estate was impressive. He was the son of upper middle-class parents who had been somewhat distant and cold in his early years. After a period of adolescent depression and rebellion, he had abandoned his temperament, his world, and had adopted theirs. His king became success, and although he maintained high professional standards, he had become somewhat cold and aloof. He had made his late adolescent transition with a lot of energy, becoming, one might say, a lion in his field. He had succeeded to a partial extent in initiating himself into adulthood, although in a somewhat one-sided and wounded manner.

By mid-life, as is often the case, he had reached a point of routine. Even though he was helping people and getting rich, he seemed to be on a demanding treadmill. Though a physician, he felt he had become a soulless machine, and the great questions of life rarely stirred him personally. He seemed completely walled off and contained in his own narrow, affluent circle where few of the primitive passions of humankind could reach him. In fact, I would later discover that he and his wife had sex rarely and little passion of any kind seemed to reach him.

Circumstances began to slowly pull the mask off his world and reveal a glimpse of a stranger and stronger face below the level of life he had constructed. He had begun to make a few mistakes in his practice. One, in his opinion, had been deadly to an elderly patient. He had always been particularly proud of his skill and now he was beginning to fear malpractice suits. The awareness of his mistakes and the fear of his inability to control them became a somber background in his daily life. This stress began to take its toll physically and several alarming symptoms appeared. By this time he felt that it would be impossible for him to continue in this career for another twenty years.

He decided to enter analysis and then to change careers. This move made sense to him as he had read Jung, thought Jungian psychology fit his mid-life predicament and a Jungian analyst would understand it. Changing careers to another specialty would take several years and cost quite a lot of money, but he could support it. It would also necessitate a family move. He presented this idea to his wife as a new adventure, a challenging and exciting opportunity for the family to move to a new place with new interests and beginnings for all. She turned him down flat. She felt that she and the children were rooted in the community, established in the schools, and this whole idea would uproot them and cost a lot of money for little gain.

When he returned to an analytic session, he felt that perhaps she was right. Maybe his whole idea was silly and that by all conventional standards their life was wonderful; they were blessed and it would be absurd to give up their success. But this line of reasoning did not assuage his fear for very long.

You may have noted that he prevented his wife from coming to grips with this problem on an emotional level by presenting it to her as an exciting new adventure. Instead of being deeply honest with her, he came off as an immature adolescent. He needed to begin the sacrifice of his lion as his king was approaching a new temple. He needed to sacrifice his self-image, that is, the image he had of himself as always strong and in charge, and to tell her that he was scared and failing on several levels. He wanted to skip on to a new self, doing new things without having to face the death of his old self. The best that can happen when we abort our transformation is to have an old self doing new things for a while before the old problems, demanding transformation, reappear. He needed to tell her how desperate he felt (which he was amazingly skillful at denying, even in his analytic sessions) and that he felt an inner split. He could go on to explain how he felt that his own disposition was turning on him and that he had some inkling, although he was not certain, that the new specialty was, in fact, truer to his nature.

Such an issue between a man and wife cannot be an issue of conventional values. It must be an issue of love. It must be personal and it must be handled with integrity and care. If a person cannot be intimate and vulnerable, and carefully talk through such serious matters in a marriage, he cannot personally value the marriage very much. The question arises as to whether he loves the image of himself more than intimacy with his wife, and if both of them love the image of their marriage and success and "the way things should be" more than they love each other. Sacrificing these images require that he, and hopefully they, will sacrifice their obsession with the external world and honor the internal world that is soliciting a deeper sense of personal integrity, vulnerability, and love. This sacrifice is one example of the unicorn's transformation as well as the lion's and the king's. Inner values and the ruling principle of his life must be sacrificed as well as his outer position. What is called for is a much greater transformation than a simple change in specialities.

There is no guarantee that he will be able to regain his conventional status or that his marriage will last. But if the full process is undertaken and he begins a transformation for a renewal of life's energy, then there is a possibility that his sacrifices will make him, and perhaps his marriage, a great deal more than they have been before. If a marriage can transform to a deeper love relationship, it may become a container where each partner challenges, nourishes, and participates in transformation with the other. A sacrifice for life, in the Garden of the Virgin, always transforms our lives to a more personal expression of ourselves.

Joe was one of the men I referred to in Chapter 1. He had problems with an emerging wife and volatile teenagers. He had turned toward his own inner work seeking to broaden and deepen himself. As he did, his life changed in many ways. He, too, had to fight a terrific battle with his self-image and the images of the way he thought life should be. In this process he had to sacrifice several make-believe relationships that he had been part of for years. Through his dreams he had come to a new realization about the "storms" in life, and realized that they are a part of nature, often destroying the structures we have built and even killing parts of us. But storms are also followed by reconstruction, re-creation and often by a renewed feeling of unity and inner cooperation.

He had come from a home with an alcoholic and abusive mother. She had hit and cursed him until, in adolescence, he became large enough to stop her. His father had been a successful businessman, generally absent as he could not tolerate his wife. Their lifestyle belied the hollow and violent reality of their true existence.

Early in life Joe wanted to be a teacher and a poet. By the time he reached college, he abandoned this idea and joined the world of his parents. Following his father's lead, he became a very successful man. He developed the fabrication that his mother had been tragic, and being who they were, his parents had done the best they could. He also developed the fiction that he and his wife had a great life and a good family and simply needed a little help to make it better. That simple thought began his inner journey.

As his analysis progressed, the volcano of rage that he had repressed began to bubble and finally he concluded that he would have to confront his father for abandoning him to an abusive mother. He went through the usual arguments of "he did the best he could," "he's too old to even understand what I'm talking about," "he thinks psychology is foolish," and so on. He did finally conclude that the confrontation should be a non-angry one in an effort to understand what happened. Still he was terrified. Why are we so afraid in these situations? For the most part, we must sacrifice our images of ourselves and our families, our whole adaptive, imaginary version of reality, in order to find out the truth of our lives; this sacrifice is not a small one. Somewhere inside we know that fictions will fall and no matter what happens, we will never be the same again.

He proceeded as planned. At first his father denied any knowledge of his abuse. Joe refused to let him off the hook, insisting that he must have known; he was too intelligent not to and even stopped the abuse in several situations. His father, 75 years old, got up and left without any apology or reconciling words. It seemed as if their relationship had moved from an appearance of closeness to one of alienation.

Joe said that he was not sure that it really mattered. He had felt something shift during this encounter. By confronting his father in a determined but non-angry manner, he felt he had moved from a son to an adult. He felt transformed into a father himself, no longer being a son who also had children. He had faced life and his fear and pain in a way he never had before. In a conscious fashion he was energized by this conversation in a manner that carried over into his family. He noted that for the first time he may be really listening to his wife and children.

A few days later his father showed up in his office and quietly handed him a twelve page letter, his version of their family life which included many of his regrets. To accept the reality of our pasts and ourselves requires a strong sacrifice. We expose our throat in the Garden of Life and allow the transforming blood to flow when we accept the grief of what happened to us, the things we missed, and the things we wish we had done and did not.

◊ ◊ ◊

To speak the "unspeakable" about our imaginary lives, the story we developed out of fear, compensation, and adaptation, is to make our sacrifice in the lap of life. We do our old people no favor by saving them from this confrontation. Their story needs to continue with truth and vitality as well as ours does. It is often our fear, the fear of our truth, that causes us to put them out in some psychic pasture where they can play golf and toddle nonsensically around. The inner voice of the Self does not retire at age 65; if we give it a chance, it will carry us in life until our life is finished.

Both the lion and the unicorn bring passion and vitality to our lives through the mediation of the king. As our individuation process grows, we create a personal story that contributes to the story of humankind. If we can break free of the peace of nonbeing fostered in the world of conventional values, then doing and being can come into relationship. When our king is expressed in our simplest and most ordinary acts which are savored and carried out with vitality, our lives become expositions of our Selves. We have made a long journey out from under the dominance of impersonal behavior—the behavior learned from our adaptation and all its supporting levels of illusion—into consciousness. We find that we have created a personality that is more solid and we are no longer a football kicked around by our inner emotions and projections or external trends and values. At this point the actions of our lives become personal and they begin disclosing our unique Selves to others in an expression that contributes to life.

Bibliography

Bradley, M. Z. *The Mists of Avalon*. New York: Ballantine, 1982.

Calvino, I. *Italian Folktales*. New York: Harcourt, Brace, Jovanovich, 1983.

Campbell, J. *The Hero with a Thousand Faces*. Princeton: Princeton University Press, Bollingen Series, 1973.

de Castillejo, I. C. *Knowing Woman*. New York: Putnam, 1973.

Castro, J. "Battling the Enemy Within: Companies Fight to Drive Illegal Drugs Out of the Workplace," *Time*, International Edition (March 17, 1986), p. 52.

Cirlot, J. E. *A Dictionary of Symbols* (2nd ed.). New York: Philosophical Library, 1971.

Davies, R. *The Deptford Trilogy*. London & New York: Penguin, 1983.

Davies, R. *What's Bred in the Bone*. New York: Viking, 1985.

Davis, M. and Wallbridge, D. *Boundary and Space: An Introduction to the Works of D. W. Winnicott*. New York: Brunner-Mazel, 1981.

Ehrenreich, B., Hess, E., Jacobs, G. "The Politics of Promiscuity," *New Age* (November/December 1986), p. 31.

Elkind, D. *The Hurried Child: Growing Up Too Fast Too Soon*. Reading, MA: Addison-Wesley, 1981.

Erikson, E. H. *The Life Cycle Completed*. New York: W. W. Norton, 1982.

Fromm, E. *The Heart of Man*. New York: HarperCollins, 1964.

Frankl, V. E. *The Doctor and the Soul: From Psychotherapy to Logotherapy*. New York: Random House, 1986.

von Franz, M-L. *The Feminine in Fairy Tales* (rev. ed.). Dallas, TX: Spring, 1976.

———. *An Introduction to the Psychology of Fairy Tales* (4th ed). Dallas, TX: Spring, 1978.

———. *Shadow and Evil in Fairy Tales* (rev. ed.). Dallas, TX: Spring, 1980.

von Franz, M-L., and Hillman, J. *Jung's Typology* (4th corrected printing). Dallas, TX: Spring, 1979.

Gendlin, E. *Let Your Body Interpret Your Dreams*. Wilmette, IL: Chiron Pub., 1986.

Gerzon, J. *A Choice of Heroes: The Changing Face of American Manhood*. Boston: Houghton Mifflin, 1982.

Greene, B. "The Man in the Gray Flannel Suit," in *Esquire: The American Man, 1946–1986* (June, 1986), p. 200.

Guggenbuhl-Craig, A. *Eros on Crutches: Reflections on Psychopathology and Amorality*. Dallas, TX: Spring, 1980.

Hillman, J. *Anima*. Dallas, TX: Spring, 1981.

Ignatius, D. "Where is the Selfless Public Servant of Yesteryear?" *The International Herald Tribune* (May 8, 1982).

Jaffe, A. *The Myth of Meaning in the Work of C. G. Jung*. Zurich: Daimon, 1984.

Johnson, R. A. *He: Understanding Masculine Psychology*. New York: Harper/Perennial, 1984.

Johnson, R. A. *Inner Work: Using Dreams & Creative Imagination*. San Francisco: HarperCollins, 1986.

Jong, E. *Parachutes and Kisses*. New York: Signet, 1984.

Jung, C. G. *The Collected Works*, trans. R. F. C. Hull, ed. H. Read, M. Fordham, G. Adler, Wm. McGuire, Bollingen Series XX, Vols. 1–20. Princeton: Princeton University Press, and London: Routledge & Kegan Paul.

Kaplan, P. W. "Dads Who Knew Best." *Esquire: The American Man, 1946–1986* (June, 1986).

Kesey, K., & Stone, R. "Blows to the Spirit: A Dialog between Ken Kesey and Robert Stone," *Esquire: The American Man, 1946–1986* (June, 1986).

Kiley, D. *The Peter Pan Syndrome: Men Who Have Never Grown Up*. New York: Avon, 1983.

Kopp, S. *Here I Am, Wasn't I: The Inevitable Disruption of Easy Times*. New York: Bantam, 1986.

Levinson, D. J. *The Seasons of a Man's Life*. New York: Ballantine, 1978.

Luke, Helen M. *The Voice Within: Love and Virtue in the Age of Spirit*. New York: Crossroads, 1988.

Maxwell, W. "Babes in Arms," *Esquire: The American Man, 1946-1986* (June, 1986).

Moore, Robert, and Douglas Gilette, *The King Within*. New York: William Morrow & Co., 1992.

Myers, I. B. *The Myers-Briggs Type Indicator* (manual). Palo Alto: Consulting Psychologist Press, 1962, 1975, 1977.

Neumann, E. *Amor and Psyche: The Psychic Development of the Feminine*. Princeton, NJ: Princeton University Press, Bollingen Series, 1956.

———. *The Great Mother: An Analysis of the Archetype*. Princeton, NJ: Princeton University Press, Bollingen Series, 1955.

Opie, Iona and Peter. *The Classic Fairy Tales*. New York & London: Oxford University Press, 1974.

Peck, M. S. *The Road Less Traveled: A New Psychology of Love, Traditional Values and Spiritual Growth*. New York: Simon & Schuster, 1978.

Peters, T. J., & Austin, N. K. *A Passion for Excellence: The Leadership Difference*. New York: Random, 1985, and London: HarperCollins, 1985.

Peters, T. J., & Waterman, R. H., Jr. *In Search of Excellence: Lessons from America's Best-Run Companies*. New York: HarperCollins, 1983; also Warner Books.

Plato. (Hamilton W., trans.) *The Symposium*. New York: Penguin, 1951.

Rowan, R. "Hailing the Eureka Factor," *Time*, International Edition (April 21, 1986), p. 65.

Rubin, L. B. *Intimate Strangers: Men and Women Together*. New York: HarperCollins, 1983.

Samuels, A. (Ed.). *The Father: Contemporary Jungian Perspectives*. London: Free Association, 1985; and New York: NYU Press, 1986.

Shain, M. *When Lovers Are Friends*. New York: J.B. Lippincott, 1978.

Sheehy, Gail. *Passages*. New York: Bantam, 1984.

Solzhenitsyn, A. I. "A World Split Apart." *Solzhenitsyn at Harvard*. Ed. Ronald Berman. Special printing by the Smithsonian Institute, Washington, D. C. 1980.

Thompson, K. "What Men Really Want: A New Age Interview with Robert Bly." *New Age* (May, 1982), pp. 30–51.

Ulanov, A. B. *Receiving Woman: Studies in the Psychology and Theology of the Feminine*. Louisville, KY: Westminster, 1981.

Underhill, Evelyn. *Mysticism: A Study in the Nature and Development of Man's Spiritual Consciousness*, New York: Doubleday, 1990.

Van Der Post, L. "Appointment with a Rhinoceros." In *A Testament to the Wilderness: Ten Essays on an Address by C. A. Meier* (pp. 111–134). Zurich: The Lapis Press, 1985.

———. *The Heart of the Hunter: A Journey into the Mind and Spirit of the Bushmen*. New York: Penguin, 1965.

———. *Jung and the Story of Our Time*. New York: Viking Penguin, 1976.

Walker, B. G. *The Woman's Encyclopedia of Myths and Secrets*. San Francisco: HarperCollins, 1983.

Whitmont, E. C. *The Symbolic Quest: Basic Concepts of Analytical Psychology*. Princeton, NJ: Princeton University Press, 1969.

Wilson, Sloan. *The Man in the Gray Flannel Suit*. New York: Simon & Schuster, 1955. Reprinted in 1991 by Buccanneer Books, Cutchogue, NY.

Wolff, T. *Structural Forms of the Feminine Psyche*. Zurich: C. G. Jung Institute, 1985.

Woodman, M. *The Pregnant Virgin*. Toronto: Inner City Books, 1985.

INDEX

Livio Piatti

Dr. C. T. B. Harris graduated from the Georgia Institute of Technology with a B.S. in Industrial Management, and received his Ph.D. in Counseling Psychology from Georgia State University. In 1989 he completed post-doctoral training at the C. G. Jung Institute in Zurich, Switzerland, where he earned a diplomate in Analytical Psychology. He combines fifteen years of business experience with over twenty years as a practicing psychotherapist, psychologist, and Jungian Analyst, bringing practicality and depth to this book. He currently lives in North Carolina where he is a Jungian Analyst.